Seed-Stage Venture Investing

The Ins and Outs for Entrepreneurs, Start-Ups, and Investors on Successfully Starting a New Business

William L. Robbins

BOOK IDEA SUBMISSIONS

If you are a C-level executive or senior lawyer interested in submitting a book idea or manuscript to the Aspatore editorial board, please e-mail authors@aspatore.com. Aspatore is especially looking for highly specific book ideas that would have a direct financial impact on behalf of a reader. Completed books can range from 20 to 2,000 pages—the topic and "need to read" aspect of the material are most important, not the length. Include your book idea, biography, and any additional pertinent information.

ARTICLE SUBMISSIONS

If you are a C-level executive or senior lawyer interested in submitting an article idea (or content from an article previously written but never formally published), please e-mail authors@aspatore.com. Aspatore is especially looking for highly specific articles that would be a part of our *Executive Reports* series. Completed reports can range from 2 to 20 pages and are distributed as coil-bound reports to bookstores nationwide. Include your article idea, biography, and any additional information.

GIVE A VIDEO LEADERSHIP SEMINAR

If you are interested in giving a Video Leadership Seminar, please e-mail the ReedLogic Speaker Board (a partner of Aspatore Books) at speakers@reedlogic.com. If selected, ReedLogic would work with you to identify the topic and create interview questions. You would then have someone videotape you answering the questions. ReedLogic producers then cut the video and turn it into a segment that is like a seminar teaching the viewer on your area of expertise. The final product is burned onto DVD and distributed to bookstores nationwide.

Published by Aspatore Inc.

For corrections, company/title updates, comments, or any other inquiries, please e-mail store@aspatore.com.

First Printing, 2006
10 9 8 7 6 5 4 3 2 1

Copyright © 2006 by Aspatore Inc. All rights reserved. Printed in the United States of America. No part of this publication may be reproduced or distributed in any form or by any means, or stored in a database or retrieval system, except as permitted under Sections 107 or 108 of the U.S. Copyright Act, without prior written permission of the publisher. This book is printed on acid-free paper.

ISBN 1-59622-543-2
Library of Congress Control Number: 2006930229

Managing Editor, Laura Kearns; edited by Eddie Fournier

Material in this book is for educational purposes only. This book is sold with the understanding that neither any of the authors nor the publisher are engaged in rendering legal, accounting, investment, or any other professional service. Neither the publisher nor the authors assume any liability for any errors or omissions, or for how this book or its contents are used or interpreted, or for any consequences resulting directly or indirectly from the use of this book. For legal advice or any other, please consult your personal lawyer or the appropriate professional.

The views expressed by the individuals in this book (or the individuals on the cover) do not necessarily reflect the views shared by the companies they are employed by (or the companies mentioned in this book). The employment status and affiliations of authors with the companies referenced are subject to change.

Aspatore Books is the largest and most exclusive publisher of C-level executives (CEO, CFO, CTO, CMO, partner) from the world's most respected companies and law firms. Aspatore annually publishes a select group of C-level executives from the Global 1,000, top 250 law firms (partners and chairs), and other leading companies of all sizes. C-level Business Intelligence™, as conceptualized and developed by Aspatore Books, provides professionals of all levels with proven business intelligence from industry insiders—direct and unfiltered insight from those who know it best—as opposed to third-party accounts offered by unknown authors and analysts. Aspatore Books is committed to publishing an innovative line of business and legal books, those which lay forth principles and offer insights that, when employed, can have a direct financial impact on the reader's business objectives, whatever they may be. In essence, Aspatore publishes critical tools—need-to-read as opposed to nice-to-read books—for all business professionals.

Contents

PREFACE 9
    Acknowledgments 11

1. **INTRODUCTION TO SEED-STAGE INVESTING**
   1.1 The Purpose of This Book 13
   1.2 Is Doing Start-Ups Right for You? 15
   1.3 What, and Who, Do You Need to Know? 16

2. **KEY TRENDS AND PLAYERS IN SEED-STAGE INVESTING**
   2.1 The Seed-Stage Funding Gap 20
   2.2 The "Mutual Fundification" of Venture Capital 21
   2.3 The Rise and Fall of the Technology Incubator 23
   2.4 Four Types of Seed Investors 25
   2.5 A Hybrid Approach to Seed-Stage Investing 30
   Chapter 2 Addendum: SEC Definition of "Accredited Investor" 34

3. **PROSPECTING FOR TECHNOLOGY AND START-UP OPPORTUNITIES**
   3.1 The Truth About Deal Flow 35
   3.2 Looking for Deals 36
   3.3 A Structured Approach to Technology Sourcing and Opportunity Development 45

4. **THE PSYCHOLOGY OF COMPANY FOUNDERS**
   4.1 Founders and the Concept of the Normal Curve 55
   4.2 What to Look for in a Founder and How to Find It 58

5. **THE DUE DILIGENCE PROCESS**
   5.1 "Hard Due Diligence" Versus "Soft Due Diligence" 61
   5.2 Personal Factors 64
   5.3 Scientific or Technical Factors 66
   5.4 Market Factors 68
   5.5 Financial and Investment Factors 70

6. FORMING AND FUNDING THE START-UP
- 6.1 Legend Versus Reality ... 73
- 6.2 The Company Formation Process ... 74
- 6.3 The Formation Agreement ... 75
- 6.4 The Semantics of the Term Sheet ... 83
- 6.5 The Term Sheet, Deconstructed ... 84
- 6.6 The Capitalization Table ... 94
- 6.7 Additional Material ... 97

7. NAVIGATING THE TECHNOLOGY TRANSFER PROCESS: ADVICE AND COMMENTARY
Contributing Author: Dr. Jonathan G. Lasch
- 7.1 Introduction to the Contributing Author ... 99
- 7.2 Technology Transfer from Academic Institutions ... 100
- 7.3 Technology Transfer and Academic Faculty ... 104
- 7.4 Advice for Technology Hunters ... 106

8. CREATING AND PROTECTING INTELLECTUAL PROPERTY: A PANEL DISCUSSION
Panelists: Mr. Nima Shiva and Dr. David Margolese
- 8.1 Introduction to the Panel ... 107
- 8.2 Panel Discussion ... 108

9. WRITING AND EVALUATING THE BUSINESS PLAN
- 9.1 The Business Plan Industry ... 117
- 9.2 Business Plan Writing as a Process ... 118
- 9.3 How Investors Review Business Plans ... 120
- 9.4 Advice on Writing Business Plans ... 122

10. WORKING WITH SERVICE PROVIDERS
- 10.1 Attorneys ... 125
- 10.2 Consultants ... 130
- 10.3 Finders ... 142

11. BUILDING THE START-UP TEAM
- 11.1 Building Teams on a Shoestring Budget ... 151
- 11.2 The Core Start-Up Team ... 152
- 11.3 Critical Early Employees ... 157

11.4 Methods of Recruitment ... 163
11.5 Compensation and Benefits ... 169
Chapter 11 Addendum: IRS Definition of an "Employee" ... 176

12. BUILDING BOARDS OF DIRECTORS AND SCIENTIFIC ADVISORY BOARDS
12.1 Criteria for Forming Boards and Selecting Directors ... 179
12.2 How Not to Form a Board ... 180
12.3 Advice on Board Size for Start-Ups ... 181
12.4 Using Boards Productively ... 182
12.5 The Value of Scientific Advisory Boards ... 185

13. CORPORATE PARTNERING
13.1 The Conventional Thinking About Corporate Partnering ... 191
13.2 The Downsides of Corporate Partnering ... 192
13.3 The Upsides of Corporate Partnering ... 201
13.4 How to Approach Potential Corporate Partners ... 203
13.5 The Corporate Partnering Proposal ... 207

14. APPENDICES
14.1 Confidentiality Agreement ... 211
14.2 Due Diligence Checklist ... 216
14.3 Certificate of Incorporation ... 220
14.4 Term Sheet ... 223
14.5 Stock Purchase Agreement ... 234
14.6 Stock Option Award ... 247
14.7 Executive Search Agreement ... 249
14.8 Letter of Invitation to Join Scientific Advisory Board ... 253
14.9 Job Offer Letter ... 256
14.10 Inventions Assignment Agreement ... 262
14.11 Useful Web Sites ... 266
14.12 Inspirational and Motivational Books ... 268

ABOUT THE AUTHOR ... 269

PREFACE

There is no shortage of textbooks and how-to manuals for entrepreneurs and venture investors. While many of these books do a good job of providing objective and practical information, most fall short in the readability department. They also tend to be rather dry, leaving out the un-censured anecdotes and tales of woe that convey what it is *really* like to create, invest in, and manage technology-based start-up companies. What inspired me to write this book was my desire to share useful, real-world knowledge about seed-stage investing and venture development, but with the candor, humor, and conversational style of an insider's guide to the wonderful world of start-ups. To the fledgling entrepreneur or first-time investor, starting a company and getting it funded can seem like a black art, shrouded in the mysterious language of private placement memoranda and term sheets. For the new company founder and the novice investor alike, and for the consultants, attorneys, accountants, and M.B.A.s that work with start-ups and venture investors, or aspire to, this book seeks to demystify the venture formation, funding, and development process.

Doing life science and technology start-ups in Los Angeles, as I do, is a lot like producing a movie. You write a screenplay (business plan), find a producer (investor) to green-light (fund) your project (company), attach (hire) a director (CEO), scout a location (lab space), assemble a production crew (start-up team), and begin the shoot (operations). If filming (product development) goes according to plan, you wrap (complete product development) in six months, pre-screen (beta test), edit and assemble the final cut (debug or optimize), roll the promotional trailer (pre-launch promotion), and hit the silver screen (launch product). However, if you are the typical entrepreneur or seed investor, this romanticized movie/start-up analogy only goes so far. Because, unlike the classic Hollywood story, six months after you finish your business plan and begin fundraising, you will see a lot of red lights but no green ones, your top choice for CEO will lose enthusiasm and join a more stable company, the great lab space you had your eye on will be leased out to another tenant, your hand-picked start-up team will disintegrate, and product development will still be at the storyboard stage.

To the star-struck entrepreneur or seed investor, I say, "So long Hollywood. Hello, Start-Up Land!"

During the heady days of dot-coms, doing start-ups was a glamorous occupation. Over-the-top networking events sponsored by trendy law firms (now defunct) and upstart venture capital firms (now disbanded) were thronged by crowds of fashion-forward M.B.A.s, Generation-X techies, and wannabe investors looking to score a job, a deal, or more likely, a cell phone number and a hot date.

If it's glamour you are looking for, don't expect to find it in a start-up. But, you may find heartbreak. With apologies to Neil Sedaka[1]:

> *Don't take your funds away from me.*
> *Don't you leave my lab in misery.*
> *If you go, then I'll be blue.*
> *'Cause starting up is hard to do.*

---

[1] Sung to the tune of his 1962 soft-pop favorite, "Breaking Up Is Hard to Do."

ACKNOWLEDGMENTS

The material for this book is derived primarily from the ongoing work and experiences of a group of professionals who have been doing start-ups together in Southern California since the late 1990s. This group includes my colleagues at Convergent Ventures, a seed-stage venture investment and development company located in Los Angeles, select faculty members and technology transfer officers from the California Institute of Technology and the University of California at Los Angeles, attorneys with substantial practices in the life sciences and high technology, and a carefully cultivated network of private equity investors, consultants, and service providers.

I would like to give my special thanks to the following individuals, without whom I could not have written this book: colleagues, present and past, at Convergent Ventures, including Dr. Jon Lasch., Nima Shiva, Ken Aldrich, Bill Adams, Winn Hong, and Dr. Curt LaBelle; Dr. Jim Conklin, ex-fighter pilot, physician, serial entrepreneur, mentor, and good friend; Dr. Henry Lester and Dr. Dennis Dougherty of the California Institute of Technology; Dr. Yang Yang of the University of California at Los Angeles; Michael Sanders Esq. and his colleagues at Reed Smith LLP; Richard Jones Esq. and his colleagues, both at O'Melveny & Myers LLP and at Nixon-Peabody LLP; Ted Humphreville, CPA, who taught me the importance of keeping good books of both the accounting and the motivational variety; Denise DeMan-Williams and Dr. Steve Williams of Bench International; Lorraine Reafsnyder and Judy Mina of HR Advisors Inc.; Dr. Mark Nowak and Kate Hawkes of Neurion Pharmaceuticals Inc.; Dr. David Margolese of ORFID Corporation; Larry Zaccaro and Dr. John Lowe of Pfizer Inc.; and the many entrepreneurs, scientists, engineers, consultants, angel investors, venture capitalists, corporate investors, corporate scientists, corporate alliance managers, and executives with whom I have interacted, successfully or otherwise, over the years.

Finally, I thank my parents for wondering when I was going to start writing a book, and my wife for wondering when I will finish the next one.

I set out to write a book that captures the world of start-ups as it really is, warts and all. I hope I got it right. Any factual errors or misrepresentations in the material that follows are entirely my own responsibility.

1

Introduction to Seed-Stage Investing

ven·ture *n.*
An undertaking that is dangerous, daring, or of uncertain outcome [2]

1.1 The Purpose of This Book

Experienced entrepreneurs and investors knowingly refer to the exciting but arduous process of creating new companies, especially those emerging from major academic, biomedical, or corporate research centers, as "doing start-ups." Doing start-ups is the subject of this book.

Investors who prefer to invest in new companies at the formative stage are known as "seed-stage investors." Sometimes, seed-stage investors are lumped together under the broader category of "early-stage investors," who may invest in one or more "rounds" of funding in a young company, including the seed round, first (or Series A), and early "follow-on" rounds. While all seed investors invest in start-ups, not all start-up investors invest as early as the seed round.

In this book, we shall focus our attention on four types of investors that typically invest in start-ups. These investors are: "friends and family," so-named because, for obvious reasons, they are the first people that many new entrepreneurs turn to for seed capital; "high net worth individual investors," sometimes known by virtue of their beneficence as "angels,"

---

[2] This and subsequent chapter-leading definitions, unless noted otherwise, are from www.dictionary.com.

and sometimes referred to as "accredited individual investors"[3]; "professional venture capitalists," who sometimes invest in seed rounds of particularly promising companies; and "corporate investors," who invest in new companies primarily for strategic reasons rather than purely for financial gain. Seed investors may be of relatively modest means, or quite affluent. They may be rank amateurs or very sophisticated when it comes to investing in start-ups. Angel investors usually practice their craft as an avocation rather than as a full-time job. Some angels are retired; others are still actively employed (often as business owners). Many angels have extensive experience as successful entrepreneurs or executives. Yet, there are plenty of angels whose only qualification is the ability to claim accredited investor status.

Entrepreneurs seeking start-up capital should be aware of the differences—sometimes subtle, sometimes painfully obvious—between the various types of investors that will consider making seed investments. These differences may be reflected in the investor's motivation for making an investment, ownership philosophy (e.g., collaborative, paternalistic, or adversarial), time horizon (or patience), desired sense of control, ability to add value (e.g., technical or management expertise), and preferred exit strategy (e.g., selling the company or going public). In Chapter 2, we will look more closely at the defining characteristics and behaviors of the four types of investors mentioned above. For now, let the company founder or entrepreneur in search of start-up capital be warned: Know thy investor, or suffer the consequences.

I count myself among a small, passionate group of professionals (some would just call us unemployable) who do start-ups for a living, playing the role of both entrepreneur and seed-stage investor. Working as a team, my partners and I scout for technology that can form the basis of a new business, initiate and lead the company formation process, invest our own money (or raise it from other accredited investors), and take on management responsibilities that would otherwise require the hiring (at great expense, assuming we could find someone with the requisite experience and appetite for risk) of permanent executives.

---

[3] The term "accredited investor" has a specific legal definition, as stated in Regulation D of the Securities Act of 1933. See Chapter 2 Addendum.

Introduction to Seed-Stage Investing

The ideas and examples discussed in this book are derived from my still-unfolding career and journey of self-discovery as an entrepreneur, start-up executive, and seed-stage investor. Having worked at companies large and small, public and private, in the pharmaceutical, biotechnology, medical device, and high technology industries, I present my thoughts in the spirit of sharing with you some of the good and not-so-good things I have learned about the world of start-ups. This includes how to identify and evaluate promising new start-up opportunities, how to create and build technology-based ventures, and how to manage the many activities that are part of the ever-eventful, always challenging process of doing start-ups.

1.2   Is Doing Start-Ups Right for You?

Most people associate start-ups and venture investing with the pursuit of wealth, but this is *not* a book about making money. Making money is the province of Wall Street and the Federal Mint. Venture formation and investing are as much about passion as they are about profit. Without the former, the latter rarely follows. To do a start-up successfully, or to invest in one intelligently, you need to be motivated by more than just the opportunity for financial gain. You need to know in your heart that starting a company, or being a start-up investor, is something you *have to do*. Not because your fellow academic scientists or your former business colleagues are doing it. Not to feed your ego or to impress your peers with your intellectual prowess, or your financial acumen, but as a matter of principle. How will you know your motivations are genuine? One way to answer this question is to consider your station in life and career. Are you truly happy with what you are doing? Are you fully applying your education, your natural talents or skills, and your expertise? Do you ever wonder whether the career path you have chosen or the position in which you are currently employed is taking you where you want to go? These questions are not just pop psychology for the entrepreneurially curious or the financially adventurous. Your answers to these questions will be telling indicators about the nature of your motivations as a professional entrepreneur or start-up investor. Be honest with yourself. To be enamored of the *idea* of doing start-ups is one thing. To be prepared to follow through is a different matter.

1.3 What, and Who, Do You Need to Know?

Whether you are an entrepreneur or an investor, you will need a team of experienced service professionals and business advisors to help you navigate the business formation and funding process and minimize the chance of mishap. Many structural, financial, strategic, and personnel problems that prove crippling or fatal to start-ups can be traced to the entrepreneur's and/or the seed investor's inexperience, lack of preparation, and failure to seek or follow the counsel of attorneys, accountants, human resource consultants, and seasoned business managers. Inexperienced entrepreneurs and inexperienced investors tend to go together, because inexperienced entrepreneurs tend to confuse capital (or the promise thereof) with competence, while inexperienced investors tend to confuse technology with business opportunity.

Unless you, as an entrepreneur—or an investor—have the combination of maturity, knowledge, and street smarts that only come from experience, you cannot afford to go it alone. Instead, build your network. If you are an academic scientist or engineer with plans to start a company, take the time to find the attorneys and financial experts who do a lot of work with start-ups originating at your institution. Resist the allure of big-name law firms and accounting firms that tout their tech-savvy "start-up practices," and instead focus on building rapport with the individual attorneys, certified public accountants, and managers-for-hire who have a track record of working successfully with start-ups. Otherwise, you may find yourself buying a firm's reputation, but not its service. In Chapter 10, we will look more closely at the professional service providers, consultants and advisors who can be invaluable members of your team, if chosen for the right reasons, and for reasonable fees.

If you are a seed investor, you will need your own inner circle of trusted attorneys, accountants, and go-to advisors. In my experience, the best members of this group are equally adept at playing both sides of the field, representing investors in some situations and entrepreneurs (or their companies) in others. My partners and I have found that an ability to play both offense and defense gives us, and our professional advisors, a better understanding of start-up situations.

The subject matter of this book, including examples of business, legal, and financial documents, is drawn directly from, or based in part, upon actual start-up companies and seed-stage investments in which my partners and I have participated, either individually, or while working together as a team. I have drawn anecdotes and examples from companies in fields including biopharmaceuticals, agricultural biotechnology, life science research tools, medical devices, advanced materials, microelectronics, computer peripherals and technical services However, the principles and practices I wish to convey are generally applicable to almost any business start-up situation.

Doing start-ups entails a considerable amount of stress, uncertainty, and tension, which can lead to a sleep-impairing and marriage-threatening syndrome called "start-up-itis." Sometimes self-induced, and occasionally inflicted by others, start-up-itis can bring an entrepreneur or seed investor to despair. Although hard to treat, start-up-itis can be prevented with a good sense of humor. Some of the funniest and most enjoyable times my partners and I have experienced together have arisen during periods when everything seemed to be going wrong. There's nothing like a sarcastic wisecrack or a cathartic dose of cynicism when things get grim. Aside from the immunizing effect of humor, the only surefire remedy I know of for start-up-itis is money. Preferably cash, and, ideally, sitting in your bank account. If you have ever been sleepless in the middle of the night, staring blankly at the ceiling and wondering where on earth the next payroll was going to come from, you have undoubtedly experienced an acute attack of start-up-itis. If you have ever rushed to your bank , investor-check-in hand, with two minutes until closing time on the afternoon before payroll is due, you have felt the healing powers of a fresh infusion of cash. Of course, that euphoric rush you felt was fleeting, but for that brief moment, life was good.

2

Key Trends and Players in Seed-Stage Investing

an gel *n.*
A typically benevolent celestial being that acts as an intermediary between heaven and earth

Seed capital may well be the hardest money you will ever try to raise. While raising a few tens of thousands of dollars to get a business off the ground can be relatively easy, raising the next $100,000 to $1,000,000 or more—to engage in business development activities, complete proof of principle, or breadboard a prototype—is notoriously challenging. A newly minted Ph.D. with little more than an idea and supportive parents can raise enough money to incorporate and print some business cards. And those start-up lenders in your wallet—Visa and MasterCard—will gladly help you get your business off the ground if you sign up for one of their ego-stroking company credit card offers, as thousands of new business owners do every year. But, let the borrower beware: Those company credit card offers that will appear miraculously in your mailbox the day after you incorporate your new business are not what they seem. Each shiny new credit card that you receive with your company name embossed in gold lettering will go right on your personal credit history along with your mortgage, your auto lease, and your student loan.

Raising capital from astute angel investors or professional seed investors entails none of the high-fiving "you've arrived" feeling depicted in television commercials for business credit cards. It is not uncommon for the seed funding round to take a year or more to close, and once your fundraising campaign gets underway, every month that ticks by, the risk increases that your offering will become stale and, therefore, less fundable.

To what may we attribute the apparent dearth of funding for seed-stage deals?

2.1   The Seed-Stage Funding Gap

Aside from the myriad reasons investors may give to decline funding any particular company (if they are considerate enough to give any reason at all), perhaps the single most important reason that securing funding for a seed round is so difficult and time-consuming is the paucity of professionally managed capital in the $1 to $3 million range available for promising but unproven new ventures. I refer to this situation as the "seed-stage funding gap." Figure 1 below illustrates the nature of this phenomenon and summarizes some of the reasons why a seed-stage funding gap exists. As I will explain, the problem is not that venture capitalists do not have enough capital to invest in seed-stage deals. Paradoxically, the problem is that venture capitalists have *too much* capital to make traditional seed investments.

Figure 1
The Seed-Stage Funding Gap

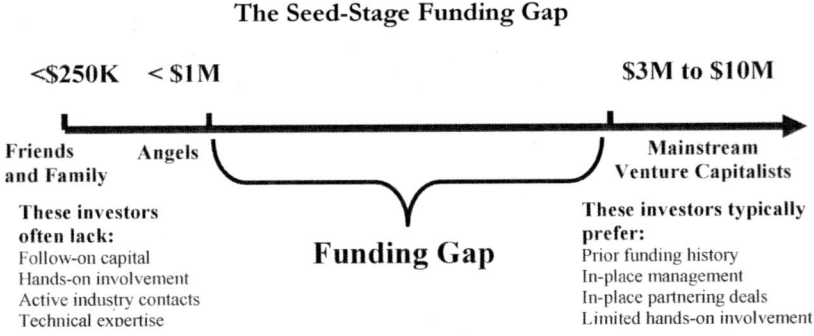

In Figure 1, friends and family are depicted as the primary source of capital for amounts less than $250,000. The typical friends and family funding round will be less complicated and less costly than an angel round or a transaction with a venture capital firm, because friends and family are less likely to require extensive due diligence and legal documentation to complete their investment (or loan). Friends and family do not have the fiduciary obligations borne by general partners of venture capital funds, and angel deals have become more venture capital-like, as angels have become more sophisticated and more highly organized. Next after friends and family, angel investors typically invest in the $250,000 to $500,000 range, and larger networks of angels may have the capacity to invest upwards of $1 million into a seed round. However, following the "anything goes" era of dot-com investing, angels seem to have developed a strong preference for companies that are near-revenue, which rules out most technology-oriented start-up companies. This is especially true in the case of start-up drug discovery or medical device companies, which are usually some years away from a marketable product.

According to the National Venture Capital Association,[4] venture capital is money provided by professionals who invest alongside management in young, rapidly growing companies that have the potential to develop into significant economic contributors. Venture capital is an important source of equity for start-up companies. That's nice, isn't it? Then why is it so difficult these days to find a mainstream venture capital firm that is willing to fund a brand new company? The answer, I believe, has to do with a trend I refer to as the "mutual fundification" of the venture capital.

2.2 The "Mutual Fundification" of Venture Capital

During the dot-com boom, venture capitalists funded anything that moved. The New Economy, ushered in by dressed-down venture capitalists in open-collared shirts and Italian leather loafers, changed everything for investors, or so it seemed. In the brave new world of the Web, traditional metrics of business analysis no longer applied. Page-views were in, paying customers were passé. Institutional investors (university endowments, public and private pension funds, and insurance companies) who bankrolled the venture capital boom of the late 1990s could hardly throw cash fast enough at new and follow-on funds investing in day-old dot-coms. Institutional investors were getting in while the getting was good, primarily because the getting out—initial public offerings (IPOs)—were the closest bet to a sure thing that most investors had seen (or will see) in their lifetime.

---

[4] www.nvca.com

Of course, we all know how the New Economy ended. All those customer eyeballs glued to sticky Web sites had, pardon the pun, detached revenues. Recently seeded start-ups failed to generate the positive cash flow needed to pay their bills. Technology vendors and equipment lessors, many with their own mounting cash flow problems, stopped selling hardware and extending easy-term leases to cash-starved start-ups. As speculative fervor rose higher, the quality of new public offerings declined. Investment bankers could no longer generate the enthusiasm in new issues that Wall Street had relied upon to float shares in untested new companies. The IPO window closed, and a huge overhang of underwater venture-backed deals, worth less than their invested capital, loomed. Limited partners (LPs) in venture capital funds, who had grown accustomed to fast exits and fat profits, stopped bankrolling new ("emerging" in limited partner-speak) venture fund managers, and the party was over. The whole capital distribution system for start-ups ground to a halt. Start-ups, needy as ever for a fix of cash, went belly-up.

Thus began the eminently logical redirection of institutional capital into only the bluest of blue chip venture capital funds. The perennial top-performing funds, those with the most seasoned general partners and the most reliable investment track records, were perfectly positioned as the last safe harbor for institutional investors seeking some semblance of safety within the venture capital asset class. Alas, as individual blue chip funds' coffers approached the once unthinkable $1 billion mark, the general partners had a new problem on their hands: too much money. Think about it. You are a general partner at a blue chip, early-stage venture capital fund, you have hundreds of millions of dollars to deploy, and all these pesky start-ups are still lobbing you business plans, asking for a measly $1 to $3 million to develop the latest and greatest "disruptive" technology. What's a blue chip venture capitalist to do? Put yourself in the general partner's shoes (those Italian loafers we mentioned at the start of this section), and let's consider some alternatives:

a) Tell your limited partners that you would prefer to return some of their capital, because investing big funds is such a bother, and besides, your management fees have gotten too big (a few praiseworthy venture firms actually did this).

b) Break your big fund into a number of smaller funds so you and your partners can return to your traditional focus: identifying great new technologies and working side by side with company founders entrepreneurs to build new companies.
c) Start investing larger amounts of capital in later-stage deals, and if you still cannot deploy capital fast enough, form a PIPE fund (Private Investment in Public Equity) and invest in undervalued public companies.

If you are like most blue chip venture capital firms, or if you want to be, the correct answer is (c): go up market, start acting like a mutual fund, but keep the venture capitalist title because it's much cooler than being just another highly compensated institutional investor. This, my friend, is what I mean by the "mutual fundification" of the venture capital industry. Mainstream venture capital firms—especially the top quartile performers—have raised larger funds and, to deploy these funds efficiently, must make larger investments in later-stage companies. Since conducting due diligence on a start-up company can take as much time as conducting due diligence on a later-stage company, and with higher risk of making a mistake, mainstream venture capitalists have become loathe to dedicate resources to seed-stage investing. It is more efficient to invest in later-stage companies with larger capital requirements. Stated another way, for larger venture funds, investing in seed-stage companies is no longer practical. When you have a $500 million fund, making $1 million to $3 million investments in seed-stage companies that may be years away from an exit will not "move the needle" on the gauge of portfolio performance.

With friends and family investors and angels having limited capacity to fund much more than $250,000 to $1 million in seed capital, and with mainstream venture capitalists funding later-stage companies requiring more than $3 million, the reason for the seed-stage funding gap becomes easy to see. But there is more to the story.

2.3 The Rise and Fall of the Technology Incubator

Another reason for the seed-stage funding gap is the demise of the New Economy Technology Incubator (NETI). During the dot-com boom, it became fashionable to assemble under one roof all the necessary services for creating start-ups. It was no longer enough to fund start-ups one by one. The really smart investors wanted to *manufacture* start-ups, assembly line-style. As the reasoning went, if all start-ups, especially dot-coms, required essentially the same types of professional and support services (human resources, accounting, legal, administrative, etc.), why not pool these services and "sell" entrepreneurs on the advantages and efficiencies of "buying" a bundled package of start-up services? And, to top it off, the incubators would invest in their tenant companies, making an incubator deal all the more attractive to first-time entrepreneurs with a year or two of work experience and a million-dollar idea. The really slick aspect of this innovation in company creation—the NETI—was that investors could form a holding company of sorts, combine all of their incubated companies into the holding company's portfolio, and then sell shares in the holding company to the public. What a great idea! By purchasing shares in one of these NETIs, the average investor on Main Street could play the start-up market, so to speak, but without the hurdle of qualifying as an accredited investor[5] and without having to do the dirty work of seeking out individual start-up opportunities and conducting due diligence. With NETIs, you could buy a diversified portfolio of start-ups and rest assured that with the NETI's own in-house start-up experts keeping careful watch over the NETI's hatchlings, each start-up in the NETI's portfolio would get the best possible nurturing at the lowest possible cost. Starting in the mid-1990s, there was an effusion of NETIs being created to incubate start-ups. To run a technology incubator during the dot-com boom was to be a veritable New Economy pied piper, charming investors and entrepreneurs alike with the wonders of company creation. The problem was that those diversified portfolios of start-up companies growing in NETI incubators were actually the antithesis of diversified. Rather than spreading risk, NETIs concentrated it. To be sure, NETIs demonstrated enough early success to entice new investors. But, as investors' ability to digest new dot-com deals soured, incubators were left with a whole kitchen full of half-baked ideas.

---

[5] Under the Securities Act of 1933, a company that offers or sells its securities must register the securities with the Securities and Exchange Commission or find an exemption from the registration requirements. Accredited investors offer one such exemption. See the Chapter 2 Addendum for the official SEC definition of an "accredited investor."

To make matters even more precarious for NETIs, their founders often liked to play the real estate market. They invested in buildings to house their incubators, all but ensuring that when the start-up market tanked, overhead costs for physical infrastructure would make the NETI business model unsustainable.

Angel investors became enamored of NETIs, because NETIs seemed to institutionalize everything angels believed. If they could just pick the right start-up opportunities, give them a shared T1 line and access to a phone switch, and force-feed them with essential services, the rest would be easy. Predictably, up popped angel-backed incubators named for all things fast and fertile, from Gazelle Labs to Greenhouse Ventures. Alas, with the demise of the NETIs, another source of professionally managed seed capital dried up, contributing further to the emergence of the seed-stage funding gap.

2.4 Four Types of Seed Investors

As we noted in Chapter 1, there are four types of investors that typically fund start-ups: friends and family (those with a penchant for alliteration will add fools to this category), angel investors, early-stage venture capitalists, and to a limited extent, corporate investors.

Friends and Family

The friends and family of company founders are often the first source of capital for start-ups, for obvious reasons. For this discussion, the salient point about friends and family is that their upper threshold for investing is typically rather modest and not sufficient to move a technology-based venture far from the starting blocks. At best, friends and family can provide the initial capital to enable the would-be entrepreneur to begin the process of forming a company, from filing incorporation papers to opening a bank account and perhaps leasing some lab space. Most observers of start-up investing set the upper limit of what friends and family typically invest in a seed funding round at about $250,000. The downside of taking money from friends and family is that, by definition, they are not professional investors. Their amateur status can put a damper on later expressions of interest from professional investors, particularly venture capitalists and corporate investors. The existence of friends and family in the capital structure of a start-up company inevitably raises questions—some valid, others perhaps not. For example, have friends or family been given board seats? Do they wield an unreasonable amount of control? Have the investment transactions between the company and friends and family investors been properly documented? Have friends and family invested at an unreasonable valuation (i.e., too high) that will be a turnoff for potential follow-on investors? For investors who are considering investing in a start-up that has taken money from friends and family, these are questions that can be answered with adequate due diligence, but other questions and issues remain. In particular, can the participants in the friends and family round add value, such as management advice or useful contacts, or is their involvement more likely to be a burden? Certainly, friends and family can provide sufficient financing to help an entrepreneur when professional funding is out of reach. Yet, their value-added contribution is usually limited. Friends and family are really a means to an end, or more accurately, a means to a beginning. Despite their good intentions, rarely can friends and family help a start-up company bridge the seed-stage funding gap on their own.

Angel Investors

The next category of start-up investors is the angels. Angel investors can be defined as high net worth individuals who invest in entrepreneurial ventures, usually at an early stage.[6] Angel investors have become an engine of creation in the U.S. economy, thanks to their numbers and the vast wealth they accumulated in the stock market and real estate market throughout the 1990s and early-to-mid 2000s. As a class, angels now constitute the *de facto* seed-stage venture capital industry. In 2005, an estimated 227,000 individual angels invested roughly $23 billion in 49,500 entrepreneurial ventures.[7] Yet, despite their name, angels are anything but saviors. Their motivations are primarily financial, not altruistic.

---

[6] Guy Kawasaki, Inc.com, December, 2000
[7] University of New Hampshire Center for Venture Research. See www.unh.edu/cvr

During the Internet boom, angels gorged themselves on quick-buck deals, and their ranks swelled dramatically. This extraordinary period of no-brainer investments and easy exits produced a fundamental change in the behavior of angel investors. Traditionally, angels avoided attracting attention and were best contacted through discreet referrals from attorneys, accountants, and personal friends. Now, many angels carry business cards, belong to investor networks with catchy names, and solicit funding proposals through highly interactive Web sites.

Having pitched my fair share of deals to angel investors, I can say frankly that angel investors are not for everyone. While the majority of inexperienced money-seekers who make a pitch to angel investors will come up empty handed, somewhere between five percent and ten percent of start-ups that go through the angel vetting process will get funded.[8] . For many company founders in search of capital—with or without prior funding from friends and family—angel investors represent the next logical source of funding and are a great way to get free feedback. Just keep your expectations in check and be prepared for a thorough grilling.

For many first-time entrepreneurs, making the first fundraising pitch to a room full of angels will be one of the defining moments of the entrepreneurial experience. For those who make it this far yet do not receive angel funding, the process will prove to be more important than the outcome. Earning a presentation slot with an organized group of angels often requires completing a detailed, Web-based application, attending a preliminary meeting (sometimes called a "screening session") with a small group of angel representatives, submitting detailed plans and projections, and honing presentations. By willingly following this rigorous process, the open-mined and patient entrepreneur can learn how to approach investors, field penetrating questions, and maintain composure in the heat of a presentation.

---

[8] The University of New Hampshire Center for Venture Research (www.unh.edu/cvr) claims a funding yield (acceptance rate) for angel-backed investments of approximately 10 percent in 2005, down from a peak of 23.3 percent at the top of the tech bubble in 2000.

My closing words of advice for pitching to angels are: Play the game. Go with the flow. See where the process takes you until you decide you have had enough—or, you get funded. There is no harm in giving it your best shot and then taking a breather if angel funding is not in the cards.

The Angel Capital Association (ACA), an organization of angel investment groups throughout North America, offers informational and educational resources for angle investors and for companies seeking investment capital from angels. The ACA Web site also includes an excellent directory of angel investment groups that is searchable by region.[9]

Early-Stage Venture Capitalists

Venture capitalists can be classified according to the stage of investment in which they typically invest. Seed investors, by definition, invest in new start-ups. Early-stage investors usually invest after the seed round (i.e., during the "A, B, or C" investment rounds, with the letters designating the seniority of shares sold). Thus Series C shares would be senior to Series B shares, and so on. Some early-stage investors will also invest in start-ups, although this has become more of a rarity in recent years (for reasons explained earlier in this chapter). Late-stage venture capitalists typically invest in more mature companies at Series C, D, or later. In favorable times, companies at this stage are often being readied for an IPO.

Most mainstream venture capital firms, regardless of stage preference, are actually structured as two entities: the "fund," which is a partnership, and the "management company," which is the general partner of the fund. As limited partners in the fund, investors have no responsibility for its management. Investment decisions are made by the managing general partners. The operating expenses and salaries of the management company are paid out of "management fees," which typically range from 2.0 to 2.5 percent of capital under management.[10] Of course, larger funds require

---

[9] See www.angelcapitalassociation.org for more details.
[10] In practice, the calculation of management fees is much more complicated than simply multiplying the fee percentage by the size of the fund. Fees can vary annually based upon the age of the fund, the compensation the general partners might receive while serving as board members of portfolio companies, and other factors.

larger management teams, and larger management teams require larger management fees. Thus, there is a built-in incentive for venture firms to grow bigger. While the existence of larger venture capital funds may be a good thing for the venture capital industry, it is not necessarily a favorable development for entrepreneurs who are trying to raise seed capital. With their larger funds, mainstream venture capitalists have little incentive to focus on relatively small seed-stage investment opportunities. Indeed, by today's standards, the idea of venture capitalists funding promising start-ups fresh out of the garage or the academic laboratory seems downright quaint. It is a fact of life in the start-up world that many venture firms have succumbed to the corporate imperative to raise bigger funds, build bigger staffs, and invest in later-stage deals. Left behind is a smaller pool of venture capitalists that remain firmly committed to true seed-stage investing.

Corporate Investors

The venture investment arms of major corporations usually function as a "window" on new technology and new companies of potential strategic interest or threat to the corporation. Major pharmaceutical, medical device, chemicals, electronics, and high-tech companies with significant corporate investing arms include Amgen, Eli Lilly, Johnson & Johnson, Merck, Novartis, Pfizer, Medtronic, Guidant, BASF, Sony, IBM, Intel, Microsoft, and Oracle, to name just a few. In a sense, corporate investment professionals are technology scouts, searching out opportunities and threats about which their parent organizations and operating subsidiaries should be aware. In another sense, corporate investors are company ambassadors, providing a point of entry for entrepreneurs who wish to solicit corporate support for research and development alliances.

Corporate investors usually have one or several of the following objectives:

A. To invest in companies or technologies that may be of immediate or future interest for collaboration, product licensing, or acquisition
B. To support a current or future source of enabling technology
C. To foster the development of new products or markets that will drive sales of the corporation's own products or services

Corporate investors are supposed to be strategic and, therefore, forward-thinking. Yet, in practice, they are very risk-averse when it comes to investing in technologies with long paths to commercialization. Corporate investors will not invest in what they perceive to be "academic science projects." They will usually solicit internal feedback from corporate scientists and business managers about the strategic value or market appeal of new technologies before pursuing more in-depth discussions with fund-seeking academic founders or business entrepreneurs. In addition, corporate investors tend to follow the lead of mainstream investors that have sector-specific expertise, and they will usually invest in a funding round as part of a syndicate of well-known venture capital firms. This investment style lowers risk and saves the corporate investor the potential embarrassment that could result from making a poor investment.

Corporate investors have certain constraints resulting from their being part of large, bureaucratic organizations. Corporate investors tend to move slowly, and their decision-making is influenced by factors unique to big companies. These factors may include annual budgeting cycles, changes in corporate priorities, and senior management changes, to name a few. It is not unusual for a corporate venture arm to go from high-profile "vanity project" with strong management support to money-squandering boondoggle and target of the budget ax as the result of serious market downturn, or a change of CEO.

Because their reasons for making venture investments tend to be more strategic than financial (although the opportunity for financial gain is certainly important), corporate investors have a reputation for paying higher valuations than private venture capital firms. In addition, corporations have a somewhat mixed track record in terms of their sense of timing. Whereas private venture investors will persist through up and down markets, corporate investors have a habit of ramping up and winding down their venture operations in reaction to, rather than in anticipation of, market conditions.

2.5   A Hybrid Approach to Seed-Stage Investing

Because mainstream venture capital investors have pulled away from funding discovery-oriented start-ups, and enthusiasm for the dot-com-style technology incubator has faded, a new approach to seed-stage investing is needed. While low-tech product or service businesses, software companies, and Web-based businesses may appeal to and be adequately served by the typical angel investor, discovery-oriented life science start-ups (biotechnology, biopharmaceuticals) and high-tech start-ups (advanced materials, microelectronics, nanotechnology) have capital requirements, technical complexities, and lengthy development timelines that exceed the financial capacity, discipline-specific expertise, and patience of most angels.

Furthermore, most life science and high-tech start-ups are not amenable to conventional venture incubation, because these sorts of companies require customized laboratories and a range of scientific or technical skills that may be company-specific. One area where venture incubation continues to have some success is in medical devices. This is because medical device design and development do not usually involve unpredictable and time-consuming biological research, and they tend to draw upon engineering skills that are transferable from one company to another.

What is needed for seed-stage life science and technology investing is a new hybrid approach. This hybrid approach, one which my partners and I have pioneered, combines elements of angel investing, venture incubation, and venture capital into a business model uniquely suited to the special needs of life science and technology-oriented start-ups. The ideal approach is that of a new type of venture investment and development company, or VIDeC (pronounced "vee-dec"), that functions simultaneously and seamlessly as a founder of, investor in, and manager of new life science and technology companies. The typical company founder of a life science or technology company is a scientist or engineer who possesses considerable academic, clinical, or industry experience but lacks the capital, financial expertise, and business experience to raise capital on his or her own. The typical venture capitalist has plenty of capital and significant knowledge about technologies and industries, but he or she no longer has the time or incentive to do seed-stage deals. Enter the VIDeC—part investment company, part operating entity, whose *raison d'être* is to create, invest in, and manage technology start-ups. As shown in Figure 2, the VIDeC's central role is to bridge the seed-stage funding gap.

Figure 2
Role of the VIDeC: Bridging the Funding Gap

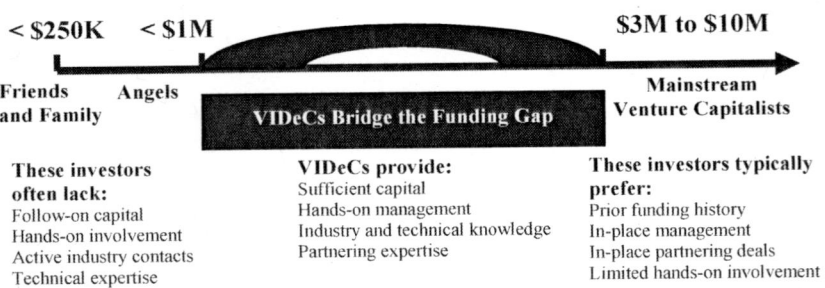

What makes VIDeCs different from NETIs is attitude. NETIs followed the "shake and bake" approach to doing start-ups: Just put all the company ingredients in a cubicle and add capital. Incubators were a product of their time, and they grew out of the hubris of investors who believed the success of a start-up company could be guaranteed by the provision of essential utilities from a wall outlet and some mentoring from a team of resident "gray-hairs." For a time, the NETI approach seemed to work. They sprung up around universities and in technology hotspots all over the United States. In retrospect, what these incubators created was the *appearance* of substance in start-ups that consisted of little more than a business plan and an impressive bank balance. Incubators conferred credibility on start-ups by providing a legitimate business address, an office, a telephone number, and a Web site. What incubators could not provide to their tenant companies were highly experienced managers who shouldered the kind of financial and career risk that make real entrepreneurs tick. Many NETIs were staffed with recently minted M.B.A.s and self-styled start-up gurus with minimal hands-on experience in founding and managing their own start-up companies.

In a sense, VIDeCs are successors to NETIs, run by experienced industry insiders, usually with significant technical backgrounds, who have a track record of founding and running companies. VIDeCs exhibit the following characteristics:

- They operate in the gap between angel investors and mainstream venture capital firms.
- They are professionally managed by industry insiders.
- They focus on the "front end" of start-ups—formation and early product development—rather than the "back end," or exit.
- They invest their own capital or have formal relationships with venture capital firms who agree to invest in VIDeC-sponsored companies.
- They offer the resources and expertise of an experienced team of product development specialists.
- They are not structured like traditional venture funds. They are more like operating companies.

The concept of the VIDeC has been put into action at several firms that specialize in the creation and early development of life science and medical device ventures, including Convergent Ventures, in Los Angeles, the Accelerator, in Seattle, and the Innovation Factory, in Atlanta.

I believe more firms based on the VIDeC model will arise to fill the void in seed-stage investing that has become a prominent feature of the start-up landscape in the mid-2000s.

Chapter 2 Addendum: SEC Definition of "Accredited Investor" [11]

Under the Securities Act of 1933, a company that offers or sells its securities must register the securities with the Securities and Exchange Commission (SEC) or find an exemption from the registration requirements. The act provides companies with a number of exemptions. For some of the exemptions, such as rules 505 and 506 of Regulation D, a company may sell its securities to what are known as "accredited investors."

The federal securities laws define the term "accredited investor" in Rule 501 of Regulation D as:

1. a bank, insurance company, registered investment company, business development company, or small business investment company;
2. an employee benefit plan, within the meaning of the Employee Retirement Income Security Act, if a bank, insurance company, or registered investment adviser makes the investment decisions, or if the plan has total assets in excess of $5 million;
3. a charitable organization, corporation, or partnership with assets exceeding $5 million;
4. a director, executive officer, or general partner of the company selling the securities;
5. a business in which all the equity owners are accredited investors;
6. a natural person who has individual net worth, or joint net worth with the person's spouse, that exceeds $1 million at the time of the purchase;
7. a natural person with income exceeding $200,000 in each of the two most recent years or joint income with a spouse exceeding $300,000 for those years and a reasonable expectation of the same income level in the current year; or
8. a trust with assets in excess of $5 million, not formed to acquire the securities offered, whose purchases a sophisticated person makes.

---

[11] Source: www.sec.gov/answers/accred.htm

3

Prospecting for Technology and Start-Up Opportunities

pros pec tor *n.*
One who explores an area for mineral deposits or oil

3.1 The Truth About Deal Flow

In some respects, a venture capital firm's popularity can be measured by its "deal flow." Simply defined, deal flow is the number of business plans, private placement memoranda, and "over the transom" funding requests that are submitted to an investor per unit of time. Having a large fund, prominent partners, or a reputation for funding successful or flashy deals is a surefire way to attract deal flow, in the same way that having a large house, being a celebrity, or driving an expensive car is a surefire way to attract solicitations from charities. When evaluating a new fund for possible investment, limited partners always ask about deal flow, because it is a metric they can easily understand. However, deal flow is an empty measure of deal *quantity* without regard to deal *quality*. The sad fact for most fund-seekers who approach angel investors or venture capitalists by mailing in business plans or e-mailing earnest requests for funding is that by doing so, they become part of that anonymous river of deal flow that sophisticated investors boast about with much fanfare and unceremoniously ignore.

How do experienced angel investors and venture capitalists really prospect for promising new technologies and investment opportunities? The answer to this question is as old as time. Seasoned investors find deals the way prospectors find gold: by digging. Whereas screening deal flow is largely a passive activity, prospecting for good deals requires pro-activity. This proactive searching can be narrowly focused, as with a miner and a pickax, broad and intensive, as in strip-mining, or purposely undirected, as in panning a stream for that elusive nugget. But regardless of the specific style of prospecting, the common thread is clear: The prospector knows what he or she is looking for and directs his or her efforts uniquely toward finding it.

3.2 Looking for Deals

3.2.1 My Own Route to Start-Up Land

I have wasted a lot of time looking for deals in all the wrong places. But if I had not done so, I never would have learned the error of my ways. This reminds me of the Waylon Jennings ballad[12], "Lookin' for Love," (with updated lyrics):

> *Looking for deals in all the wrong places*
> *Looking for deals in too many spaces*
> *Searching in plans, looking for traces*
> *Of what I'm dreaming of*

When I was just getting started as a seed-stage investor, I never really knew what I was dreaming of until I found it. When you don't have much capital to invest and no one knows for sure whether you are for real, every phone call from an entrepreneur seems to deserve your attention and every business plan sent your way looks like an opportunity. This was all part of my education, and I consider the first $25,000 I invested (and lost) as a co-founder and investor in an ill-fated computer peripheral company as my tuition in the school of hard knocks. I met the founder of this company at a breakfast networking session for a local venture association (more on this in a moment).

I had recently informed my then full-time employer—a company in which I had been the seventh employee and that went public several months into my tenure as director, and later vice president, of business development—that I had formed my own consulting firm to work with start-ups and that I

---

[12] Lookin' for Love, © Waylon Jennings

was going out on my own. I told my employer I had found a client that was developing a new type of medical imaging device, and that I wished to continue my relationship with my employer, but as a consultant rather than as an employee. My employer agreed. So, in 1997, I left behind the relative safety of a steady paycheck (in any young technology company, "safety" and "paycheck" are relative terms), planning to develop a consulting practice for life science and technology start-ups as a springboard to a career in venture investing.

At the time I founded my first company, Convergent Management Inc., my credentials consisted of an Ivy League undergraduate degree in psychology and biology, three years of New York City work experience with the health care division of a leading Madison Avenue advertising agency, an M.B.A. from another Ivy League institution, four years of corporate experience with a major pharmaceutical and consumer health care products company, and five years on the start-up rollercoaster at a medical image processing company. At the medical imaging company, I had been part of, and lived through, an IPO, growth from seven to over forty employees, the opening of satellite offices in Europe and California, the selling of $6 million in new business contracts, three rounds of layoffs, and the nuclear winter in the pharmaceutical and biotech industries brought on by the threat of Hillary Clinton's health care reform initiative, announced by President Bill Clinton in his State of the Union address of 1993. Having spent time pitching my company's newly public shares to stockbrokers at second-tier brokerage firms, having done business development in Silicon Valley and San Diego—where, in the mid to late 1990s, a drive through towns near Stanford University or the University of San Diego was like an automobile tour of NASDAQ—and having made some pitches to Sand Hill Road venture capitalists, I figured I had what it would take to become a successful advisor to fledgling biotech and medical technology companies, and, eventually, a venture capitalist in my own right. Wrong. Well, right on the consulting part. My client roster grew to more than two dozen companies, mostly in California but also in Canada and Israel. As for my venture capital aspirations, that would take time.

3.2.2 Don't Look Here

Networking Sessions

Back to the computer peripheral company that was my first seed investment. As I was saying, I met the founder of this company at a networking breakfast sponsored by a local venture association. In Silicon Valley, in the second half of the 1990s, a breakfast for a venture association might bring out dozens of venture capitalists, a retinue of attorneys and accountants with active start-up practices, and an entourage of fund-hungry entrepreneurs expecting the opportunity to make acquaintance with some investors and swap business cards. But in Los Angeles, not exactly a hot bed of mainstream venture capital (but Mecca for movie deals), a venture association breakfast circa 1998 was a gathering place for newly self-declared angel investors, not-so-experienced consultants, representatives from local law firms and accounting firms trawling for new business, and hordes of inexperienced, first-time entrepreneurs. Newbies. Novices. Tyros. For better or worse, this was my initial hunting ground.

University Technology Transfer Offices

One of my partners, a former technology transfer officer at a leading private research institution, has taught me a thing or two about doing business with academic centers. One of his pearls of wisdom is: If you are looking for good start-up opportunities, do not waste your time hanging around the local university technology transfer office. On its face, this would seem like odd advice. Technology transfer offices are repositories for a university's intellectual property (IP). It is the technology transfer office's responsibility to encourage faculty members, graduate students, and post-docs to disclose new discoveries and inventions, and to decide which of these disclosures merits the filing of patent applications. The technology transfer office retains outside patent counsel to prepare and submit filings to the U.S. Patent and Trademark Office (and the USPTO's international counterparts) and pays the legal fees for this work. To recover the cost of protecting the university's IP and recoup the university's investment in its personnel and facilities, the technology transfer office seeks to generate option fees, licensing fees, royalties, and capital gains from university spin-outs. Some top-tier, research-based academic institutions—such as the

Massachusetts Institute of Technology, Columbia University, and the California Institute of Technology—are quite successful at generating substantial returns on their IP assets. These and other institutions receive hundreds of millions of dollars in federal funding annually for basic and applied research from federal granting agencies such as the National Institutes of Health, the Department of Defense, the Defense Advanced Research Projects Agency, the Office of Naval Research, and the Department of Energy attract substantial corporate funding. With this government and corporate largesse, research institutions go about their business, which of course, is to create knowledge, make new discoveries, and invent new technologies. It is a big job for a university to keep track of all the IP generated by its faculty and students under the auspices of government grants or privately funded projects, and the task falls on the technology transfer office. Perhaps you can see where I am going with all this. Due to the nature of their work, technology transfer offices at big universities are bureaucratic organizations. It is the job of the university tech transfer office to administer the never-ending flow of IP being generated every day at its parent institution. To complicate matters, the technology transfer office must ensure that its handling of IP assets—of the parceling out of licenses and the assignment of rights—adheres to state and federal regulatory guidelines that govern the proper management of IP created with state or federal dollars.

Although the role of the technology transfer office is primarily administrative, it is also responsible for marketing the university's IP to potential licensees in the private sector, including corporations, start-ups, and venture investors. The marketing task is usually accomplished through the publishing of Web-based listings of available technologies, the production of scientific conferences and technology fairs, and personal outreach to companies and investors. Technology transfer offices at private universities are typically smaller, less bureaucratic, and less constrained than their public university counterparts by state regulations, budgets, and politics. Consequently, most entrepreneurs, investors, and start-up executives would probably agree that it is easier to do a licensing deal with the technology transfer office of a private institution than a public one.

Aside from reasons of inaccessibility and bureaucracy, especially at public institutions, it is not advisable to spend a lot of time prospecting for start-up-worthy technology at technology transfer offices, because the best technology is usually found at the source—individual faculty members and graduate students—rather than at the repository—the technology transfer office. Ultimately, the technology transfer office functions as a clearinghouse of technology. All of an institution's potentially patentable discoveries and inventions make their way to the technology transfer office. However, more often than not, the "good stuff," the most interesting and potentially valuable IP, is found and captured by corporate research or licensing executives, venture investors, and savvy entrepreneurs before it makes its way to the technology transfer office. There are two reasons why this is true. First, as already explained, in-the-know investors and corporate licensing executives will go directly to faculty members to find interesting technology and interface with the technology transfer office after some interesting technology has been found. Second, faculty members and graduate students who are more experienced with the ways of the business world will seek out and interact with potential investors and corporate licensees before surrendering their most commercially interesting discoveries and inventions to the technology transfer office. This is not to say business-wise faculty willfully circumvent the technology transfer office (although, sometimes, they do). But, the more experienced faculty members have learned that the right time to go to the technology transfer office about licensing out a piece of technology is *after* a deal has been put on the table, and not before. Thus, if you are an inexperienced entrepreneur or seed investor, starting your search for interesting technology at your local university's technology transfer office will virtually guarantee that what you will find has either been submitted by less commercially savvy faculty members, or has already been picked over and rejected by more experienced industry representatives or investors.

Thus, while it is a good idea to familiarize yourself with the tech transfer office at your local university, it would not be the most productive use of your time to prospect for start-up opportunities there.

Another reason not to start your technology prospecting at the technology transfer office is that, as a new investor or entrepreneur, you are not likely to be in a position—either financially, or in terms of your limited track record—to establish early control of a piece of technology. Gaining control of IP, or of a negotiation with the technology transfer office, usually requires proof of the ability to fund a company, conduct a research and development program, and commercialize a technology. Experienced technology transfer officers know what to look for in a prospective licensee and will not want to expend much effort providing information, working out a non-disclosure agreement, or negotiating terms of a technology transfer and licensing agreement with investors or entrepreneurs that lacks a track record. In addition, technology transfer officers will usually direct their efforts to those potential licensing deals or start-up opportunities that have the full support of the faculty member(s) whose technology is the subject of interest. Thus, if you, as an investor or entrepreneur, approach the technology transfer office and express an interest in starting a company around a particular piece of technology, the first person the technology transfer officer will contact about your inquiry is likely to be the faculty member who invented the technology. If you have not previously spent time building a relationship with this faculty member, establishing a rapport, and building trust, you have little likelihood of gaining his or her cooperation or that of the technology transfer officer.

Faculty Mixers, "Venture Capital Days," and Start-Up "Boot Camps"

It can certainly be helpful to get to know faculty members and graduate students at university-sponsored or departmental events that are designed to facilitate networking between individuals in the academic, business, and investment communities. I have attended many such events, and they are a good way to get a feel for the territory and to do some fact finding by what the legendary stock market investor, Phil Fisher[13], referred to as the "scuttlebutt approach." According to Fisher, some of the most valuable information about companies and stocks can be found simply by picking up the phone or walking around and talking to people. The same can be said for investors in start-ups. Start-up investors can analyze market reports and scrutinize scientific publications all day long, but the really useful information is found by getting out and talking to scientists, and picking up the "vibe" about which faculty members and which academic labs are generating the most exciting work.

I recommend networking on the campuses of leading academic centers. I just caution against going overboard. The problem with on-campus

---

[13] Fisher's investment classic, *Common Stocks for Uncommon Profits*, was first published in 1958.

networking events is that they tend not to attract the busiest, most experienced, and most sought-after faculty members. These top-performing faculty members are too busy running their labs, writing grant proposals, traveling to conferences, and meeting with corporate collaborators to burn valuable time attending the latest university-sponsored "venture capitalist roundtable" or "start-up boot camp." I used to go out of my way to attend such events, thinking I would make important contacts and generate valuable leads, but more often than not, I found I had blown another few hours meeting perfectly nice people who could not help me get to where I wanted to go. The business-savvy faculty members—the ones with the well-funded labs, the most consulting gigs, and the most active involvement with start-ups—simply have better things to do with their time than to be frequent attendees at on-campus mixers. In sum, the faculty members you really want to meet at campus mixers are the ones who aren't there.

Consultants and Advisors without a Track Record of Success

Start-Up Land is populated by a host of independent consultants, advisors, and colorful posers. What unites these characters with their prey, the entrepreneur, is a never-ending search for money: nobody has it, and everybody wants it. The sorry truth in Start-Up Land is that most people who do not already have money are likely to stay that way. While it was obvious to Willy Sutton why people rob banks, it fails to dawn on a lot of people that doing business with start-ups is not, in general, a lucrative proposition. Thus, in Start-Up Land, there are a lot of consultants and advisors who are hoping to hitch their wagon to a promising start-up, but can barely make their own ends meet. If you are an entrepreneur looking for help, or a seed investor looking for leads, are consultants and advisors without a track record of success the kind of people from whom you should be getting your start-up intelligence? I don't think so. If you seek the advice and counsel of consultants or advisors about starting a new company or investing in one, be sure to engage people who are more experienced and successful than you are. But you need to keep in mind that you are unlikely to find successful consultants and advisors hanging around networking sessions and informational events intended for new entrepreneurs. Experienced entrepreneurs and seed investors learn about start-up opportunities by doing their own spade work and trusting their own judgment.

Conferences Featuring "How To" Panels and Start-Up "Case Studies"

Conferences for entrepreneurs and venture investors, with their panels of speakers and their case studies of high-profile deals, generate the proverbial background radiation of the start-up universe. By the time the interesting news reaches the audience, the source from which it has emanated has long burned out. That is to say, to hear the really interesting information at start-up conferences, the best place to be is by the coffee urn, not in the meeting room. There was a time when I would eagerly attend industry and investment conferences to hear about the latest technology trends and investment themes. Now, I can barely sit still for five minutes at one of these conferences before I need to escape to the coffee urn, check my voicemail, and scan name tags for useful contacts. The best way to make use of conferences is to make new acquaintances, pick up scuttlebutt, collect business cards for later follow-up, and avoid burning all your time listening to venture capitalists and start-up CEOs prattle on about their latest conquests and over-subscribed funding rounds.

Seed-stage investors and entrepreneurs in search of opportunities need to be close to the action. The action can be found by chatting informally with academic scientists, reading scientific publications, mining the Web, and by networking with industry insiders.

3.2.3 Do Look Here

Established Faculty

If you are looking for technology and want to know which university faculty members are doing the most interesting research, just ask other faculty members. It should come as no surprise that faculty members would be an excellent source of feedback and referrals for investors and entrepreneurs who are prospecting for promising technology on which to base a new company. My partners and I rely upon this method of technology prospecting, because it is highly personal and relatively reliable. When my partners and I go looking for technology, what we are really looking for is scientists or engineers with whom we would be very comfortable co-founding a new company. Faculty members, particularly senior faculty members, are usually quite familiar with the research interests of all their departmental colleagues. Indeed, faculty members probably know more about the personalities and idiosyncrasies of their colleagues than anyone else outside of their colleagues' immediate families. For this reason more than any other, I strongly recommend that you get to know faculty members well enough that you can solicit their candid advice and feedback about their colleagues, because looking for great technology is really about looking for great people.

Referrals from Other Investors

Basically, there are two types of investor referrals: useful ones and throw-aways. The useful ones come from other investors who know you personally or professionally, respect your time and interests, and are sincere about being helpful to both you and the scientist or entrepreneur who seeks funding. The throw-aways come from investors who do not know you very well and are probably just looking to unload some annoying entrepreneur while appearing to be helpful. Whenever I get an unexpected telephone call that begins with "Josh So-and-So from Such-and-Such Investment Company suggested I call you because you firm invests in start-ups...," I feel like I have once again become an unwitting participant in a game of telephone tag. "Josh mentioned that he heard you invest in life science deals, and my company is looking for funding to launch a new line of proprietary neutraceuticals based upon all natural herbal remedies from China." Tag. I'm it.

Happily, on more than a few occasions, I have received legitimate and interesting referrals from venture capitalists or corporate investors. These referrals have typically involved investment opportunities that the venture capitalist or corporate investor considered to be too early-stage for a mainstream venture firm or corporate investor, but perhaps just right for a seed-stage investor like myself whose firm focuses on the creation and early development of companies that may ultimately become attractive Series A or B investment opportunities. These are the kinds of referrals that seed-stage investors appreciate. I view these well-considered referrals as evidence that I have established a useful niche for myself in the minds of my fellow investors. These "good" referrals also create an opportunity for me and my partners to show what we can do, which usually means talking with the referred scientist or entrepreneur, providing some constructive feedback, and occasionally arranging a follow-up meeting. Taking these simple steps in response to a referral from another investor makes me look good, makes the other investor look good, and generates the sort of mutual respect and goodwill that will eventually pay dividends.

In one such case, I received a referral from a major corporate investor regarding a group of academic and government scientists who were trying to develop a robotic system for the rehabilitation of people with spinal cord injuries. I was informed by the corporate investor that the technology in question was still too early for corporate investment, but that it might be an ideal situation for a firm like my own to consider, given the need for seed capital and hands-on start-up management. Beginning with this initial telephone referral, I and several of my colleagues made some preliminary phone calls to the scientists who were leading the rehabilitation project, which then led to a two-month series of meetings, technology demonstrations, and business development discussions involving neuroscientists, bioengineers, robotics engineers, medical device experts, and a handful of major health care and medical device companies. Although my partners and I eventually found that some of the technology and personnel issues associated with this start-up opportunity were too complicated for our liking, we learned some valuable lessons about evaluating start-up opportunities involving academic and government scientists, about interacting with corporate investors, and about investing (or not investing, as this case turned out) in the field of rehabilitative medicine. In addition, my colleagues and I were able to share the results of our business plan development and due diligence process with the corporate investor who originally referred the opportunity to us, thus affording us the opportunity to demonstrate our capabilities.

Attorneys

Attorneys can be another good source of referrals and feedback regarding technologies and start-up opportunities worthy of consideration. But for the restrictions of attorney-client confidentiality, who better to know and convey the prospects of a scientific founder or entrepreneur than his or her legal counsel? Of course, it is essential that you respect the referring attorney's opinions enough to give credence to his or her referrals.

3.3 A Structured Approach to Technology Sourcing and Opportunity Development

You may conclude from the foregoing discussion that prospecting for technology and start-up opportunities is basically a matter of effective networking and searching in the right places. For amateur investors or entrepreneurs, this may well be true, and it may even work. But professional seed-stage investors cannot build a solid track record without a plan.

Having been intimately involved in the creation, funding, and early management of more than a dozen technology-based start-up companies over the past ten years, either individually or as part of our current team, my partners and I have devised a structured approach to technology sourcing and opportunity development that is illustrated in Figure 3. Even though our day-to-day work of prospecting for technology and managing our portfolio companies does not follow a fixed pattern of activity, we have found that nearly everything we do to develop our investment opportunities and build our companies falls within the five boxes in Figure 3 that are aligned beneath the heading "Value Creation." Value creation is what it takes to turn raw science and technology into a fundable business proposition.

It will be instructive to look at each of the major headings in Figure 3—"Technology Sourcing," "Value Creation," "Seed Funding," and "Series A Funding"—to understand the venture prospecting, development, and investment process.

Figure 3 [14]
The Company Sourcing, Creation, and Funding Process

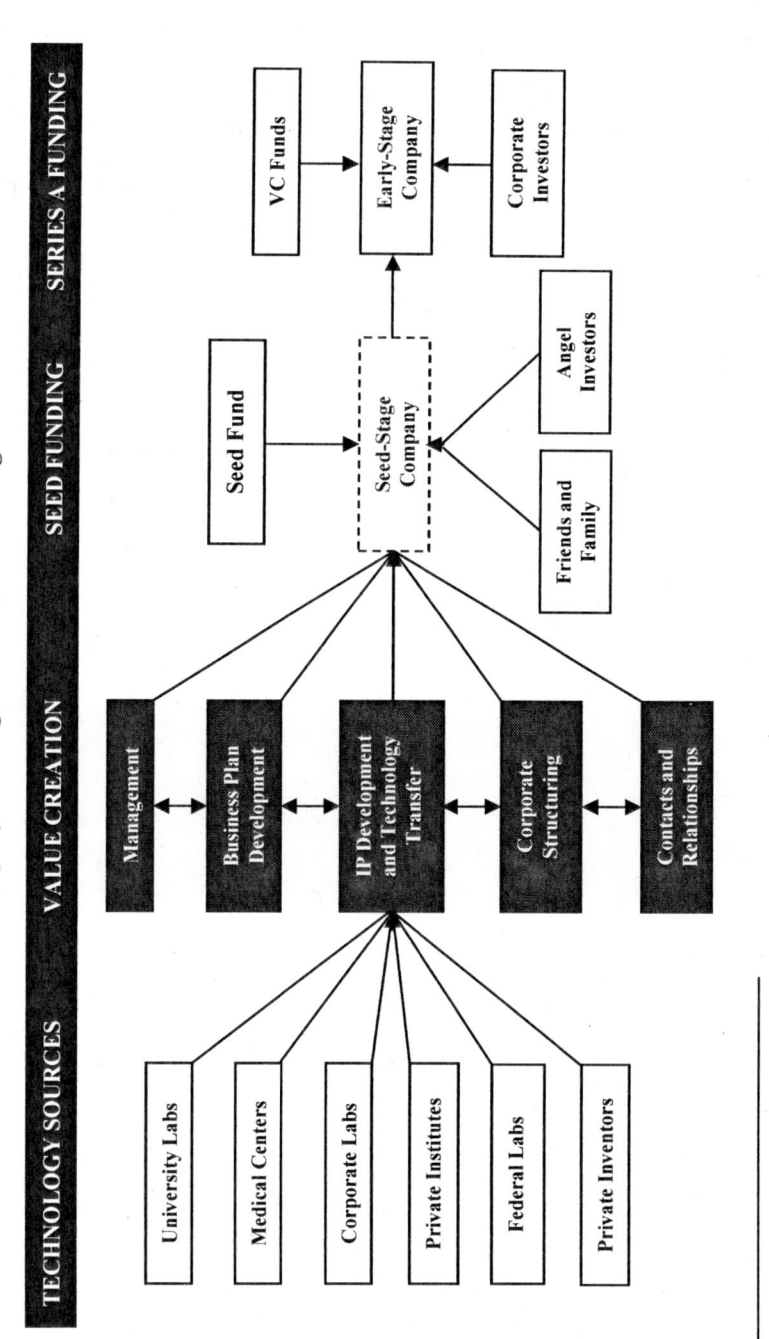

| TECHNOLOGY SOURCES | VALUE CREATION | SEED FUNDING | SERIES A FUNDING |

Technology Sources:
- University Labs
- Medical Centers
- Corporate Labs
- Private Institutes
- Federal Labs
- Private Inventors

Value Creation:
- Management
- Business Plan Development
- IP Development and Technology Transfer
- Corporate Structuring
- Contacts and Relationships

Seed Funding:
- Seed Fund → Seed-Stage Company
- Angel Investors → Seed-Stage Company
- Friends and Family → Seed-Stage Company

Series A Funding:
- VC Funds → Early-Stage Company
- Corporate Investors → Early-Stage Company

---

[14] © Convergent Ventures LLC.

Technology Sourcing

Seed-stage investors and start-up entrepreneurs should become familiar with each of the six sources of almost all innovation in the life sciences and technology: university labs, medical centers, corporate labs, private institutes, federal labs, and private inventors. If you are fortunate enough to live in a geographic area with one or more major academic centers, odds are that you are going to have access to multiple sources of promising technologies. It is no coincidence that the greatest concentration of start-up activity and venture investment can be found in the three geographic regions that have by far the greatest number of world-class academic centers: the San Francisco Bay area (with Stanford, UCSF, and UC Berkeley), Boston/Cambridge (with Harvard and MIT), and Southern California (with UCLA, UCSD, UCI, UCSB, USC, and Caltech).

For the purpose of this discussion, I will focus more closely on Southern California. The four University of California campuses between Santa Barbara and San Diego constitute some of the most fertile hunting grounds for new technology to be found anywhere. These four campuses, their affiliated medical centers, the federal laboratories they manage (for example, Lawrence Livermore, Los Alamos, and NASA's Jet Propulsion Laboratory, which is managed by Caltech) receive billions of dollars in federal, state, corporate, and non-profit funding. Where money flows, business grows, and consequently, if you live in Southern California, you need not look further than your own backyard to find a virtually limitless supply of start-up opportunities, almost all of which (at least those sourced from universities) have benefited from prior funding from Uncle Sam or the State of California. Thanks largely to funding from the National Institutes of Health[15] and the Department of Defense,[16] and from state programs in the emerging fields of nanotechnology and stem cells, Southern California

---

[15] In 2005, the greater Los Angeles and San Diego areas pulled in a whopping $1,786,759,336 in NIH grants, accounting for 8.51 percent of all NIH funding in the United States. The same areas raked in another $60,710,673 in SBIR grants, or 9.7 percent of the United States total. In 2005, the Los Angeles area alone blew away the San Francisco area in NIH grants, $996.8 million to $786.6 million. That's a $210 million difference, but who's counting?

[16] In 2002, five Southern California universities ranked among the top twelve academic recipients of DOD grants, with a combined total of $121.1 million in grant funding.

is arguably the richest source of scientific and technological innovation anywhere in the world. The best way to mine this territory is to become as familiar with its university campuses as you are with the campus of your own *alma mater*. Perhaps the single most important reason I enjoy being a seed-stage investor and start-up entrepreneur is that I am a student at heart and I feel completely at home walking around university campuses and wandering the halls of academic buildings. To be specific, when I find myself walking along the tree-shaded pathway of Caltech's main pathway on my way to a meeting with a faculty member, or heading to some on-campus meeting at UCLA, I feel as if I am in my element—back at school, in an intensely intellectual environment, with my mind racing, and happy as a clam. This is the feeling I spent the first fifteen years of my career searching for, and it was not until I became a seed-stage investor that I recaptured it. I would do this work without getting paid for it. And I have.

So, where were we? Ah, yes. Prospecting at universities. Aside from having your own contacts with or referrals to university faculty members, a great way to get started is the Web. Say you consider drug discovery an interesting area for investment, because the population in western societies is aging, people want to preserve their active lifestyles, and federal grants ensure a constant source of funding for academic research. If you live near a major academic center that includes a medical school and a hospital, all you need to do is type some keywords into a Web search engine, including the name of your university of interest, and you will turn up the names of academic scientists doing research in specific areas of drug discovery. Of course, if you know what you are looking for, you can zero in on those research groups and individual scientists who are doing relevant work. With this information, you are a phone call or an e-mail away from a meeting with the scientists who could be sources of technology for or scientific founders of a new company. This is not just a conceptual approach to finding promising technology. This is exactly the way my partners and I identified the technology and the scientific founders for the first portfolio company that we created together. We had spent six months rummaging around the field of membrane proteins—which are important but difficult targets for drug discovery—and one of my colleagues happened upon the Web sites for several university research groups that were engaged in a multi-year collaboration to study the structure and function of a particular class of membrane proteins called ion channels. Based upon a closer review of departmental and faculty Web pages, it was clear that the two professors who led this research collaboration were highly respected scientists, prolific authors of peer-reviewed scientific publications, and leaders in their field of research, which straddled the disciplines of molecular biology, synthetic organic chemistry, electrophysiology, and computational chemistry. In other words, the two faculty members appeared to be exactly the kinds of scientists with whom a seed-stage life science investor would want to meet. Meet we did, and approximately four months later, my partners and I and these two university professors founded a new drug discovery company together.

I recount this story to illustrate several key points about sourcing technology and start-up opportunities from universities. First, you need to know what you are looking for. Otherwise, your search will be unfocused, you will cast your net too wide, and you will be overwhelmed by what you haul in. Start with areas you know a lot about due to your own academic background, research interests, industry experience, and aptitude for learning. I like to stick to areas that interest me intellectually. Thus, a litmus test I use routinely is to ask myself whether I could read about the subject matter of my potential investment day and night and still not get bored. Second, you need to look for highly credible scientists as the source of your technology and, potentially, as the scientific co-founders for your new company. Doing start-ups is difficult enough under the best of circumstances, but doing a start-up with technology that comes from an unknown lab or from scientists who are going to have a hard time passing the credibility test—with other scientists in their field, with potential corporate partners, and with seasoned investors—is out of the question. My partners and I simply will not do start-ups without a founding scientist, engineer, or medical practitioner whose reputation is both well established and universally credible. To do less is asking for trouble. This is why my partners and I now follow a general rule, based upon our own bad experiences, that when searching for technology and scientific founders, we steer clear of junior faculty, newly minted Ph.D.s, and post-docs with entrepreneurial aspirations.

Value Creation

Once you have set your sights on a particular area of interest for a start-up and have found technology that addresses your chosen market, the real work begins. Not that prospecting for technology isn't hard work, but prospecting has a beginning and an end. Value creation never stops. If it does, it will only be a matter of time before your once-promising start-up goes south, and you will be looking for a steady paycheck. In Exhibit 1, value creation is broken down into five elements, working outward from the first: IP Development and Technology Transfer (Chapters 6 and 7 are devoted to these topics). We could argue about whether the first step in value creation should be business plan development, but until you can identify and gain control of some proprietary technology or know-how, or the means to create them, having a business plan will not get you very far.

**Exhibit 1
The Five Elements of Seed-Stage Value Creation**

1. IP Development and Technology Transfer Value creation begins with the identification of unique and commercially attractive technology that can be protected. Short of having a physical technology asset (e.g., a prototype) or an asset that can be reduced to writing (e.g., a verifiable discovery or reproducible methodology), value creation could also begin with the existence of trade secrets or know-how. You need not have issued patents to start a company, although having patents does help establish the start-up company's initial valuation (i.e., the dollar amount of what the company is worth at the time of initial capitalization).
2. Business Plan Development The value of a business plan is often misunderstood by inexperienced entrepreneurs and investors. Commonly, people place far too much emphasis on quantity rather than quality. Verbosity and excessive detail cannot compensate for the lack of clear thought and concision. More than just a description of a business model, a good business plan speaks volumes about a company's ability to communicate effectively with its target audience.

3. Corporate Structuring
Inexperienced entrepreneurs and investors tend to underestimate the importance of creating a corporate structure (appropriate formation documents, board composition, capitalization plan, etc.) that creates a solid legal, financial, and governance foundation for the start-up company. Thus, when properly considered by experienced company founders with access to expert counsel, proper corporate structuring is an important step in value creation for a start-up.
4. Management
Start-ups are of little value without sound management, but inexperienced entrepreneurs and investors often make the dangerous mistake of not spending enough time learning and implementing good management principles and practices. Good management adds value by ensuring that all five elements of seed-stage value creation receive the proper amount of expert attention.
5. Contacts and Relationships
Seasoned entrepreneurs and investors are valued not just for *what* they know, but *who* they know. Contacts and relationships are the force multipliers that enable a highly engaged seed investor to take an amorphous pile of technology and ideas and turn it into a business.

This may not be the case for certain service businesses or for companies based on hard assets such as real estate or natural resources, but for the kinds of start-ups that concern us here, the need for technology is self-evident.

By combining the five elements of value creation, the seed-stage investor and the entrepreneur or founding scientist(s) can convert raw technology, ideas, and vision into a fundable business entity.

Seed Funding

Inexperienced entrepreneurs and investors often believe the seed funding event leads to value creation. In theory, this sounds logical enough. In practice, exactly the opposite is true. Value creation leads to seed funding. Until the five elements of value creation are in place, there is no business to fund. This is why my partners and I spend so much time thinking about a business opportunity and how we would put a company together *before* we invest. Planning precedes funding. Execution follows. This may be the most valuable lesson I have learned since I became a seed-stage investor. Most first-time entrepreneurs and seed investors assume money is required to create value, which is why new entrepreneurs are always in a rush to put a fundraising document in front of investors, and new investors spend too much time reviewing business plans. Experienced entrepreneurs and investors recognize that it is putting the cart before the horse to slap together a seed funding round before adequate attention has been paid to each of the five steps of value creation. The seed funding event should mark the culmination, not the commencement, of the value creation process. If one follows the structured approach to technology prospecting and opportunity development I have described thus far, the seed funding event should require little more than the preparation, review, and execution of the requisite legal and financial documents. The fundable business entity should be ready to receive start-up capital and commence operations.

Series A Funding

As you can see from the flow of events in Figure 3, I have chosen to delay the participation of venture capital investors and corporate investors in the venture development process until after the seed round (i.e., until the Series A round). This timing of initial investment participation by mainstream venture capitalists and corporate investors has become the norm in the mid-2000s. After the dot-com bubble burst, mainstream venture capitalists and corporate investors reigned in their seed-stage investing activities significantly, to the point where seed-stage investments constitute just a tiny fraction of all investments made by traditional venture capital firms and corporate investors. For example, of the $6.66 billion in health care venture capital investments made in 2005, a paltry $102 million were committed to seed-stage investments. That is just 1.5 percent. By contrast, in 2005, health care venture investors committed $4.1 billion to product development-stage companies, $2.1 billion to companies shipping product, and $334 million to profitable companies.[17] These figures should dispel any remaining doubt about the existence of a seed-stage funding gap.

---

[17] VentureOne, Dow Jones & Company Inc., 2006

4

The Psychology of Company Founders

psy·chol·o·gy *n.*
The science that deals with mental processes and behavior

4.1   Founders and the Concept of the Normal Curve

To understand the motivations and behaviors of a company founder, you either have to be one or be very good at reading people. Choosing founders with whom to start a company may well be the most important decision an investor will make. To fail in this decision is to risk not only one's money, but worse, one's sanity. Once, I almost lost both. If you are going to be a seed investor for long, it is imperative that you hone your skills at sizing up potential founders and that you develop the confidence to trust your own instincts. As Napolean Hill, author of *Think and Grow Rich*, proclaimed during one of his famously homespun lectures: "Fool me once, shame on you. Fool me twice, shame on me."[18]

Evaluating founders is not a process that can be reduced to a spreadsheet, but some statistical principles and a degree in psychology help. An apt concept is that of the Gaussian distribution, also called the normal distribution, or simply, the normal curve. Statistical Principle Number One: Few founders are normal. I do not mean founders are not good people; the kind you can drink a beer with after work. I am talking about aptitudes and

---

[18] "Your Right to be Rich" lecture series. Napolean Hill. High Roads Media, Arden, NC. © 2001 by the Napolean Hill Foundation.

attitudes. The best and worst of founders are "off the chart" in one or the other direction. Versus the general population, founders, good or bad, deviate from the mean. Most people in the general population simply do not contemplate being a company founder. Even fewer actually take the steps necessary to earn the title.

Figure 4 [19]
The Standard Normal Distribution of Founders

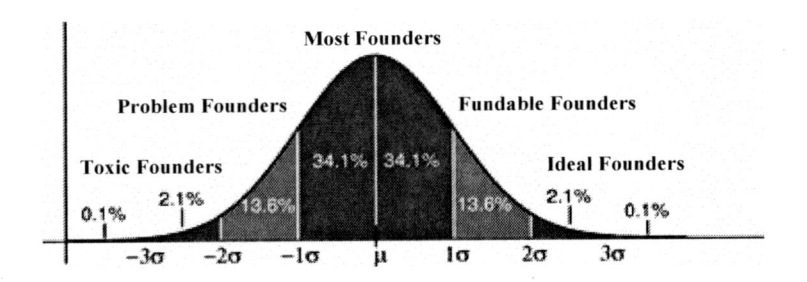

[Bell curve diagram showing the standard normal distribution with the following labels: Most Founders (center), Problem Founders (left of center), Fundable Founders (right of center), Toxic Founders (far left), Ideal Founders (far right). Percentages shown: 0.1%, 2.1%, 13.6%, 34.1%, 34.1%, 13.6%, 2.1%, 0.1%. X-axis labeled: -3σ, -2σ, -1σ, μ, 1σ, 2σ, 3σ.]

It can be helpful to think of potential or actual company founders that you meet in terms of where you would place them on the normal curve.

Toxic Founders

These will threaten any investor's sanity. Toxic founders lurk out there on the left tail of the normal curve, two or more standard deviations (σ) below the mean (μ). Toxic founders are the egomaniacs and control freaks that will make your life a living hell until either you get rid of them or they get rid of you. The problem with toxic founders is that they can be like chameleons. In social situations, they may be charming, cordial, perhaps even fun. In public engagements, they may project leadership qualities and great intelligence. But, in private, they may be egotistical and intransigent. The only way to acquire immunity to toxic founders is through sustained and painful exposure. Once immunity is established, exposure to a new toxic founder may provoke reactions ranging from mild redness and itching to full-blown anaphylactic shock, including hives, airway obstruction, and

---

[19] Illustration of a normal curve reproduced from www.wikipedia.org, with labels added by the author.

an irresistible urge to change careers. If you have had your own unfortunate encounter with a toxic founder, you know what I mean.

Problem Founders

These will consume most of an investor's time and patience. Problem founders lie between one and two standard deviations below the mean. Identifying problem founders before it's too late can pose a real challenge for inexperienced investors, because problem behavior may not come to the surface until after an investment has been made, when all the romancing and the honeymoon are over and the day-to-day grind of building a company reveal the founder's true colors. What kind of behavior marks a problem founder? Any kind that finds you spending an inordinate amount of time trying to correct it. And there's the rub: Problem behavior in problem founders cannot be corrected. Problem behavior in a founder is generally incurable. You can marginalize a problem founder, but the only real solution is to remove him or her from the company.

Most Founders

These are within one standard deviation of the mean, and they are not fundable. They are perfectly decent people, but they suffer from being too normal and have few (if any) remarkable characteristics that make them stand out in a crowd of money-seekers.

Fundable Founders

These will receive the bulk of venture dollars (seed or later). Most fundable founders fall between one and two standard deviations above the mean. Fundable founders stand out because they have special aptitudes or attributes. For example, they are particularly talented chemists or electrical engineers, are entrepreneurial in spirit, or they are highly charismatic deal-makers. Fundable founders tend to be well balanced, relatively cool under pressure, and, above all, reasonable.

Ideal Founders

These attract funding from the best venture funds. Ideal founders are exceedingly rare, falling more than two standard deviations above the mean. The real outliers are founders such as Bill Gates, Steve Jobs and Michael Dell, who are six-sigma events (i.e., way out there on the right side of the curve, where it nearly touches the X-axis). Ideal founders are flat-out smarter than everyone else, which by itself does not make them ideal. What makes them ideal is that they excel not only in their specialized disciplines (i.e., science, technology, systems), but also in business (especially marketing) and leadership.

4.2 What to Look for in a Founder and How to Find it

Understanding the concept of the normal curve will certainly help you in your search for fundable, or better yet, ideal founders. But just as some coursework in geometry won't make you a Euclid, a working knowledge of the normal curve of founders will not make you king of Sand Hill Road. Sizing up founders is part art, part science, but mostly instinct. Some investors have a special gift for finding great founders in a crowd. The rest of us have to work at it and may still do no better than average. Fortunately, seed-stage investors can learn from experience how to spot better-than-average founders. I claim no extraordinary ability in the founder-finding department, but here is what I have learned:

Finding Fundable Founders Takes Time

Getting to know a potential founder can be a months-long process, and it should not be rushed. Successful seed-stage investing depends upon establishing and building a relationship of credibility and trust between the seed investor and the company founder(s). To get to know a company's founder(s), the investor should seek to engage the founder(s) in a variety of situations ranging from scientific meetings, to business gatherings, to social get-togethers. The investor should also meet the founder on his or her "home turf" (the founder's lab, for example), at the investor's office, and at a neutral location such as a restaurant. The goal for the investor should be to become familiar with the founder's personality in situations that can be expected to elicit or test different behaviors and reactions. An investor may wish to see if the founder acts uncomfortable or is intimidated in business situations, or whether the founder lacks tact or conversational ability during social interactions.

Look for Founders Who Have Nothing to Prove

Seed investors should be wary of founders who have something to prove, such as newly minted Ph.D.s or post-docs seeking to make the transition from academia to industry. Warning signs to look for are a founder's expressed desire to be CEO, a less than fully forthcoming nature when it comes to disclosing information that should be shared, or a passive-aggressive attitude that seems to flip between "I'm in charge" and "I'm not responsible" depending on who is likely to get the accolades or the blame in a given situation.

Having had several unpleasant experiences with first-time founders who could not seem to let go of authority, my partners and I have developed a preference for scientific or technical founders who are senior faculty members or seasoned practitioners who have nothing to prove. Ideally, such a founder has already reached the top of his or her academic field or profession and has held positions of authority, published widely, and achieved recognition among his or her peers. Under these conditions, the investor can be reasonably confident that the founder is not seeking to start a company simply to make a name for him or herself. Such founders are usually too deeply engaged in their careers to have any desire to be a CEO or hold any sort of day-to-to day operating role in a company. As a matter of fact, most academic institutions prohibit their faculty members from holding officer positions in start-ups in which they are involved as founders.

5

The Due Diligence Process

caveat emp·tor *n.*
The axiom or principle in commerce that the buyer alone is responsible for assessing the quality of a purchase before buying

5.1   "Hard Due Diligence" Versus "Soft Due Diligence"

In the basic relationship between entrepreneur and investor, it is axiomatic that the investor is the buyer and the entrepreneur is the seller. But the transaction between seed investor and start-up entrepreneur is not just the culmination of a negotiation between a buyer and a seller. In start-ups, the complex interaction between investor and entrepreneur that culminates in a financial transaction is more like a marriage than a sale. So, what kind of marriage matches your style? Whirlwind romance followed by a honeymoon in Vegas, or the built-to-last kind, progressing at its own natural pace from casual courtship to stable union? In start-ups, whether you are the suitor (investor) or the object of affection (entrepreneur), if you and your counterpart do not share the goal of a built-to-last union, I wish you the best and hope you negotiate a good prenuptial agreement (term sheet) because, odds are, you will need it.

In the built-to-last marriage of seed investor and start-up entrepreneur, most of what you should be looking for (or avoiding) will not be found on a standard due diligence checklist. (See Appendix 14.2 for an example of just such a checklist.) This is because most of what makes or breaks a lasting relationship between two consenting individuals are the intangibles—the endearing quirks of personality or the troubling faults of character—and not the dry facts that can be found in a résumé, *curriculum vitae*, or personal financial statement.

Ordinarily, the term sheet provided by an investor to an entrepreneur, or to the management of a start-up company, will specify that the financing in question is predicated upon satisfactory due diligence. This means the entrepreneur or company seeking financing must be able to deliver to the investor—or demonstrate the existence of—formal documentation, personal information, and other data verifying that the entity receiving financing has been formed properly and maintains appropriate corporate, legal, financial, operational, technical, and personal records. The due diligence checklist found as Appendix 14.2 lists more than seventy-five items in ten separate categories. These categories are:

1. Promotional and fundraising materials
2. Corporate formation documents and records
3. Employment and consulting agreements
4. Landlord, vendor, and service provider agreements and contracts
5. Technology transfer and IP agreements and documents
6. Insurance policies and benefits plans
7. Banking and financial information
8. Personal information about founders and senior executives
9. Personnel and operations
10. Market, scientific, business development, and investor prospecting information

It is important to point out that, depending upon the stage of the company seeking funding, some or many of the more than seventy-five items listed in the due diligence checklist that is Appendix 14.2 may not be available or, for that matter, relevant. At the true seed stage, it is possible that the corporate entity that will receive seed funding has not yet been formed and, therefore, that items such as articles of incorporation, company banking statements, and insurance policies will not exist. However, if a corporate entity has been formed prior to the financing, these and other documents had better be available for inspection by the investor, or something is seriously wrong.

The due diligence process for previously incorporated entities is well covered in other places, and I will not go into further detail here on the requirements of standard due diligence checklists. I will refer to the standard due diligence process for start-up companies as "hard due diligence," because it relies largely upon hard-copy documents and objective data. However, there is another kind of due diligence that is of great importance and utility for true seed-stage situations, which I shall refer to as "soft due diligence." For true seed-stage situations, it is entirely possible that the corporate entity to receive funding has not yet been legally formed, that little if any official documentation (e.g., banking statements, technology transfer agreements) exists, and that the scientific or technical founders do not have the business expertise to know what sort of documents would be required for a hard due diligence process, no less how to arrange for the preparation of such documents (which are usually drafted by attorneys, paralegals, experts in venture finance, technology transfer officers, etc.)

In true seed-stage situations, it must be assumed that the investor, if experienced, will have sufficient knowledge of the due diligence process or, if inexperienced, can access appropriate counsel, to conduct hard due diligence. What cannot be assumed is that the inexperienced investor will know how to conduct soft due diligence or will have access to other people who have enough experience with true seed-stage situations to offer advice about soft due diligence.

Soft due diligence is more subtle and nuanced than hard due diligence, because it is primarily experience-based rather than evidence-based. Soft due diligence relies more upon subjective evaluation than quantitative analysis, and upon intangibles that cannot be directly observed rather than upon such physical items as documents and spreadsheets. Hard due diligence can be reduced almost to an administrative function—a box-checking process that can be delegated to underlings. In stark contrast, soft due diligence is a management function, must be learned through experience, and is not easily delegated to subordinates.

A critical distinction between hard due diligence and soft due diligence is that whereas the hard type is usually completed *after* the preparation and delivery of a term sheet, the soft type should be completed *before* the preparation of a term sheet. By definition, once a term sheet has been drafted and delivered to the fund-seeker, the decision to propose an investment has already been made. Only then is hard due diligence initiated in earnest. On the other hand, soft due diligence is the informal but essential evaluation process through which the seed-stage investor decides whether to pursue an investment opportunity in the first place. Thus, to prepare and deliver a term sheet to a seed-stage fund-seeker before conducting a thorough soft due diligence process is to put the proverbial cart before the horse.

To aid in the teaching of soft due diligence, I have organized the soft due diligence process around four sets of factors: personal, scientific/technical, market, and investment.

5.2 Personal Factors

Soft due diligence always begins with personal factors, because personal factors ultimately determine the outcome of any relationship. Many inexperienced investors make the mistake of putting technology before people, on the assumption that there is no business without good technology, while people come and go. But because seed-stage investing usually involves a close, long-term, and productive working relationship between investor and entrepreneur (or scientific/technical founder), there is no use investing in and going into business with someone if you are not fully convinced you could tolerate being in the same room with your fund-seeking counterpart(s) for longer than the typical board meeting. If you are going to be a successful seed-stage investor, it is an undeniable fact of life that you will be spending countless hours, months on end, and probably for several years, interacting up close and personally with your co-founding entrepreneur(s) or scientific/technical founder(s).

Now, to return to our analogy between seed-stage investing and getting married, how long did it take you to get to know that your significant other was the "right one" for you? How many blind dates, false starts, dead-end relationships, and messy breakups did you go through before reaching your current state of marital bliss? My guess is that you have had your share of, shall we say, less-than-ideal relationships, and it is the same way with seed-stage investors who do start-ups. You've got to go through it yourself to know what it's like, and you may not get it right until you get it wrong a few times. Only then will you come to savor those moments of relief when you realize that the reason you could not bring an otherwise attractive start-up opportunity to fruition was because the scientific founder who you had once pursued with the reckless abandon of youth turned out to be a complete loser and would have been an absolute Pain with a capital P to work with.

This is why soft personal factors are so important. So, what should your soft due diligence checklist of personal factors look like?

Exhibit 2
Soft Due Diligence Checklist: Personal Factors

Personal Factors of Entrepreneur(s) or Scientific/Technical Founder(s)

The entrepreneur or founder...

- [ ] Is extremely smart, has the credentials to prove it, but is unpretentious
- [ ] Is at the top of his or her profession, or has the ability and drive to get there
- [ ] Is a likable person
- [ ] Is trustworthy and reliable
- [ ] Behaves consistently across multiple interactions and in a variety of situations
- [ ] Has complete self-confidence, is authoritative, but is not egotistical
- [ ] Speaks and writes very well
- [ ] Is presentable among strangers and is an excellent presenter
- [ ] Is at ease in social situations
- [ ] Has the respect of his or her academic and/or professional peers
- [ ] Is well liked by others, has no apparent enemies (at least none you would like)
- [ ] Has patience but also sets and acts on priorities
- [ ] Has a sense of humor and knows when to use it
- [ ] Has a sense of perspective
- [ ] Is candid and keeps no secrets inappropriately

The last item on this checklist reminds me to mention the concept of the "secret fax," the existence of which one of my partners has often cited as a major cause for concern for any seed-stage investor. The secret fax is that one little piece of critical information the prospective entrepreneur or founder somehow "forgets" to mention to you until you are well into discussions about investing in a seed-stage venture. To avoid any surprises, be sure to ask your prospective company founder(s) whether he, she, or they have any secret faxes or other pieces of information to disclose that may have any bearing, however minor, on your investment decision.

5.3 Scientific or Technical Factors

When evaluating science and technology, the first things that probably come to mind are experimental data, peer-reviewed publications, patent applications, and issued patents. These are hard due diligence checklist items. So are laboratory tours, the inspection of prototypes, and the gathering of feedback from expert consultants. But before getting into hard due diligence on technology, the seed-stage investor should run through a checklist of soft technology factors, which are not typically found in documents or in physical samples. Soft technology factors are usually found right there in the open, for everyone to see, without access to confidential information or outside consultants. All you need to know is what to look for and what questions to ask. To use the analogy of buying a newly constructed house, hard technology factors are the things you look at *after* your offer has been accepted, with the help of a licensed inspector. For example: Does the house construction meet all applicable building codes? Is the foundation free of unusual moisture? Is there any evidence of roof leaks? Has the basement passed a radon test? Is electrical wiring properly installed? These are questions that can be answered by physical inspection by someone with appropriate credentials. If you have ever bought a house, by the time you get to pre-closing inspection, you are already pretty heavily committed emotionally, legally, and probably, financially. Pulling out can be difficult and costly, barring discovery of serious deficiencies in the condition of the property. Continuing the house purchase analogy, soft technology factors are what you evaluate *before* making a serious offer. For example: Is the builder known for good workmanship? Does the physical layout of the house and property suit your family's needs? Will the house cost a fortune to heat and air condition? Will you need to hire a gardener?

Is there adequate closet space? In the foregoing analogy, checking off hard technical factors will tell you whether the house meets certain specifications and is well constructed, but will tell you nothing about whether the house suits your needs. On the other hand, checking off soft technical factors will give you all the information you need to determine whether you should even consider making a firm offer.

Following is a "soft due diligence" list of scientific or technical factors:

Exhibit 3
Soft Due Diligence Checklist: Scientific or Technical Factors

<u>Soft Scientific or Technical Factors</u>

- [ ] Scientific or technical founder(s) has (have) strong credentials in his/her/their field
- [ ] Science or technology can/cannot be scaled up in a reasonable period of time
- [ ] Science or technology are/are not in a field in which investor has some competence
- [ ] Science or technology are/are not broadly applicable (is/is not a "one-trick pony")
- [ ] Science or technology are/are not advanced past basic research and ready to be commercialized
- [ ] Science or technology will/will not require heavy investment in expensive laboratory equipment
- [ ] Science or technology will/will not depend heavily on involvement of original founders
- [ ] Science or technology can/cannot easily be transferred from an academic to a commercial setting
- [ ] IP landscape is/is not heavily contested or staked out by competitors
- [ ] Science or technology can/cannot be outsourced to reduce internal resource requirements
- [ ] Science or technology will/will not require in-house manufacturing capabilities

5.4 Market Factors

In the housing market, hard market factors concern sales figures for new construction and existing homes, median purchase prices, forecasts of mortgage rates, and projections of macroeconomic conditions. Soft market factors are all about curb appeal and the quality of the neighborhood. Seed-stage investors need to focus on soft market factors first, because what really matters to the seed-stage investor is whether he or she has a good roof over his or her head, and not what everyone else is buying.

One of the foremost hard market factors is market size. Today, most mainstream venture capitalists look for companies or products that will address a potential market of $500 million to $1 billion or more. Companies or products that address smaller markets may represent perfectly good opportunities, but for venture capitalists with funds of, say, $250 million and above, performing due diligence on smaller opportunities can take just as much time as evaluating larger opportunities. Thus, why expend resources on sub-$500 million opportunities? Furthermore, the larger opportunities afford a greater margin of safety. Not that they are safe, but if an investor's market estimate turns out to be too high by 50 percent, there is an obvious advantage to starting from a higher base. For most seed investors, however, I think it is not critical to set a high bar on market size when seeking and evaluating investment opportunities. More important for the seed investor is whether he or she can gain control of a high-quality opportunity in which he or she has the ability to add real value in a reasonable period of time and at a reasonable cost in terms of required capital, resource requirements, and personal time commitment. Thus, for seed-stage investors, I would say market size is important, but not in absolute terms. Market size should be evaluated *relative to* other factors, such as market maturity, ease of market penetration, degree of competition, ability to influence market development, and cost of addressing the market.

Following is my checklist of soft due diligence market factors:

Exhibit 4
Soft Due Diligence Checklist: Market Factors

<u>Market Factors</u>

- [ ] Is the market size sufficiently large relative to the size of investment contemplated, the cumulative amount of capital that might be necessary to reach the market, and the amount of time the seed investor expects to commit to the project?
- [ ] Can the company or product generate early cash flow to offset development costs?
- [ ] Can the company/product attract early corporate funding to support development?
- [ ] Is the company pursuing markets that benefit from government grants?
- [ ] Is the market/product aided or impeded by government regulations? Will this make product development and market penetration slower? More costly? More complicated?
- [ ] Does the existence/lack of technical standards aid/impede market penetration?
- [ ] Does the company have an ability to influence the pace or direction of market development? If not, will the company be at the mercy of outside market forces?
- [ ] Is the market heavily concentrated or highly fragmented? Will this benefit or impede market entry?
- [ ] Are purchase decisions in the market based primarily on price? Value content? Service? Where does the company fall relative to these and other key determinants of purchasing behavior?
- [ ] Does the company have a sustainable competitive advantage?

As you can see, the foregoing market factors are more qualitative (soft) than quantitative (hard). With experience, evaluating soft market factors becomes second nature and requires neither a calculator nor a spreadsheet.

5.5 Financial and Investment Factors

During my two years at Columbia Business School, while many of my classmates were preparing themselves for careers on Wall Street, I took exactly one finance course and could barely program my standard-issue HP-12C[20] to calculate net present values. The concept of net present value was easy enough to understand, but the NPV formulas, simple as they were for any business school student with a few years of investment banking or accounting experience, eluded me. I got my M.B.A. in 1988, graduating Columbia unable to calculate net present value without the aid of an HP-12C user's manual. To this day, I still consult my trusty user's manual on those rare occasions when I need to calculate anything more complicated than my bank balance. So, I offer the following disclaimer: I am woefully unqualified to instruct my readers about quantitative financial analysis. Therefore, it should come as no surprise to you that I find "crunching the numbers" to be about as useful to the seed-stage investor as a briefcase full of HP-12Cs.

I consider quantitative financial analysis—number crunching—to be hard due diligence. Inexperienced investors, and some experienced ones, tend to believe that anything to which you can attach a number somehow gains validity. The same goes for start-up entrepreneurs who present business plans with page after page of elaborate financial projections in the mistaken belief that the more numbers, the better. How do you quantify something as fluid and unpredictable as a start-up opportunity? By no means do I recommend that you ignore financial planning and analysis. You need to estimate start-up costs, evaluate cash requirements for operations and capital equipment purchases, and consider ways to generate revenue. But don't waste time cranking out net present values before you have done some soft due diligence on more fundamental financial issues.

One aspect of any technology-based start-up that investors should evaluate is the degree of "hotness" of the start-up's technology. By hotness, I mean: Is the technology in a field a lot of investors are talking about? Hotness can

---

[20] A business school student's first HP-12C programmable financial calculator was like a medical school student's first stethoscope—a tool of the profession that set the owner apart from those with lesser training.

be measured in terms of the degree to which the money-seeking entrepreneur or the boastful investor will go to link his or her darling start-up company's technology the "buzz word" of the moment. Instant tip-off: if *Fortune* magazine has devoted a feature article to some emerging technology that "has venture capitalists clamoring to get in on the ground floor of a whole new industry," the real story is about a buzz word. Figure 5 below contains a sampling of terms that have enabled entrepreneurs and investors to raise billions of dollars, in no small part by associating their companies with a buzz word.

Figure 5
Buzz-Word Investing, 1996–2006, by Sector

Internet	Biotech	High-Tech
B2B	BioMEMS	Broadband
B2C	Combinatorial Chemistry	Digital (anything)
e-Business	Computational (anything)	RFID
e-Commerce	Genomics	MEMS
e-Healthcare	Glycomics	Nano (anything)
New Media	High-Throughput (anything)	Optical (anything)
Portal	Metabolomics	Organic Electronics
P2P	Microfluidics	Printable Electronics
VoIP	Pharmacogenomics	Virtual (anything)
	Proteomics	Wireless (anything)
	Systems Biology	

Buzz-word investing has both positive and negative aspects. If buzz is on the rise and your timing is good, why not invest with some wind (or, more precisely, hot air) at your back? If buzz is peaking and you are an investor, you might buy into an overvalued deal. If buzz is on the decline, you could end up investing in a once-hot area just as more sophisticated investors lose interest.

Once again, from the foregoing discussion about buzz-word investing, you can see that soft due diligence, even if it concerns financial and investment factors, tends to emphasize qualitative rather than quantitative analysis.

Following is a checklist of soft due diligence topics and questions regarding financial and investment factors:

Exhibit 5
Soft Due Diligence Checklist: Financial and Investment Factors

Financial and Investment Factors

- [ ] Degree of "hotness" of the investment opportunity with the venture investment community
- [ ] Existence of buzz words and excessive hype in the field of investment
- [ ] Viability of exit options (Are alternatives limited or numerous?)
- [ ] Timing of exit opportunities (How long will your money be tied up?)
- [ ] Time to the next round of investment (How long will your money last?)
- [ ] Existence of co-investors to share the risk (Yes? No?)
- [ ] Quality of co-investors (Will they benefit or impair your own reputation?)
- [ ] Involvement of competent legal counsel (Is the company well represented?)
- [ ] Quality of investment documentation (Does the company know what it is doing?)
- [ ] Reasonableness and real-world nature of the company's financial projections
- [ ] Degree of entrepreneur's and investor's familiarity with the types and amounts of expenses typically incurred in the normal equipping and operation of the subject business
- [ ] Reasonableness and real-world level of company valuation given investment environment, comparable situations, and stage of company development

6

Forming and Funding the Start-Up

cor·po·ra·tion *n.*
A body that is granted a charter recognizing it as a separate legal entity having its own rights, privileges, and liabilities distinct from those of its members

6.1 Legend Versus Reality

According to legend, some great technology-based companies can trace their beginnings to business plans sketched out on coffee-stained paper napkins. The legend goes something like this: A venture capitalist and a university professor meet over breakfast at some earthy-crunchy coffeehouse frequented by, you guessed it, venture capitalists and university professors. The venture capitalist and the professor sink into intense conversation about a hot new technology, feverishly sketch out some business ideas on a napkin, and, lo and behold, a start-up company is born. A few phone calls are made, some documents are drawn up, and it's off to the races. Things start out just swell, then go sideways for a while, but just as the investors are ready to pull the plug, the company makes a fateful technological breakthrough and launches its first product to great acclaim. The company goes public, the early investors reap millions, and *Fortune* magazine does a cover story about how the latest darling of Wall Street got started on a paper napkin.

For every magazine article or business book written about some entertainingly improbable success story in Start-Up Land, there are 999 other articles and books that were never written about the start-ups that tried hard and failed, joined the ranks of the "living dead," achieved a modicum of success, or hit a grand-slam home run in blissful obscurity. Truth be told, almost every company founder and seed investor goes into a business with high hopes for success. No matter what the ultimate outcome, all company founders and investors in start-ups share the experience of company formation.

6.2 The Company Formation Process

The decision to start a company should only be made after thorough consideration, and never in haste. While start-up formation has become idealized in popular culture, it is in reality a demanding, legalistic, and sometimes tedious process. Done properly, forming a company entails a lot more work than simply filling out an application through some low-cost, incorporation service, charging a few hundred dollars to a credit card, and specifying the color of the newly formed entity's stock certificates. For a few hundred bucks, almost anyone can experience the thrill of being a company founder, but all this really buys you is a few minutes of self-satisfaction. If your goal is to attract experienced investors and corporate partners, dialing 1-800-INC-4YOU or logging on to www.incorpor8.com may save you a few bucks, but do not assume the company formation process is done once you receive your Deluxe Corporate Start-Up Kit, complete with corporate minutes binder (in its very own protective sleeve), articles of incorporation, fifty official stock certificate blanks, and a corporate seal embossing stamp (with convenient leatherette carrying pouch).

As a venture investor, I have occasionally been asked by a prospective founder (usually a young academic scientist who is thinking of forming a company) why he or she should go through the expense of using an attorney to form a company when his or her sibling/best friend/colleague/cousin/brother-in-law said that the whole thing could be done through a do-it-yourself incorporation service for under $1,000. My point is not that forming a company cannot be done economically or without an attorney, but for a company founder and seed investors, forming a company properly should only be done with the help of an attorney experienced in doing start-ups. Unless the lawyer is a solo practitioner, he or she is likely to delegate most steps of company formation to associates, paralegals, or support staff members, but a number of questions are likely to arise along the way for which the input of an experienced attorney will be invaluable.

It is not within the scope of this book or my professional expertise to give legal advice on the fine points of company formation. However, it is my objective in this chapter to demystify the company formation process and render it comprehensible to the first-time company founder, entrepreneur, or seed-stage investor.

6.3   The Formation Agreement

In the narrowest sense, company formation refers to the creation of a new business entity with all the rights, privileges, and obligations as allowed or required by law. However, before setting the administrative and legal steps in motion that are necessary to form a new company, some fundamental decisions must be made. These decisions are conceptual, strategic, and financial, and they address the following important questions:

- What is the general nature of the business?
- What is the company's specific purpose?
- How will the company be funded?
- Who will own the company?
- How will ownership of the company be divided?
- How will the company be governed?
- What IP will the company own?
- How will the company be managed?
- How will the company compensate its owners/managers?

Answering these questions to the mutual satisfaction of all parties involved in a company's formation requires many hours of frank discussion between the principals. For the sake of our discussion, and in the following example of a formation agreement, we will assume a company's founders include several academic scientists and a seed-stage venture investment and development firm.

Exhibit 6 below is an example of a memorandum of agreement my partners and I have used (with modifications, as appropriate) to document the terms of company formation in businessmen's language. The goal of this agreement is to codify for all founding parties and their attorneys the intentions of the founders without complicated legal language so that, once executed, the document can be used as a universal roadmap to guide company formation and initial capitalization.

Exhibit 6
Sample Memorandum of Agreement for Company Formation

Section 1

The first section of the agreement spells out the general nature of the business that is being formed, as well as the purpose of the document.

Memorandum of Agreement

The parties to this agreement intend that it shall constitute an agreement to form a new corporation focused on __(area of business)__ and related to work on __(specific technology)__. For convenience, that corporation shall be referred to herein as "the Company." The Company shall be incorporated under a name to be determined.

It is intended that this agreement shall be a binding contract between the parties until such time as a more formal documentation of this agreement and other documents (including articles of incorporation and bylaws) can be prepared by counsel for the parties and executed by the parties, each of whom agrees to cooperate in good faith in the preparation and execution of such documentation.

Therefore, in consideration of the mutual agreements and obligations herein, the parties executing this document agree to the following:

Section 2

This section defines where the company will incorporate and where it will do business.

<u>Incorporation</u>: A _____(name of state)___ Corporation, authorized to do business in _____(name of state)_____.

Section 3

This section provides a specific statement of the primary business and may refer to an executive summary or business plan, attached as Exhibit A. The executive summary or business plan should be developed jointly by the founders or by the founding management/investment team and approved in principle before the memorandum of agreement for company formation is executed.

Business Purpose: _____(statement of specific field of business)_____, by implementing insofar as possible the business model reflected in the business summary attached hereto as Exhibit A, subject to such changes and development of that model as further research and development may make appropriate. The business summary is intended as a guideline, not as a definitive set of requirements, and the parties recognize that it will evolve and change with time.

Section 4

This section specifies exactly how ownership of the new company will be divided among the founding scientists, founding investors, start-up managers, future employees, scientific advisory board, and originating university (licensor of the founding IP). Obviously, the capital structure of the company should be fully discussed among all the principals before the numbers, percentages, and share figures are filled in.

Many inexperienced founders and inexperienced investors get themselves and their companies into trouble by making decisions about company ownership unilaterally or by dividing up a company's equity without the input of more seasoned start-up specialists and attorneys. Being smart, independent-minded people, academic founders often assume wrongly that allocating a company's ownership is a straightforward quantitative exercise. Far from it, designing a capitalization table for a start-up should take a host of factors into account that may only be apparent to experienced company founders, veteran investors, and attorneys who are fully informed about the latest trends in venture financings, compensation, option plans, securities regulations, taxation, and other matters.

<u>Initial Capitalization</u>: The initial capitalization shall be as follows:

		No. of Shares
"Founders Stock"		
Co-Founder A	(__%)	___ shares
Co-Founder B	(__%)	___ shares
Seed-Stage Ventures, LLC	(__%)	___ shares
"Management, Employees, Advisors, University"		
Start-Up Management	(__%)	___ shares
Future Employees	(__%)	___ shares
Scientific and Business Advisors	(__%)	___ shares
License from University	(__%)	___ shares
"Initial Funding"		
Seed-Stage Investment	(__%)	___ shares
Total	**(100.0%)**	**___ shares**

Founders stock shall be issued for nominal consideration and fully vested at issuance, but shall be subject to a purchase agreement in favor of the other founders in the event a founder ceases to be actively employed or engaged in company activities. The repurchase shall be at cost, but the number of shares subject to repurchase shall decrease on a monthly basis so that at the end of ___ years, no founders stock will be subject to purchase rights by the other founders.

Section 5

This section specifies the amount of capital to be raised and the form in which funds will be committed (i.e., equity, debt). Let the attorneys specify—and explain—the details.

<u>Initial Funding</u>: Upon formation of the Company and completion of formal documentation reasonably required, Seed-Stage Ventures, LLC shall provide to the Company the sum of $_____ (funding according to a schedule of benchmarks) to cover operating costs until such time as institutional financing can be obtained as described below. Such funds shall be in the form of convertible preferred stock, which shall be convertible to common stock on a one-to-one basis with customary covenants and other provisions relating to liquidation preferences, anti-dilution, etc.

Forming and Funding the Start-Up

Section 6

This section addresses special terms conditioned upon a follow-on investment by outside (third-party) investors. Thus, the following text is customized for a specific purpose and should not be viewed as being standard.

<u>Institutional Funding</u>: As soon as practical after formation, the Company shall seek "institutional financing" in the amount expected to be not less than $___ nor more than $___ (or such other sum as the board of directors shall determine appropriate). The anticipated structure and ratio of investment is anticipated to be as follows:

Type of Security:	Series A Preferred Stock
Seed-Stage Ventures, LLC's Portion:	$_____
Other Investors:	$_____ to $_____
Estimated Pre-Money Valuation:	$_____

Seed-Stage Ventures, LLC shall use reasonable efforts to obtain the proposed financing on the best available terms, but shall not be obligated to fund more than $___ nor obligated to fund unless at least $___ of third-party funds can be obtained. It may, however, elect to fund more than $___ as it sees fit. The terms of the financing shall be determined by market conditions, and such financing may be derived from any source, including corporations and individual investors.

Section 7

This section addresses corporate governance issues and may be brief or more detailed.

<u>Board of Directors</u>: The initial board of directors shall consist of ___ individual representatives from Seed-Stage Ventures, LLC, one of whom shall be replaced by a director named by the principal outside investor at the time of the Series A round funding described above, and founders A and B. Additionally, founders A and B may elect two co-chairmen of the scientific advisory board.

Section 8

This section defines the company's founding IP and the nature of its ownership. Note that this section provides an escape for the investor if the company fails to secure rights to the IP that are satisfactory to the investor.

<u>Intellectual Property</u>: All patents, patent applications, trade secrets, copyrights, and other items of intellectual property developed by the Company after execution of this agreement, and which fall within the scope of intended activities of the Company (as described in Exhibit A) shall be assigned to and be at all times the exclusive property of the Company, subject only to such rights as may be granted by agreement of the Company or by law or prior agreement to a third party. In the event any third party has or claims rights covered by this paragraph, Seed-Stage Ventures, LLC shall not be obligated to make any funding otherwise required hereunder until an agreement satisfactory to it shall have been entered into with respect to such third-party rights or claims. In addition, the parties acknowledge that Seed-Stage Ventures, LLC is in the business of founding and funding life science and technology companies and agree that not intellectual property developed by any such company shall be deemed subject to this agreement, whether or not competitive in form or function with intellectual property owned by the Company. Upon execution of this agreement, the founders agree to assign all present and future intellectual property that directly relates to (i) the Company's core business, (ii) the demonstrated research and development activities of the Company, or (iii) results from consulting or scientific advisory board activities within the Company except to the extent such intellectual property is subject to preexisting agreements the founders have with their university employer or other consulting relationships listed in Exhibit B. Copies of any such consulting agreements will be provided to the Company, with numbers redacted, for review of the scope of the intellectual property rights.

Forming and Funding the Start-Up 81

Section 9

This section sets certain conditions on the scientific founders, the investors, and managers with regard to non-competition and non-disclosure of proprietary information.

<u>Non-Competition</u>: The _____(number of founders)____ individual founders agree to enter into non-competition and non-disclosure agreements with the Company precluding disclosure of any proprietary information about the Company or competition (directly or through employment or advisory services to others) with the Company during any period in which they are actively engaged in Company activities, are on its board of directors or an advisory board, and, to the extent permitted by law, for a period of one year following termination of relations with the Company. Seed-Stage Ventures, LLC and its managers and employees who may be engaged in business of or with the Company, shall also execute similar non-competition and non-disclosure agreements, but these shall not prohibit service to or financing of other companies financed directly or indirectly by Seed-Stage Ventures, LLC or its affiliates, except to prohibit disclosure of any trade secrets of the Company under any circumstances, without the approval of the board of directors.

Section 10

This section defines how the scientific founders and the founding managers may be compensated. Once the company is formed, its board of directors would be free to make changes to the compensation structure.

<u>Compensation</u>: No founder shall be compensated other than through equity ownership for being a founder. However, it is expected that formation of the Company may cause the founders to lose some of the outside consulting fees enjoyed by them. Therefore, the Company will enter into consulting agreements with founders A and B, providing for consulting fees sufficient to replace the amount of fees currently being generated by any contracts that are terminated because of this agreement. Following the first round of institutional financing described above, founders A and B shall also enter into consulting agreements for additional compensation in amounts to be determined by mutual agreement of the board of directors and founders A and B. Founders A and B shall also be free to enter into new consulting agreements with other companies that do not compete or

conflict with the business of the Company on such basis as they choose. All such agreements shall be promptly disclosed to the board of directors.

Venture Investment and Development Company shall provide the services of one or more of its managers as directors. Managers of Venture Investment and Development Company hired to act as officers or employees may be compensated separately at rates not to exceed fair market value for such functions, as determined by the board of directors. The CEO identified in Exhibit A will propose an operating budget and compensation amounts to the board of directors for review and approval. In addition, it is recognized that founders A and B may incur personal expenses associated with the founding and conduction of business of the Company, including but not limited to legal fees. The Company, subject to approval of the CEO, will reimburse these expenses.

Section 11

This section warrants that the scientific founders are not precluded by other agreements from performing their obligations to the company under this agreement.

Conflicts of Interest: Each individual founder warrants that at the time of first funding by Venture Investment and Development Company, he will have no conflicting agreements with any other entity that would preclude his performance of the obligations hereunder, including specifically the consulting services contemplated by this agreement. Exhibit B (attached) discloses all outstanding agreements between individual founders and third parties.

Section 12

This "catch-all" section covers any other terms that may not be addressed in the memorandum of agreement but which are expected to be covered in a more formal agreement, as prepared by counsel at a later time. This section also specifies how disputes between the founders will be handled.

Other Provisions: Any items requiring agreement of the parties and not covered specifically by this agreement shall be addressed in the more formal documentation to be prepared by counsel, and the parties shall act in good faith an in a manner consistent with customs and practices in the life sciences and technology venture capital industries in resolving any disputes relating to the drafting of such

Forming and Funding the Start-Up

agreements. Any matter essential to the operations of the Company, which cannot be resolved by this agreement, shall first be subject to mediation, and if that does not result in agreement, shall be submitted to binding arbitration under the rules of the American Arbitration Association.

This agreement is executed as of the __(day)__ of __(month)__, 200X and shall be effective as of that date.

_____   _____
Founder A   Founder B
Seed-Stage Ventures, LLC

By:_____
Managing Member

6.4 The Semantics of the Term Sheet

In his book, *Term Sheets and Valuations*, Alex Wilmerding, a venture capitalist at Boston Capital Ventures, defines a term sheet as "a letter of intent given to a company seeking an investment by a venture firm in order to outline the proposed terms for an investment transaction between two parties."[21] What is the difference between a company formation agreement and a term sheet? For starters, the formation agreement is a founder-driven document, whereas the term sheet is investor-driven. By founder-driven, I mean the founders themselves need to initiate creation of the document. Indeed, without willing founders, there is no company. Investors may participate in the drafting of a formation agreement, but by definition, any investor that participates in a company's formation is also a founder. On the other hand, as an investor-driven document, the term sheet is initiated and drafted by the investors and *delivered to* the company or its founders. To some readers, the distinction between a formation agreement and a term sheet may seem pedantic, but I believe the distinction is quite important. The words "formation agreement" imply a mutual understanding or meeting of the minds between willing founders. By contrast, the words "term sheet" imply a one-sided statement of conditions, as in "terms of surrender." Term sheets may not be binding and may be negotiable, but they are symbolic instruments of power wielded by investors and intended to show the recipient who is boss. I don't like that. If venture investors were truly

---

[21] *Term Sheets and Valuations*, Alex Wilmerding, Aspatore, Inc., 2004

interested in "being partners" with prospective portfolio companies (and remember, we are talking about start-ups) and in "working together to build the business," wouldn't it be better for the term sheet to be called an "investment proposal" or, better yet, a "request to invest?" And, wouldn't it be better if term sheets were written in language founders and start-up entrepreneurs could understand?

My aim in having a little fun with the semantics of term sheets is to encourage company founders and start-up entrepreneurs to look beyond the size of an investor's fund and consider the investor's attitude when presented with a term sheet. Consider whether the investor would be a real partner with a win-win attitude or just another person with money looking to come out on top.

6.5 The Term Sheet, Deconstructed

It is unfortunate that term sheets are about as easy for inexperienced founders and entrepreneurs to translate as hieroglyphics. For a detailed discussion about term sheets, I highly recommend Wilmerding's *Term Sheets and Valuations*. For a top-level overview, Exhibit 7, which follows, provides an outline of a typical term sheet, with simple definitions and explanations. The complete version can be found as Appendix 14.4.

Exhibit 7
Term Sheet Outline

MEMORANDUM OF TERMS FOR THE PRIVATE PLACEMENT OF SERIES A CONVERTIBLE PREFERRED STOCK

Section 1

The opening section of a typical term sheet usually starts with a boxed disclaimer stating that neither party is obligated to complete the transaction until a definitive agreement is signed. The rest of the section simply lists the particulars of the deal such as the amount raised, the number of shares, the type of security to be purchased, and the valuation of the company at the completion of the financing. Just the facts, and nothing fancy.

> THIS BOX CONTAINS A STANDARD "BOILERPLATE" DISCLAIMER, STATING THAT NEITHER THE COMPANY NOR THE INVESTOR SHALL BE OBLIGATED TO COMPLETE A TRANSACTION UNTIL A DEFINITIVE AGREEMENT IS SIGNED. THE INVESTOR ALSO WILL STATE THAT ITS COMPLETION OF A DEAL DEPENDS UPON SATISFACTORY DUE DILIGENCE. THIS GIVES THE INVESTOR A FACE-SAVING WAY OUT IF IT FINDS SOMETHING IT DOES NOT LIKE.

FIRST ROUND OF FINANCING:

Amount to be Raised:	$_____
Type of Security:	_____
Number of Shares:	_____ shares
Purchase Price:	$_____ per share (the "Purchase Price")
Investors:	_____
Closing Date:	On or before_____

Post-Financing Capitalization:	Class	Number of Shares	Percent
	Common Stock	________	____%
The new investors propose to purchase "Series A preferred stock." These shares carry certain "preferences," or special rights and privileges, ahead of the common stock.	**Stock Option Pool**	________ (________ un-issued)	____%
	Series A Preferred Stock	________	____%
	Total	________	100%

Forming and Funding the Start-Up 87

Section 2

This section explains the rights, preferences, privileges, and restrictions of the particular class of stock the investors wish to purchase.

Rights, Preferences, Privileges, and Restrictions of the Preferred Stock:

Following are brief descriptions (in plain English) of what the recipient(s) of the term sheet can expect to find in each section:

Dividends: The Series A Preferred stockholders will expect to be paid a dividend, expressed as an annual percentage rate, on their invested capital. The dividends may have different terms, depending upon whether the term sheet is investor-favorable, neutral, or company-favorable.

Voluntary Conversion: The Series A Preferred shareholders are usually granted a right, at their option, to convert their preferred stock into common stock, typically on a one-to-one ratio, as explained below.

Automatic Conversion: Preferred shares will typically convert to common stock either (i) when a majority of preferred shareholders vote to approve a conversion or (ii) upon the closing of an underwritten IPO of the company's common stock. Usually, the preferred shareholders will set some conditions on the IPO (called a "qualified IPO"), such as a minimum amount that must be raised and a minimum purchase price, before an automatic conversion will take place. This prevents the company from doing a sub-optimal IPO for too little money and/or at an unreasonably low price.

Redemption: The term sheet will specify here that after a certain period of time (for example, five years) and at the request of the holders of a certain majority of the preferred stock, the company will redeem the preferred stock at the original purchase price, plus any accrued and unpaid dividends. The company will wish to avoid redemption by meeting its development and financing milestones.

Anti-Dilution Provisions: Anti-dilution provisions can be a topic of great debate, because they protect the new investor's position at the expense of the company and previous investors. Since one group's gain is the other's loss, a battle may ensue over how much anti-dilution protection the new investors will be entitled to receive.

The wording in this section can be quite technical and hard to follow, and the company should be sure to request a thorough explanation.

Liquidation Preference: The ominous-sounding heading for this section simply refers to the preferences and protections to which the investor will be entitled in the event that the company is sold, merged into another entity, winds up its business, or looses voting control. Basically, in the event of one of these events, the preferred shareholders will stand in line ahead of the common shareholders.

Voting Rights: This section will simply explain how the number of shares that the preferred shareholder may vote will be determined.

Section 3

Protective Provisions:

This section specifies that certain significant events may not take place without the consent of the preferred shareholders, as determined by a vote. These events may include, for example:
- Sale or merger
- Change of shareholder rights or preferences
- Change in the number of authorized shares of any class of stock

Forming and Funding the Start-Up

- Creation of a new class of stock with preference over or parity with the existing preferred stock
- An amendment or revision to the company's charter or bylaw that may affect the preferred shareholders
- Share purchases or redemptions
- Issuance of dividends to common stockholders

Section 4

Information Rights:

The preferred shareholders will require that the company provide financial statements or other information in a generally accepted format and at a particular frequency.

Section 5

Right of First Offer:

This section can be lengthy and complicated, with the kind of paragraph-long sentences lawyers love to write, but the basic purpose is to specify the conditions under which the company must offer the preferred shareholder the first right of offer in the event of a sale of common stock or other event involving the issuance and sale of shares.

Section 6

This section contains a number of paragraphs that address preparations for and execution of an IPO. As this section gets into matters covered by securities law, the language can get rather technical. It is advisable to have an attorney experienced in securities law to explain this section in detail.

Registration Rights:

Registrable Securities: This short section defines what is meant by a "Registrable Securities."

Demand Registration: As with redemption, this section gives the preferred shareholders the right to demand, after a specified period of time or when the company has completed an IPO, that the preferred shareholders be permitted to register their shares for sale.

Piggyback Registration Rights: A technical term, "piggyback registration rights" simply require that the preferred shareholders be permitted to register their shares for sale when any other class of shareholder registers its shares. The effect is to "piggyback" along with another group of shareholders.

Registration on Form S-3: This section refers to a particular type of SEC form that must be completed to register the investor's shares. This is a technical detail only.

Registration Expenses: It is customary for the investor to ask that the company being funded cover the costs to register securities for sale in the public markets. The language in this section usually puts some restrictions or upward bounds on the costs to be borne by the company.

Transfer of Rights: Another technicality, this section allows the preferred shareholder to assign its registration rights to a transferee or assignee, provided the company is given written notice and certain other conditions exist.

Lock-Up Provision: A lock-up provision prevents pre-IPO investors from selling their shares immediately upon commencement of trading once shares are listed on a public exchange, which would put downward pressure on the public share price. This section tries to put a limit on the length of time preferred investors' shares will be subject to a lock-up but is not likely to stand if investment bankers demand a longer lock-up period.

Forming and Funding the Start-Up

Termination of Registration Rights: This is another technicality concerning the expiration of registration rights.

Other Provisions: This catch-all section may refer to other rights the preferred shareholder may require and that may be written into a separate rights agreement. One example would be cross-indemnification.

Section 7 *Board of Directors:*	This section specifies the total number of board seats and the composition of the board, including the number of board seats that shall be provided for the preferred shareholders and the common shareholders.
Section 8 *Option Pool:*	This section specifies the number of shares of common stock that shall be reserved and made available through issuance of stock option to employee, directors, consultants, and other service providers.
Section 9 *Stock Options:*	This section specifies the vesting schedule to apply under the company's stock option plan. Three-year or four-year vesting in monthly increments is typical.
Section 10 *Employee and Consultant Agreements:*	This section protects the company and its investors by requiring that each employee or consultant of the company shall have entered into an acceptable proprietary information and inventions agreement.
Section 11 *Purchase Agreement:*	This section states that the sale of the Series A preferred stock will be made pursuant to a stock purchase agreement reasonably acceptable to the company and the investors. The company's attorneys

will be responsible for preparing the stock purchase agreement.

Section 12

Finders:

This section sets restrictions on or forbids payment of fees to finders in connection with the transaction, and is meant to prevent investor funds being used to pay finders.

Section 13

Held in Confidence:

This section confirms that the term sheet and any related information will be treated by the investor and the company as confidential and will not be disclosed without the investor's approval. This prevents the company from "shopping around" the term sheet without prior approval of the investor.

Section 14

Legal Counsel and Fees:

This section specifies that the term sheet is not legally binding until certain conditions are met, including completion of satisfactory due diligence by the investor and completion of formal legal documentation of the terms, to the satisfaction of the investor. Basically, it says that, at the investor's sole discretion, "It's not a deal until it's a deal."

The investors will also typically require that, assuming a deal is brought to fruition, the company will pay all reasonable and customary legal fees associated with completion of the transaction, within some specified limit.

Finally, space will be provided for the company and the investor to sign off on the term sheet.

COMPANY

By: _____

Name: _____

Title: _____

Date: _____

INVESTOR

By: _____

Name: _____

Title: _____

Date: _____

6.6 The Capitalization Table

Before a company is legally formed, it is a good idea for the founders and investors to draw up a capitalization table (or "cap" table). The cap table is typically prepared as a spreadsheet to enable easy recalculation of "what if" scenarios, as well as to allow for the addition of new equity-holders as the company grows. Exhibit 8 below presents a cap table for a hypothetical start-up company that has just one seed investor, an initial scientific advisory board, and a few initial employees. Purely for illustration, Exhibit 8 presents a cap table with three sections:

- Section 1 shows the capital structure for shareholders.
- Section 2 shows the capital structure for holders of non-qualified stock options, which are the type of options set aside for directors, scientific advisory board members, and service providers.
- Section 3 shows the capital structure for holders of incentive stock options, which is the type of option set aside for employees.

When all three of these sections are presented together—shareholders, non-qualified stock option holders, and incentive stock option holders—the reader of the cap table will have a complete picture of the company's current and fully diluted ownership.

Exhibit 8
Example of a Capitalization Table

Section 1

Listed in this first section are all current holders of common stock. This example makes several unconventional assumptions, which are based upon the venture investment and development company (VIDeC) model. First, the seed investor, acting as both a co-founder and investor, also holds common stock so as to be "in the same boat" with the scientific co-founders. Next, the seed investor, being a VIDeC, contributes its own hands-on managers as part of the newly capitalized company. Lastly, the seed investor holds a convertible note. This note will convert to Series A preferred stock, priced at the same valuation paid by the new (outside)

Series A investors (presumably, one or more mainstream venture capital firms). This unconventional capital structure puts the seed investor on the same footing as the founding scientists, because the seed investor holds the same class of stock (common) as the scientific founders at the time of the company's initial capitalization.

As licensor of the company's founding technology, a university is also listed as a shareholder, presumably because the university received common shares as part of a licensing agreement with the company.

Summing up Section 1, out of 20,000,000 shares authorized by the company, 5,950,000 (39.7 percent) have been issued and 14,050,000 (60.3 percent) remain available for issuance.

Common Stock Name	Title	Issue Date	# of Shares	% of Issued	% of Total
Scientist A	Scientific Co-Founder		1,500,000	18.9%	7.5%
Scientist B	Scientific Co-Founder		1,500,000	18.9%	7.5%
Seed Investor	Investor Co-Founder		1,500,000	18.9%	7.5%
Seed Investor	Start-Up Manager		1,050,000	13.2%	5.3%
Seed Investor	Convertible Note Holder		2,000,000	25.2%	10.0%
University	Licensor		400,000	5.0%	2.0%
	Total Issued Common Stock		5,950,000	100.0%	39.7%
	Shares Still Available from 20M Share Pool		14,050,000		60.3%

Section 2

Section 2 lists all holders of non-qualified stock options, which, in this case, includes only scientific advisory board members. Later, this list would likely expand to include directors, consultants, and perhaps other service providers, including those willing to accept options as part of their compensation.

Starts-up should be careful about doling out options to company outsiders, as the tendency early on is to be too generous, thereby causing excess dilution and limiting the company's flexibility in the future.

The reader will notice at the bottom of the table in this section that non-qualified stock options represent 73.4 percent of the issued stock options but only 10 percent of total stock options issued or available for issuance.

Non-Qualified Stock Options Name	Title	Award Date	# of Options	% of Issued	% of Total
Scientist A	Co-Chair, SAB		50,000	18.3%	2.5%
Scientist B	Co-Chair, SAB		50,000	18.3%	2.5%
Scientist C	SAB Member		50,000	18.3%	2.5%
Scientist D	SAB Member		50,000	18.3%	2.5%
	Sub-Total NQSO Issued Options		200,000	73.4%	10.0%

Section 3

Section 3 lists incentive stock options for employees, but otherwise the presentation is identical to Section 2. Start-ups often have difficulty deciding how many options to grant to employees and may get themselves into trouble by "winging it" and making up stock option award allocations as they go along. To avoid making this mistake, start-up founders or senior executives responsible for compensation should consult with outside experts, including experienced founders, investors, compensation consultants, and attorneys, about setting up an option allocation plan that is appropriate for the company's size, stage of development, industry, and hiring environment.

Section 3 shows that the company's four employees have been awarded a total of 72,500 options, representing 26.6 percent of issued options and 3.6 percent of all options authorized and issuable.

Finally, we see that 1,727,500 options remain to be issued, representing 86.4 percent of the total option pool authorized. Out of 20,000,000 total shares authorized by the company for issuance, a total of 8,222,500 shares,

Forming and Funding the Start-Up

including those issued and those underlying options that have been awarded, have been issued.

Incentive Stock Options Name	Title	Award Date	# of Options	% of Issued	% of Total
Employee 1	Director, Research		40,000	14.7%	2.0%
Employee 2	Scientist, Chemistry		15,000	5.5%	0.8%
Employee 3	Scientist, Biology		15,000	5.5%	0.8%
Employee 4	Research Associate		2,500	0.9%	0.1%
	Sub-Total ISO Issued Options		72,500	26.6%	3.6%
	Total Issued Options		**272,500**	**100.0%**	**13.6%**
	Options still available from 20M pool		1,727,500		86.4%
	Total Issued Shares and Options		**8,222,500**		**37.4%**

6.7 Additional Material

Formation of a new company is a multi-step process that can be somewhat overwhelming if not handled in an organized fashion and with the assistance of an experienced law firm or corporate attorney. Most documents that are associated with company formation are formulaic and do not leave a lot of room for creativity. Much of the material in these documents constitutes "legal boilerplate" containing language required by law or regulation, or included by custom. Some of the specifics may change from company to company, but the basic language changes infrequently.

As a reference for readers, examples of the following documents can be found in the Appendices:

- Articles of Incorporation
- Term Sheet
- Stock Purchase Agreement
- Stock Option Award

7

Navigating the Technology Transfer Process: Advice and Commentary

Contributing Author: Dr. Jonathan G. Lasch

---

li·cense *n.*
A right or permission granted by a competent authority (as of a government or a business) to engage in some business or occupation, do some act, or engage in some transaction which would be unlawful without such right or permission [22]

7.1 Introduction to the Contributing Author

Technology transfer is a fundamental process in the creation of companies that are based on technology invented by scientists and engineers at academic centers. Yet, despite the importance of technology transfer, there are relatively few start-up entrepreneurs and investors who can claim to have an insider's knowledge of every step of the technology transfer process. As contributing author for this chapter, Dr. Jonathan Lasch, a *bona fide* expert in technology transfer, provides the reader with an insider's guide to this important topic.

Dr. Jonathan G. Lasch has more than twenty-five years of experience as a product development scientist, industrial research manager, academic technology transfer officer, consultant, entrepreneur, venture investor, and start-up executive. In addition, Dr. Lasch teaches graduate students in the fully employed and executive M.B.A. programs at UCLA's Anderson

---

[22] *Merriam-Webster's Dictionary of Law* © 1996 Merriam-Webster Inc.

School of Business and at the Keck Graduate Institute for Applied Life Sciences. From 1992 to 1997, Dr. Lasch served as vice president of technology development and technology transfer at the Scripps Research Institute in La Jolla, California, the world's largest private research institute in the life sciences. Prior to the Scripps Research Institute, Dr. Lasch was a scientist and research director at PPG Industries. Since the late 1990s, Dr. Lasch has consulted for, co-founded, and/or managed more than a dozen life science and high-tech companies through his consulting firm, Prosortium Inc., and through Convergent Ventures, of which he is a founder and managing director.

7.2 Technology Transfer from Academic Institutions

Transfer of technology from academic and government research institutions to commercial entities for the purpose of development of goods and services is a key component to economic growth and vitality within the United States and elsewhere. Nowhere is this critical component of the economic cycle better exemplified than in technology-based start-up companies. Most of these development-stage companies are the recipients of licenses of intellectual property (IP) from academic institutions, which serve to form the first (and often core) technology that underpins their business.

Slightly over a quarter of a century ago, landmark legislation changed the way the U.S. government treated the disposition of IP developed from government grants. In 1980, the Bayh-Dole Act, named after the sponsors of the legislation, Senators Birch Bayh of Indiana and Robert Dole of Kansas, placed responsibility for management and transfer of technology into the hands of the institution that was a recipient of grant funding from government agencies such as the National Science Foundation, the National Institutes of Health, the Department of Defense, and the Department of Energy, amongst others. The governing regulations pertaining to the Bayh-Dole Act can be found within the United States Code Title 35, Patents, and the Code of Federal Regulations Title 37, Patents, Trademarks, and Copyrights.

Amongst other obligations, incumbent upon the academic institution that is recipient to government agency grants is the responsibility to move technology into appropriate commercial pipelines from start-ups to large corporations—albeit with a preference for small companies—while preserving the rights of the U.S. government to use the IP for non-commercial purposes, royalty-free. This is why issued patents must be marked to acknowledge U.S. government funding and why academic institutions will agree to license, but not usually to assign,[23] patents that evolve from government-sponsored research. By licensing rather than assigning patents for technology developed in part or in whole with federal funding, academic institutions preserve their control over patent prosecution and protect the government's rights.

The technology transfer offices of academic institutions have great latitude in terms of license agreements they negotiate with companies. Terms often include field of use, geographic regions, exclusivity or non-exclusivity, development milestones, and limits of liability and indemnification. Consideration (compensation) received by the licensor may include recovery of past costs and payment of ongoing patent costs, up-front fees, annual payments, royalties, milestone payments, and equity. Prospective agreements and terms may include specific funded research within a specific area within academic laboratories, with the sponsor given a first right to new inventions. Often, licensees are obligated to provide a grant back of improvements to the IP to the licensor.

Technology transfer officers often work with other administrative groups on campus, such as the offices of general and patent counsel and the office of grants and contracts, to coordinate the management of funding, collaborations, and transfer of technology while remaining within applicable federal laws and institutional regulations. In addition to license agreements, research proposals, and grants, the technology transfer staff must administer invention disclosures, patent applications, material transfer agreements, consulting agreements, and confidentiality agreements while managing information flow in and out of laboratories. Also, the technology transfer staff must be watchful to avoid inadvertent conflicts of interest and breaches in ethics by the personnel of their institution as a consequence of licensing and other funding arrangements. With all of these responsibilities,

---

[23] Licensing of IP confers rights of use, whereas assignment confers ownership. Licensing is, therefore, a means by which the owner of the technology can maintain some element of control over the technology's use.

technology transfer departments are typically understaffed and have limited time and resources to engage in protracted negotiations with every potential licensee that arrives at their doors. The solution is their use of boilerplate agreements for the various types of transactions they encounter on a regular basis.

Boilerplate agreements are templates that have been prepared, reviewed, and approved by the institution's general counsel. The licensee that wishes to use a different license agreement or make significant modifications to the boilerplate risks, at best, protracted negotiation times and, at worst, no deal at all. This is because deviations from the boilerplate agreement will require review by counsel, who is likely to be busy on higher-priority activities and transactions. The academic institution's counsel must review the language in the licensing agreement to protect the institution from engendering risk that is out of proportion to the somewhat limited, and often unachieved, potential rewards from completing the licensing transaction. The technology transfer officers are bound by their fiduciary responsibilities to protect their institution from the consequences of doing many licensing deals over many years. Hence, significant changes to clauses in agreements that pertain to liability, indemnification, and insurance are likely to kill a deal. While the individual licensee may have good arguments for flexibility of language within a specific agreement, the technology transfer department must manage a portfolio of licenses and must, therefore, consider the implications of modifications made to each and every licensing agreement. Although each individual technology transfer agreement may seem important at the time of execution, no one can predict which agreement will be a large contributor to the future financial health of the institution and is hence particularly worth additional risk.

While it is likely in the course of any licensing transaction that small modifications to the language of the boilerplate agreement will be made, the negotiation of financial terms is a different story. Each institution has its own range of acceptable terms, with private institutions having considerably more latitude than publicly funded universities, where policies may be more rigid and subject to more oversight. The personal incentives and motivations for technology transfer staff members can be very different from those of start-up entrepreneurs or business development executives in for-profit corporations. For example, the business development manager within a corporation will be necessarily concerned with the impact his or her technology transfer agreements have on the short-term earnings and long-term business trajectory of the company. Thus, he or she may prefer to do a smaller number of larger-sized technology transfer deals, because larger deals can make a greater contribution to the company. Larger deals may also have a more favorable impact on the business development manager's career advancement and year-end bonus. Contrast this situation with that of the academic technology transfer officer who may prefer to complete a higher volume of deals, even small ones, because the success of any one deal may not be known for many years and the impact of any one deal on an academic institution's future is not likely to be significant, with rare and noteworthy exceptions.[24] Furthermore, unlike his or her for-profit counterpart, the academic technology transfer officer has little to no opportunity to profit individually from a favorable technology transfer deal, whereas deals with negative outcomes are likely to have a direct negative impact on his or her opportunities for career advancement. Consequently, the technology transfer officer is well advised to move as many pieces of IP as possible into appropriate commercial pipelines within the given timeframe while trying to avoid high-risk or "dumb" deals. In institutions where oversight of technology transfer is constant and certain, the experienced technology transfer office will look to the licensee to provide at least some positive return in all or most areas such as up-front payments, royalties, milestone payments, and annual payments. Receiving a portion of consideration in the form of equity is almost always important to the technology transfer officer, who wishes to avoid having to answer the question, "Why didn't you get equity?" when the occasional start-up company makes it to an IPO or is acquired. At publicly funded academic institutions where oversight of technology transfer deals carries with it the responsibility for protecting the public interest, technology transfer officers may place more emphasis on "checking off each box" in a technology transfer agreement rather than worrying about how much each box may be worth in terms of total deal value. By contrast, technology transfer officers

---

[24] For example, an academic institution may control (or believe it controls) critical patents for cloning genes used to produce commercially important therapeutic proteins, as was the case with City of Hope National Medical Center in its legal dispute with Genentech Inc. over the production of human insulin. The outcome of this dispute ultimately proved to be worth hundreds of millions of dollars to City of Hope.

at private academic institutions may have more latitude to negotiate terms based on the unique circumstances of the deal rather than on the need to "check off each box" of a boilerplate technology transfer agreement. That said, either situation (public institution or private) is workable; however, it is always useful to understand the needs and limitations of the organization within which the transaction is being negotiated. Speaking plainly with the technology transfer officer about his or her institution's preferred deal structure and key terms, as well as working within the framework of the institution's own boilerplate agreements, can make the licensing experience much more pleasant, faster, and successful for all parties.

7.3 Technology Transfer and Academic Faculty

Another force in the academic technology transfer universe comes from the constituency of scientists and engineers, namely the faculty and postgraduate researchers, that generate the IP that is the subject of the license agreements. Since turnover of faculty in academic institutions is relatively low and open technology transfer positions are rare, the technology transfer officer would do well to pay close attention to his or her customer base. In other words, service is the key, and more than one technology transfer officer has felt the wrath of faculty members caused by ineffective technology transfer practices and poor service. In the early days after the Bayh-Dole Act, academic faculty members at academic institutions were often confused about who owned the rights to the IP they generated. This confusion sometimes resulted in the technology "walking out the back door" of the institution and into various commercial enterprises, with the faculty member receiving compensation in some situations, but not in others. Start-up entrepreneurs and seed investors are often surprised to learn that some academic scientists and engineers are willing to forego large personal financial gain from their inventions, because they are more interested in the development of their technologies than in making a profit from them. Whatever their motivations, academic faculty members, as well as start-up entrepreneurs and investors, have become aware and better educated about the technology transfer process and usually know to negotiate *through* the academic technology transfer department rather than around it.

When academic technology is licensed into a start-up company, the academic inventor may serve the company in a number of different capacities, such as a consultant, a chairperson, a member of the scientific advisory board, or a member of the board of directors. They do not usually serve as corporate officers or executives, as they are already employed by the licensor and this can set the stage for conflicts of interest. In fact, the academic inventor may hold equity in and receive cash compensation from a start-up company that has licensed the inventor's technology, as long as this compensation falls within the rules of the academic institution. When an academic inventor has a personal or financial stake in a start-up company that has licensed his or her technology, the inventor is strongly advised to recuse himself or herself from all negotiations between the academic institution and the company, lest they be found at odds with one or both organizations. The Federal regulations allow for the inventors to share in the revenues received by their licensing institution but, the specific formula for sharing is determined by each institution.

Because academic inventors' relationships with start-ups and larger corporations hold the potential to be financially lucrative and beneficial from a career development standpoint, faculty members often rush to disclose to technology transfer departments, with great spirit and enthusiasm, ideas and inventions that have not yet been fully vetted. Faculty members make these disclosures enthusiastically with the hope that their technology will become the basis of a successful new company or a licensing deal with a large corporation. However, most single technology disclosures will not be enough, on their own merits, to form a company. Add to the faculty member's visions of fortune the fact that he or she can always site examples of other faculty members "down the hall" whose technology has been licensed to a hot new start-up company or a well-known corporation, and the academic inventor's desire to move his or her technology "out the door" often trumps reason. During the contributing author's tenure as the head of technology development and transfer at The Scripps Research Institute, the phrase "I have the billion-dollar molecule" was heard so often that the contributing author often remarked, "Yes, of course you do, and would that billion dollars be in revenues or expenses?" Sarcasm aside, and in all fairness to academic inventors, the best scientific work is done by those individuals who eat, drink, and sleep their work, and their unbridled enthusiasm is to be commended very highly. In fact, academic scientists and engineers that do not act this way are probably not pushing as hard as they need to in order to be successful in commercializing their technology. However, that does not mean the enthusiastic scientist is necessarily able to put forth unbiased and expert advice as to the business opportunity at hand. Indeed, some of the best technology found in journals such as *Science* and *Nature* may never make it through the non-linear process of technology transfer and development to achieve commercial success, while some weaker technologies, coupled with experienced management and the appropriate resources and execution, may succeed.

7.4   Advice for Technology Hunters

To hunt for licensable technologies at academic institutions, it is advisable to do two things. First, scan through Web pages and other materials such as journal articles and meeting announcements for insights into the research efforts of academic scientists and engineers who are doing interesting research. Also, speak with those faculty members who are in areas of interest. Next, contact the technology transfer office for information regarding available technologies. Often, the technology transfer office has a list of invention disclosures, patent applications, and issued patents that are available for licensing. Additionally, technology transfer officers can help you begin the process of working with the faculty member and licensing technology. In the end, technology transfer officers are the professionals who are there to help move technology towards commercial reality.

8

Creating and Protecting Intellectual Property: A Panel Discussion

Panelists: Mr. Nima Shiva and Dr. David Margolese

pat·ent *n.*
A grant made by a government that confers upon the creator of an invention the sole right to make, use, and sell that invention for a set period of time

8.1 Introduction to the Panel

The creation and protection of IP is a complex field that calls for the expertise of a patent attorney. Most brand new start-ups do not have a patent attorney on staff and will need to hire one from among the ranks of solo practitioners, boutique IP firms, or the IP departments of larger law firms.

Discussing the legal aspects of IP protection is beyond the scope of this book. Instead, it is my aim in this chapter to share some of the practical knowledge I have gathered during a "panel discussion" with two start-up veterans, one a molecular biologist and M.B.A. with extensive biotech start-up experience, and the second a Ph.D. chemist with years of experience "in the trenches" as an engineer, technology manager, and co-founder of several venture capitalist-backed high-tech companies. Both of these individuals have had primary responsibility for managing the IP development process within their respective companies. Their comments, recorded by me during several face-to-face interview sessions and presented below, are likely to be more immediately relevant to new company founders and entrepreneurs than would be a legal treatise on the patent process.

Acknowledgements

I would like to thank Mr. Nima Shiva and Dr. David Margolese for their assistance in the preparation of the following material. Mr. Shiva is co-founder, chairman, and CEO of Encode Bio Inc. and was a co-founder and start-up executive at Neurion Pharmaceuticals Inc. and ORFID Corporation. He is also a managing director at Convergent Ventures in Los Angeles, which he joined after a brief stint as a biotech and medical device equity analyst, following an early career as a bench scientist and research manager in academia and in the biotech industry.

Dr. Margolese currently serves as vice president of technology development at ORFID Corporation, an organic electronics company. Dr. Margolese earned his Ph.D. in chemistry at the University of California at Santa Barbara after an early career as a staff engineer at TRW. Since then, he has been a consultant, process development and design engineer, and a co-founder of several venture-backed start-ups. Dr. Margolese has worked with diverse technologies ranging from semiconductor processing equipment to self-assembling materials, conductive polymers, thin-film displays, and radio frequency identification.

8.2   Panel Discussion

Mr. Robbins: Nima and Dave, can you explain for us how you came to handle IP matters at your companies? Was there something in particular about your respective backgrounds that made you the "go-to" people for IP at your companies?

Mr. Shiva: Company founders and start-up executives have to play many roles. In the early days at Neurion Pharmaceuticals, because I had strong knowledge of the life science business, a scientist's knowledge of the company's core technology, and a basic knowledge of the patent process, I started managing the IP development process somewhat by default. I worked closely with outside patent attorneys to develop our initial patent applications. In the process of interacting with the lawyers and making decisions, I developed the practical, management-level knowledge that is needed to file patent applications, first in the United States and then internationally, via the Patent Cooperation Treaty, or PCT, process. With each subsequent company for which I have managed IP development, the process has become more deliberate, but the basic steps are the same. But the legal work, and dealing with the U.S. Patent and Trademark Office, should always fall on the attorneys. That's what you pay them for—their expertise and their experience working with the U.S. Patent and Trademark Office.

Dr. Margolese: ORFID is a technology company with IP matters that cut across materials, semiconductor device physics and engineering, as well as electrical engineering, all of which are focused on organic electronic applications. To wrap one's head around these topics and to see how the company's IP fits within the general IP landscape of organic electronics requires a diverse technology background. In addition, IP cannot be developed usefully without paying attention to the business plan of the company. I have some experience in all the relevant areas: I have a technical background in semiconductor engineering and material science, and I have participated in previous start-up companies doing technology and business development in these areas.

Mr. Robbins: Could you tell me a little about what your companies do and where their IP originated?

Mr. Shiva: What is interesting about Neurion, as a case study for early IP development, is that the company's founding technology was not a specific drug but a platform for developing new drugs. Ultimately, it is much easier to think of IP in terms of a specific drug, because you know what it looks like—its structure—and you know exactly what diseases the drug is intended to treat. With a platform technology, it can be hard to know up front what the technology can be used for. Some uses are not readily apparent at the outset. Thus, you can end up spending more money developing IP for a platform technology, because you file applications on a number of different uses, but you may not know which ones will be important to the business down the line. With another one of our companies, Encode Bio, we were developing a specific research tool, so the initial IP development was more straightforward. We had very specific uses in mind right from the start.

Dr. Margolese: ORFID is working to commercialize display and radio frequency identification technologies based on organic electronics. Some of ORFID's original IP was licensed from a university, and some was licensed from another company, albeit a much larger company. At ORFID, we are specifically interested in protecting device technology, because devices made from organic electronics will form the foundation for the products people ultimately will use. We are interested in establishing patent claims on materials and device architectures, which are key to the fabrication of the devices. It's all about protecting how the devices are made. As we evolve, we will start to claim specific design circuitry. Eventually, we will patent entire applications.

Mr. Robbins: I understand that Neurion got its start as an academic spin-out, whereas some of ORFID's technology came from a university and other technology came from a corporate partner. Were there any differences in how IP issues were handled in each situation?

Mr. Shiva: Yes. In your average university spin-out, you are probably dealing with having to license IP, which means you will need to work out a licensing agreement with the university. Negotiating a licensing deal with a university is not always straightforward. You may not wish to give away too much in terms of product royalties. You might not have a lot of cash to pay up front, so you might need to give away more equity. It's really the university's patent or patent application, and the university has its own IP attorneys, so it's really up to the university to decide what the IP covers. If you have a company co-founder who is also a faculty member "on the inside" at a university, this is a nicer situation, because you have someone who can look after how the university treats you. Entrepreneurs can run into trouble with universities when they do not have someone on the inside looking out for their interests.

Dr. Margolese: Generally, academic institutions do not commercialize their own technologies, and this point is reflected in the licensing agreements. The licensing agreement from the academic partner goes one way: out to the licensee. With ORFID's corporate partner, the agreement

Creating and Protecting Intellectual Property

goes both ways. We license technology from them, and they license technology back from us. With our corporate partner, we have to carefully define the fields of use in each of our agreements. In technology we license back to our corporate partner, the field must be narrow enough and the markets restricted enough so we can do collaborations with other corporate partners in order to do co-development work as well as to raise money from outside investors. As a cautionary note, in a cross-licensing arrangement, you have to be careful not to out-license anything that is critical to your business plan.

Mr. Robbins: What do you look for when choosing an IP attorney? Do you have any advice on how to work with an IP attorney?

Mr. Shiva: Personally, I believe it is not worth picking an IP attorney on price alone. Better to pick people who have a personal interest in what you are doing, are responsive, understand your business, and have comfort with your technology. The worst situation is dealing with attorneys who are too busy and do not get back to you, or dealing with someone who is more junior and you have to go through him or her to get to someone with more experience who will also be more expensive. I prefer to deal with one person who is experienced and an expert. In bigger firms, to be more efficient, they have more attorneys and more resources, but this makes it more time-consuming and expensive when you need to get answers.

To keep costs down, and to ensure fidelity of information, I believe it is preferable to write your own technology disclosures, rather than to delegate this work to an outside IP attorney. The IP attorney will never understand your company's technology as much as you do. But it is best to leave filings with the U.S. Patent and Trademark Office and other patent agencies to the attorneys, because this is what they know best. It is an inefficient use of IP attorneys' time to have them do their own searches to understand your technology. Explaining to the IP attorney where the prior art is and why your company's technology is useful and novel, can be more cost-effective than having the attorney figure it out for himself or herself.

Dr. Margolese: The choice of IP attorney is very important. The attorney needs to understand the time and money constraints peculiar to your particular start-up. He or she must know the technology. It is too costly to engage an attorney that needs to climb a steep learning curve. In addition, a technologically astute attorney can add value to a patent with properly crafted claims and can help to determine how your company's IP fits into the IP landscape in your field.

As I mentioned above, money is at a premium in a start-up. A good way to cut costs with an IP attorney is to minimize the use of their time. Do not use them for business matters, for example. When engaged in putting together licensing agreements, business matters can be handled substantially in-house. Many of the key issues in licensing agreements are business-related, such as royalty rates, fees, sublicenses, scope of the field, and so on. Legal counsel should be brought in intermittently throughout the process to assure that the licensing document reads as intended and that your business objectives are represented in the correct legal framework.

Another way to use an IP attorney's time most efficiently is to provide all the necessary background information needed to construct a patent, write a draft of the claims in-house, and lay out what you wish to accomplish with the claims in the application. The attorney should take it from this point.

Mr. Robbins: Nima, can you outline a typical patent application process and explain some of the terminology?

Mr. Shiva: I could do that in general, but I would refer people to the U.S. Patent and Trademark Office Web site for a detailed explanation. I do not think it is efficient for an entrepreneur to learn all the details of the patent application process.

Basically, at the beginning, the entrepreneur needs to make a decision about whether he or she wants to do a provisional or non-provisional application, the difference being that a provisional application is less expensive up-front and does not have to have claims. What's important is providing specifications of the technology and to establish a priority date for the invention. Usually, you would use a provisional application when you need more time to develop the technology and make sure it's for real. If you feel strongly about the value of your technology, and would prefer to have your patent published and issued sooner,, you can go directly into a non-provisional application process, but it costs more, it is a longer application

Creating and Protecting Intellectual Property

process, and it involves all the details—the claims, the drawings. Also, with a provisional application, you have one year to decide upon entering the Patent Cooperation Treaty process for international coverage, whereas with a non-provisional, you need to make that decision up front, which increases up-front costs. You really do a non-provisional application when you know for sure what you want to do. The advantage is that you save yourself up to a year of time at the patent office, which starts reviewing your patent application a year earlier. This is important, because as soon as your patent issues, you can begin to go after infringers.

Mr. Robbins: Dave, can you offer some helpful tips about dealing with the U.S. Patent and Trademark Office?

Dr. Margolese: Yes. Let your IP attorney guide you through the process! Virtually all patents are challenged by the examiners at the U.S. Patent and Trademark Office. Objections can be on many fronts but particularly with the rejection of claims based on prior art. Experience in handling these objections is quite valuable in either overriding the objections raised or narrowing the scope of the patent as little as possible. Attorneys are in their element here. Let them do it.

Mr. Robbins: What about international IP filings. How is that done? How do you decide where to file? Who handles the actual work of filing internationally?

Mr. Shiva: The biggest decision you have to make is whether international protection is important to you, and if so, what country or what region in which you want coverage. It's very expensive. Not just the fees you need to pay to be considered, but also maintenance costs. Every country will charge you a certain amount every year to maintain your patent. But most of the cost arises from negotiating with individual countries, because each time your attorney is charging you for the time spent. The biggest cost is the attorney fees for all the back-and-forth interaction with the various international patent offices.

The decision to go international, and what countries to protect, has to do with what's important to your business. It's a case-by-case decision, and you should involve your attorney in that decision.

Dr. Margolese: There are many countries in which you could file for patent protection, but the cost of filing in all of them would be sizable. I would suggest only filing in those countries in which a significant market exists or is likely to exist for your products. The work of filing internationally is handled by your IP attorney through the use of foreign patent agents familiar with patent prosecution in the countries where protection is needed.

Mr. Robbins: Aside from yourselves, are there any other people at your companies who get involved with IP development?

Mr. Shiva: The only other person that would get involved is the actual inventor of the technology.

Dr. Margolese: Yes. The founding scientist and senior scientists generate many ideas that are potentially patentable. Consultants may also be hired to develop patents to protect a particular field.

Mr. Robbins: How do you handle disclosure issues such as academic publications or new IP that gets developed as part of a corporate collaboration? Can you recommend any special agreement terms that deal with these particular issues?

Mr. Shiva: I can generally say that with academic institutions, the interest is always publication, so prior to a publication being accepted or going into press, the university or company should at least file a provisional patent application, which could be as simple as submitting the actual manuscript or just rewriting the manuscript in a way the attorney can do very quickly. It is not very expensive.

If you are in business and your company is inventing new technology in-house, you need processes in place so your employees know how to submit a technology disclosure either to the in-house IP manager or the company's IP attorney. If you want to protect the technology, you need to describe how you arrived at the invention, why it is novel, what the prior art is, and what its utility is.

Creating and Protecting Intellectual Property 115

In many ways, preparing a patent application is like writing a manuscript. But there are specific formats for technology disclosure, which you can read about in books or get from your IP counsel.

Dr. Margolese: Disclosure issues with academic and corporate partners are handled under collaborative research and development agreements that are put in place at the beginning of the relationship. For example, our academic partner needs to publish. So, our agreements allow this but give us the opportunity to file before publication if we choose. For example, ORFID has a thirty-day period to review publications for identification of any enabling disclosure of patentable inventions, and publication can be delayed an additional sixty days in order to file a patent application.

With our corporate partners, the situation is quite different. Publications are not at issue, but both we and our partner on occasion have the need to disclose IP to third parties for business development reasons. This is taken care of in the research and development agreement prior to disclosure, and the third parties must be covered under a non-disclosure agreement.

Mr. Robbins: Nima and Dave, can you offer closing words of advice for seed investors about what to look for when it comes to IP?

Mr. Shiva: There are several things that are important. First, you need to know that the IP is broad, or in other words, will have an ability to properly protect the business. Also, what you should look for is IP that can be used to grow the business. Plus, you should think in terms of whether a technology can be protected by a combination of trade secrets and patents. It all comes down to whether barriers to competition can be raised through protection of the IP. For example, in the life sciences, IP may be of limited value if you are marketing so-called "tools" to the end user, and the end user could simply practice your art without paying for it.

Dr. Margolese: Examine the IP to be sure it advances the company's business plan. This requires a fair amount of due diligence on the part of the investor, but it is necessary. Examine the licensing agreements. Are they exclusive or non-exclusive, for example? Also, look out for out-licensed technology that interferes with the company's business plan by creating a competitor or by giving away markets. Also, do the patents have value? Are they obsolete? Are the products that are being produced different from the IP? Can competitors engineer around the IP? Are there other patents that block the IP that would require the acquisition of a license? These are the kinds of questions investors need to ask.

9

Writing and Evaluating the Business Plan

plan *n.*
A scheme, program, or method worked out beforehand for the accomplishment of an objective: *a plan of attack*.

9.1 The Business Plan Industry

Almost everyone offers advice about writing business plans, from friends, consultants, and publishers, to the U.S. government[25]. If you didn't know any better, you might believe that, with a good book or software package about writing business plans, you could "write a powerful, high-impact business plan in six weeks," or, in "thirty days," or, in "twelve easy steps," and "win big money." An entire cottage industry of freelancers and ghost authors will help company founders and entrepreneurs draft business plans that will make investors sit up and take notice. Like desperate self-help junkies, fledgling company founders and first-time entrepreneurs spend millions of dollars every year on business plan instruction manuals, do-it-yourself software, and how-to courses. Armed with confidence-boosting outlines, checklists, and templates, seekers of start-up funding will then spend many thousands of hours agonizing over executive summaries, situation analyses, technical rationales and financial projections, all in pursuit of the perfect business plan. Everyone knows that before you approach an investor to ask for funding, you have to have a business plan.

---

[25] See www.sba.gov and navigate to business plans

Here is my tongue-in-cheek definition of a business plan: A business plan is a very important document that most company founders or entrepreneurs take great care to write, and few, if any, experienced investors ever read. Yes, the ironic truth about business plans is that, important as they are in the writing, they play a relatively minor role in the investor's decision about whether to fund a new venture. This truth is hard for people new to the start-up scene to grasp, because it flies in the face of everything we are told in business school, at start-up "boot camps," at the bookstore, and by start-up business consultants about the almost religious significance of a professionally prepared business plan. To say that business plans are not important for start-ups is blasphemy. It also misses the point. Of course, business plans are important, but as a *process* more than as a finished *product*.

9.2 Business Plan Writing as a Process

Business plans are works in progress. They evolve but are never truly "done." The real importance of the business plan is in the process of its writing rather than its completion. The most difficult part of writing a business plan is getting started, because staring at a blank computer screen is discouraging, and if you have ever written a business plan before, you know what you are in for. Hours spent with your fingertips massaging your brow, searching for the right words, the appealing turn of phrase, the pithy statement that will impel the reader (i.e., investors) to give you an encouraging call, send you an inviting e-mail, and grant you a meeting. The business plan is thought by most company founders and entrepreneurs to be a carefully crafted door-opener, a compelling description of a technology and a business opportunity that will motivate the reader to action. Thus, an extraordinary amount of attention is devoted to the business plan, and, to its packaging.

When I first got serious about doing start-ups (at the time, as a consultant), I invested in (i.e., charged on my shiny new American Express Gold Business Card, embossed with my own company's name), a series of binding machines of increasing size and cost. Back then, I was convinced that no business plan was presentable until neatly and professionally bound with a colored plastic spine and clear acetate cover. A thick, slick, Velo-bound business plan was a thing of envy. Fast forward to the present day, and I cannot remember the last time I used a binding machine to package a business plan. A staple will do just fine. Or, more commonly, an electronic version, sent by e-mail.

I no longer view the business plan as a work product unto itself. A business plan, at its best, is a clear, concise, and well-written description of a business opportunity and justification for an investment. A business plan does not have to be a magnum opus, consuming acres of old-growth timber and weighing in at a hefty three pounds (minus supplementary financials).

I do not believe that my current sentiment about business plans is simply a matter of having become jaded through experience. Instead, I blame technology. Specifically, I blame Microsoft Word®, Excel®, and PowerPoint®, aided and abetted by Hewlett Packard, Xerox, Kinko's, and Staples. Back in the 1980s and even the early-to-mid 1990s, producing a nice-looking business plan took significant effort. Back then, many senior partners at venture capital firms and senior executives in big companies couldn't even type, no less create an impressive-looking spreadsheet, or design an eye-catching PowerPoint slide. Now, anyone can produce a decent-looking printed document. Back then, printing in color required a hefty investment in a painfully slow color pen plotter (late 80s to early 90s) or early-generation inkjet printer (mid-90s). Now, a few hundred bucks will buy you a full-color print shop. (It's the ink cartridges they stick you for.) Back then, if you cared enough about professional word processing or graphic design, you might hire a consultant to create a business plan template or produce computer illustrations. Now, you fire up Microsoft Office®, snap some digital photos, Photoshop® a few enhancements, and bingo! You have business plan glitz at your fingertips. The mass distribution of low-cost, easy-to-use technology for producing documents and graphics has made business plans a commodity. Plus, to make matters worse (well, not worse, necessarily, but certainly different), the Internet, the Web, and e-mail have made hard-copy documents old-fashioned, even wasteful, inefficient, and dumb. There are fewer and fewer good reasons to produce a hard-copy business plan these days, and to do so is expensive. The paper costs money. The ink costs money. Delivering documents via postal mail or FedEx® costs money, and the upshot of all this expense is that investors and other targets of business plans would rather receive plans electronically, because it takes less time, uses less desk space, and weighs less in one's briefcase. So, today, when investors receive business plans as hard copy, the first reaction may be, "Why bother?"

Getting back to the original point for this section, the reason to bother with writing a business plan is that writing ideas on paper (sorry about the anachronism; I meant on the computer) takes a depth and precision of thought that, for most people, cannot be achieved by other methods. No matter the extent of one's eloquence with the spoken word, or one's powers of verbal persuasion, writing a business plan is a valuable exercise. Drafting a business plan forces the writer to think logically, linearly, and comprehensively about the path the company will take to develop its technology, commercialize it, and make money. It should take no more than a few pages to lay out everything important that a reader of a business plan would need to know to understand the nature of the business opportunity. The rest is details.

9.3 How Investors Review Business Plans

Sorry to burst your bubble, all you eager founders and entrepreneurs out there, but angel investors and venture capitalists are not sitting in their offices eagerly awaiting your business plan. Most investors only pay attention to what other investors are paying attention to, and you can bet that does not include your business plan. The submission of unsolicited business plans to experienced angels or professional investors by unknown parties is not an effective means of prospecting for investors. But the unsolicited business plans keep pouring in. They come in through the mail, through e-mail, over the transom, and under the door. They arrive by FedEx, UPS, and DHL. They get dropped off, winged in, uploaded, downloaded, passed along, and handed over.

Most venture capital firms allow money-seekers to submit business plans online. This is a polite way of saying: "Although we probably won't even look at your plan, to avoid giving you the (largely truthful) impression that we only consider opportunities we source internally or that come from our coterie trusted contacts and co-investors, send us what you've got, and if one of our overworked associates isn't busy, maybe she'll give it a look-see."

Writing and Evaluating the Business Plan

Thus, visit most venture capital firms' Web sites, and you find a statement like the following:

> If you don't have a personal contact at or referral to XYZ Ventures and would like to submit an opportunity for review by one of our investment professionals, you may send a non-confidential business plan or executive summary, along with your contact information, to businessplan@xyzventures.com.

What you won't find on any venture capital firm's Web site is an additional statement reading something like this:

> If you do not hear back from us within one week, it's because we are not interested. If you do not hear back from us within two weeks, it's because we are really not interested. If you do not hear back from us in three weeks, it's because we never read your plan.

Many angel investor networks have developed elaborate online plan submission procedures that give money-seekers the impression that angels are different from mainstream venture capital firms and really care about what start-up founders and entrepreneurs have to say. Thus, many Web sites for angel networks feature an online form for submitting business plan information, accompanied by a statement such as the following:

> Angels-R-Us employs a rigorous and objective process to ensure that all investment opportunities we receive are evaluated promptly and thoroughly. Before submitting your opportunity for consideration by our screening committee, please review our **Statement of Investment Criteria** and our **Guidelines for Plan Submission**. To be considered for review by our members, please refer to the **Application Form**, enter the requested information, and attach a copy of your executive summary.

If you have ever submitted a business plan to an angel network, only to have your start-up opportunity summarily dismissed and your ego bruised, you probably wish the angel network's Web site had provided the following disclaimer:

> **Warning:** While most members of our investor network will do their best to give you honest, well-balanced feedback and advice, you are bound to encounter a few know-it-alls, attention-grabbers and power-trippers in our midst that will make your experience less than pleasant. Applicants who are not prepared to receive unvarnished criticism are advised to turn back.

When investors do read business plans, it is done with a specific purpose. Investors are looking for the telltale signs that distinguish a legitimate business opportunity from just another un-fundable request for funding. Specifically, investors are looking for the following:

- Good writing and critical thinking
- An intriguing and compelling executive summary
- A logical plan for addressing a large, existing market
- Validated technology that can be protected
- Scientific or technical founders with excellent credentials
- A business team with a proven track record
- A well-reasoned funding request
- A clear path to value creation and exit

It's not much more complicated than that. The length of the plan does not matter. Writing a novel gets no extra points when a novella will do just fine, and a short story would be even better.

9.4 Advice on Writing Business Plans

My advice to would-be writers of business plans is the following:

Write It Yourself

Hiring a consultant to write a business plan tends not to work well. No consultant can capture the inner passion of a founder, nor is it a good idea

Writing and Evaluating the Business Plan

to write a business plan by committee. I have drafted business plans as a consultant-for-hire, and have found the process to be all-consuming. Writing a good business plan takes a great deal of focused effort. Unfortunately, no consultant's effort ever seems to satisfy the client that lacks sufficient ability and business insight to write a business plan without outside help. If a start-up's founder or a key member of the founding team cannot handle the task of writing a business plan, there is a problem.

Focus on the Executive Summary

A really good executive summary is better than a mediocre full plan. In recent years, I have concluded that about six pages is usually sufficient. The rest can go into a separate technical backgrounder, or an appendix of business information, financial projections, and assumptions.

Buy a Copy of Strunk & White, and Don't Misspell

Just because a business plan is not a work of literature does not mean it cannot be written well. If you do not consider yourself to be a good writer, or even if you do, buy a copy of *The Elements of Style* by Strunk and White.[26] This classic style guide is a small treasure trove of practical guidelines about good writing. Read it. Keep it on your desk. And while you are at it, use your spell-checker.

Don't Overuse Superlatives

Business plans that lean heavily on tired adjectives such as "revolutionary," "groundbreaking," and "disruptive" are a turnoff. If the significance of a new technology or business opportunity does not speak for itself, pumping up the volume with empty superlatives is not going to help.

Don't Go Overboard with Numbers

Writers of business plans often assume that throwing around a lot of market statistics, technological performance data, and financial projections

---

[26] *The Elements of Style*, Fourth Edition, William Strunk Jr. and E.B. White. Allyn & Bacon, Needham Heights, MA, 2000

demonstrates a command of the business opportunity at hand. Sometimes, excessive use of data just shows an inability to separate the wheat from the chaff. Experienced investors are not impressed or swayed by numbers. What they focus on is people and a well-communicated story. Too many numbers can get in the way of communication.

10

Working with Service Providers

The purpose of this chapter is to provide some helpful guidelines for hiring and working with service providers and professional advisors. While there is no foolproof method for selecting good law firms, consultants, marketing agencies, and other service professionals, there are some helpful principles and practices that company founders, entrepreneurs, and seed-stage investors can follow. Let's focus our attention on just a few of the most important classes of services providers that start-ups usually need to hire.

10.1 Attorneys

Effects of Post-Dot-Com Consolidation

Start-ups will need a variety of legal services that may or may not be provided by a single firm. There are two countervailing trends in legal services that have bearing on whether a start-up is likely to obtain most of its legal services from one firm, from a group of boutique firms, or from solo practitioners. One trend has to do with consolidation of firms within the legal profession, and the other with increased specialization. Following the dot-com bust, the major law firms serving start-ups in high-tech and the life sciences underwent a period of dramatic consolidation. Some of the more aggressive law firms in major technology-heavy regions such as Silicon Valley, Boston, and San Diego expanded rapidly during the heady days of the Internet boom, often taking large portions of their compensation from start-up clients in the form of equity rather than old-fashioned legal tender. During the mid to late 1990s, national law firms and regional powerhouses were practically falling over each other to compete for the accounts of venture-backed start-ups, and the marketing of legal services became a bit of a circus. Law firms hired business development specialists and tech-savvy "rainmakers" to drum up new business. Law firms plastered their logos on conference marketing materials, sponsored trendy networking events, placed print advertisements in the hot technology business publications of the day, and, in at least one case, launched a multimillion-dollar network television advertising campaign. For a while, start-up attorneys ranked right up there after venture capitalists as the movers and shakers of the start-up world. This situation was an aberration, another distortion of reality caused by that huge spinning black hole known as the New Economy. The New Economy sucked some very respectable law firms into its vortex along with once respectable consulting firms and technology providers. When the New Economy imploded, a lot of law firms that had expanded too rapidly, spent too much on marketing, and taken too much compensation in the form of worthless equity vanished literally overnight. The same fate was suffered by smaller regional or local firms whose business dried up and by boutique patent law firms whose rosters of patent-filing clients shrank precipitously. In the wake of this carnage, larger and more conservative law firms that had maintained a stable roster of Old Economy clients began to gobble up New Economy law firms that had fallen on hard times. By the mid-2000s, the consolidation of major law firms has left start-up companies in the nation's leading technology centers with a dramatically smaller group of law firms from which to choose.

Legal Fees

For start-ups, the consolidation of leading law firms made it easier to do one-stop shopping, but it also resulted in a period of escalating fees. Retaining a major law firm for legal services can be a good move for start-ups that want the convenience of one-stop shopping and the credibility that can be gained from working with a well-known law firm. However, working with a major law firm is very expensive. The division of labor in major firms between senior partners, specialists in areas such as taxation and securities, associates, and paralegals leads to a multi-tiered fee structure that seems to encourage delegation of responsibilities, parsing of services, and consequently, "piling on" of legal fees (at least from the client's perspective). When reviewing legal bills, billable items that make me raise my eyebrow and grit my teeth include "researching issues related to...," "conferring with partners regarding...," and "drafting e-mail to..."

Working with Service Providers

Consolidation within the legal profession has brought with it revenue-maximizing specialization and computerized billing systems that capture every billable minute of every specialist. Smaller, old-school law firms used to be casual about billing. Now, big firms' monthly statements seem to arrive every two weeks, and their accounts receivable departments accept all major credit cards. Just think of all the American Express Rewards Points you would rack up by charging your legal fees to your Gold Card. Not a bad idea.

In large law firms, the role played by corporate counsel has become less like a general practitioner and more like a general contractor. Rather than servicing most of their start-up clients' legal needs on their own, outside corporate counsel now parses out the start-ups' legal work to specialists in the areas of securities law, taxation, patents, trademarks and copyrights, employment law, immigration law, and if an office lease is needed, commercial real estate law. The specialist-partners, in turn, may delegate to junior associates or paralegals. All these specialists and underlings represent a lot of overhead for the law firm to cover and a large inventory of billable hours to apply somewhere—anywhere—in fifteen-minute increments.

Advice on Working with Law Firms

Everyone likes to complain about lawyers and legal fees, but working with an experienced, conscientious attorney who is backed by an efficient team is worth every dollar. Besides, who else is going to do all the work that the lawyers in Congress, and at the Securities and Exchange Commission, the Internal Revenue Service, the U.S. Patent and Trademark Office, the Food and Drug Administration, your secretary of state, and your business-friendly state legislature dreamed up, in the form of new laws and regulations?

Following are a few guidelines for working with law firms that are worth considering:

Keep Your Corporate Law Firm and Your Patent Firm Separate

This is not some Machiavellian stratagem to divide and conquer. It's a way to avoid having to pitch the baby out with the bathwater if you become dissatisfied with the service of your corporate counsel or your patent counsel. Post-consolidation, most major law firms have built up substantial patent law departments and would be more than happy to provide patent and trademark counsel to start-ups along with the standard corporate legal services. The problem with this arrangement is that, somewhere along the line, you may decide you would like to take some of your legal business elsewhere, or perhaps your favorite corporate counsel or patent attorney decides to move on to another firm. If you have all of your legal business—corporate and intellectual property—at the same firm, moving just a portion of the business to another firm can lead to touchy situations. For example; how do you tell your corporate counsel, who has also become a good personal friend, that his colleagues in the legal department are doing a lousy job and that you would like to take your patent business elsewhere? What if your patent counsel, who you would never leave, decides to start her own boutique firm and has a messy falling out with her previous employer, which also happens to handle all of your corporate work? Would you let your loyalty to your patent attorney disrupt your relationship with the rest of your legal team? These may seem like remote, hypothetical situations, but if you are in the thick of important legal work such as a private placement or a string of critical patent filings and things suddenly go sour with your corporate or your patent counsel, you can minimize the potential for work disruption or disruption of personal relationships if you make it a policy not to place your corporate legal work and your patent work at the same law firm.

Only Request Work You Need Right Now—or Soon

Law firms seem to respond best to requests with event-driven or time-driven deadlines. Otherwise, they just spin their wheels or do nothing. Also, be specific with requests. For example, if you are preparing for a stock offering, ask for advice on documents that need to be prepared and the order of priority. Be specific about your schedule, but do not waste your time and the law firm's time by having papers drawn up ahead of time for which key information is still needed or that may become unnecessary.

Ask Attorneys for Advice, but Make Your Own Decisions

Attorneys offer advice and render opinions, but they are not paid to make business decisions. Company founders, entrepreneurs, and investors must make business decisions, and they can make more informed and, therefore, better decisions by seeking legal advice. Attorneys can provide counsel on legal matters and help businesspeople understand risks, but in the end, lawyers are not there to tell you what you can or cannot do. They are only there to tell you about the implications of your actions. Businesspeople make decisions. Lawyers render advice.

Keep Your Corporate Counsel in the Loop

It is a good idea to copy your corporate counsel on the e-mails you send to board members and for the board members to know counsel is being copied, so that board matters are out in the open and you, as the sender of an e-mail, do not create the impression that you are compartmentalizing information. I have found this to be especially true when corporate counsel is on personally friendly terms with a start-up's founder(s) or when you, when sending e-mail to board members, wish to avoid appearing to favor one particular point of view or one subgroup of board members. Copying corporate counsel on e-mail correspondence has the effect of keeping everyone honest. It also avoids having to bring corporate counsel up to speed every time some new board matter arises.

It is also a good idea to keep corporate counsel informed about daily operational matters and special situations that may require an attorney's input in the future. Doing so will save vital time when some simmering personnel dispute or squabble with the landlord suddenly boils over and requires prompt action.

Pick Up the Phone or Meet Informally

Every once in awhile, it is helpful simply to pick up the phone just to catch up with corporate counsel and shoot the breeze. For example, you might talk about start-up activity in your area, or companies that are hiring. These informal conversations can also be held over a meal, out on the golf course, or if you are lucky, in your law firm's well-provisioned hospitality suite at a ball game.

10.2 Consultants

"We don't actually do the things we recommend; we just recommend them."[27]

Start-up consultants fall into two broad categories: business consultants and scientific/technical consultants. Let's take a look at some of the defining characteristics of these two types of consultants:

Business Consultants

Tech start-ups are often founded by scientists and engineers with little to no experience raising capital or running a business. If scientific and technical founders do not have the connections to attract experienced entrepreneurs or senior executives to handle the business end of the start-up, nor the credentials to attract mainstream venture investors, consultants can help fill the management gap. Technology hubs like Boston/Cambridge, San Francisco, and San Diego are crawling with start-up business development and management consultants whose ranks include industry veterans, serial entrepreneurs, semi-retired professionals, Ph.D.s who escaped from the lab bench, laid-off managers, career changers, and recent M.B.A.s looking to gain start-up experience. Indeed, any town with a major academic or biomedical research center is likely to have an active pool of consultants who specialize in helping technology start-ups develop business plans, raise capital, manage business development, or provide coaching on general management issues. The challenge for company founders, inexperienced entrepreneurs, and seed-stage investors is to pick the right consultants to handle the tasks at hand and to avoid wasting time and money in the process.

To choose a good consultant and limit the risk of making a hiring mistake, start slow, and start small. When meeting a potential new consultant for the first time, there is a natural tendency to get swept away by initial enthusiasm. The consultant is likely to be on his or her best behavior, and to show great interest in the start-up's business. And for their part, the start-up's founders and/or senior executives are likely to feel a rush of excitement in finding someone who expresses an eager interest in their

---

[27] Quote from a humorous television commercial, poking fun at consultants.

business. All the warm fuzziness of a first "get to know" meeting with a potential consultant can lead to errors in judgment. The start-up may confuse the consultant's enthusiasm for talent or overlook little warning signs that might become obvious in later meetings. Such things can only be validated through follow-up meetings, reference checking, and other due diligence. Thus, no significant decisions about hiring a consultant should be made at the first meeting. Furthermore, when initiating a consulting engagement, I recommend starting with a trial engagement such as a half-day consultation or a short-term assignment. By starting slowly, the start-up can "test drive" the consultant to determine whether to continue and expand the consulting relationship. This trial process may be more important for business consultants than for technical consultants, because technical consultants have certain objective qualifications such as academic degrees, faculty appointments, publications, and patents that are easier to assess than a business consultant's work history.

Scientific/Technical Consultants

Technical or scientific consultants usually fall into one of the following categories, each of which brings its own things to watch out for:

Academic Consultants

Academic consultants generally include university faculty members from the scientific, engineering, or medical fields. University professors vary widely in the degree to which they consult. Some could make it a full-time job. Others consult rarely, if at all. Most universities limit their faculty members to the equivalent of one day per week of outside consulting. If you wish to hire an academic consultant, be sure to inquire about other companies with which he or she is, or has been, engaged by as a consultant, and whether he or she has any exclusive engagements, outstanding non-compete agreements, secrecy agreements, or agreements with other companies concerning intellectual property rights. Sometimes, faculty members may not recall the terms of their prior consulting engagements. If you have any concerns, it is usually appropriate to ask if the faculty member can provide a copy of a potentially conflicting consulting agreement, with any confidential information redacted.

Start-ups should request that their academic consultants sign confidentiality agreements, although it may be necessary to loosen the terms, particularly with regards to topics such as rights to make use of or publish data. It is also standard practice to request that the academic consultant sign an invention assignment agreement, although the consultant may need to run the terms of an assignment agreement by his or her institution's attorneys to avoid impeding academic research or other business pursuits with which the consultant might be engaged.

Start-ups should be cautious about engaging extremely busy faculty members as consultants, because these faculty members may be so heavily committed that they are rarely available.

Specialized Consulting Firms

Every industry has its own cadre of specialized technical consulting firms. Usually, a start-up would seek outside consulting support to provide advice on or hands-on services for research, product development, regulatory affairs, process design, process scale-up, manufacturing, operations, logistics, sales support, customer support, or other technical tasks for which the company does not have internal personnel.

The same basic advice about securing formal agreements with academic consultants applies to industry consultants, but start-ups should expect industry consultants to be completely familiar with the scope and terms of their prior consulting engagements. Start-ups might cut an absent-minded professor a little slack when it comes to business agreements, but not so for industry consultants. Industry consultants should adhere to certain customary practices within their industry, should be compliant with relevant state, federal, or commercial regulations, and should warrant such compliance within their consulting agreements.

Independent Scientific/Technical Consultants

Independent scientific or technical consultants are usually scientists with doctoral degrees or engineers with commercial experience. Independent consultants may derive most of their experience from working at or with big companies, or they may have considerable experience with start-ups.

When choosing among independent consultants, start-ups should place more emphasis on an independent's start-up experience than on his or her big company experience. Nine times out of ten, an independent consultant who has spent most of his or her career working for corporate giants will seek to apply big company solutions to small company problems, and will flounder in the absence of big company resources. There have been instances when my partners and I have considered hiring independent consultants because of their experience working at big high-tech, electronics, computing, or drug companies, and we have almost always concluded—sometimes after making a hiring mistake—that an independent consultant's ability to adapt to and work productively within that start-up environment is inversely proportional to the amount of time he or she has spent working in big companies.

When searching for good independent consultants, look for big company refugees—the consultants who bailed out of corporate positions as a matter of personal choice, but only after having built up a good knowledge base and having earned a few battle scars. Some independent consultants prefer ad-hoc situations. Others may prefer longer-term engagements as stand-ins for full-time employees.

Semi-Retired Scientific or Technical Executives

I have put semi-retired scientific or technical executives into a separate category, because they can play a distinct role as advisors to management on scientific or technical matters of strategic importance. This is one area where hiring should favor consultants or recent retirees with extensive big company experience. Start-ups should look to former scientific or technical executives not to do start-up work, but to help start-ups look, act, and perform more like the big companies with which they wish to do business. Thus, if a start-up's management wants to know "how the big companies do it" or wants to give members of their own scientific or technical team access to an industry veteran with deep knowledge of how big companies do research, develop products, and make management-level decisions about scientific or technical issues, look to the ranks of recent or semi-retirees from big companies.

Evaluating Consultants

When evaluating industry consultants for hire, bigger is not necessarily better. The need for size and scope of services depends on the nature of the start-up's business and its need for local, regional, national, or global reach. Aside from size and scope of their operations, industry consultants should be compared on the factors such as:

- Reputation for excellent service
- Expertise in a start-up's particular technology and business
- Depth of experience (i.e., Does the consulting firm have just one extremely knowledgeable expert or a whole team of specialists and sub-specialists that can handle a start-up's every need?)
- Ability to provide on-site or on-demand service
- Ability to deliver services remotely or electronically
- Capacity
- Scale-up and turnaround time
- Documentation and report generation
- Data management
- Quality assurance/quality control
- Project management
- Security

Start-ups can get themselves into budget trouble by assuming automatically that they will be better served by hiring technical consulting firms rather than independent consultants simply because consulting firms have a recognizable name, a large staff, or global reach. Larger consulting firms tend to focus most of their attention on big corporate clients, because that's where the money is. Larger consulting firms may promote their interest in working with start-ups because they like to appear "cutting-edge," and entrepreneurial, but the larger the consulting firm, the more it will emulate the bureaucratic, slow-moving behavior of its larger clients

Working with Service Providers

How to Be a Good Client for Consultants

Having served as a business consultant in more than thirty start-up situations during the past ten years, I would like to share some observations about how to be a good client:

Use Professional Agreements

When hiring a professional consultant, a start-up can use its own template for a consulting agreement or ask the consultant to submit his or her standard contract. Either way, the contract should be reviewed (if not prepared by) the client's attorney.

Following as Exhibit 9 is an example of a typical consulting agreement:

Exhibit 9
Consulting Agreement

Consulting Agreement

TECHNO-WIDGETS, INC., a Delaware Corporation with principal offices at _____ (hereinafter "COMPANY") and Dr. _____, of TECH CONSULTING, LLC, with principal offices at _____ (hereinafter "CONSULTANT") agree that CONSULTANT will advise COMPANY on matters relating to the field of organic electronics (hereinafter "Field") under the following terms and conditions ("this Agreement"):

1. **Consulting Services.** CONSULTANT's responsibilities shall include, without limitation, the following activities (hereinafter collectively referred to as "Services"):

   Meeting with and advising COMPANY's management and technical team members to prepare a product development plan for TECHNO-WIDGETS's Super-Chip and related intellectual property.

   The Services shall be performed for the most part in person during meetings at COMPANY or via telephone, e-mail or other correspondence, and may include meetings with personnel and other consultants at times and locations to be mutually agreed upon. In each instance, CONSULTANT shall perform the Services only upon COMPANY's request and after the scope of the Services has been approved by COMPANY. In the event that CONSULTANT believes that consulting services provided by CONSULTANT for other parties may be inconsistent with the terms of this Agreement, CONSULTANT shall promptly notify COMPANY, to the extent that such notification does not breach confidentiality provisions or understandings between the CONSULTANT and any third party. COMPANY and CONSULTANT will jointly determine whether or not to terminate this Agreement as a result of aforementioned notification.

2. **Compensation.** As consideration for CONSULTANT's services hereunder, COMPANY shall pay CONSULTANT as follows:

   $_____ per day for up to_____ days of service. CONSULTANT agrees to inform COMPANY in the event that services requested by

COMPANY will require more than _____ days, and in the event CONSULTANT will require additional compensation for this extra time.

COMPANY shall be under no obligation to pay for Services other than those actually requested and scheduled by COMPANY.

The COMPANY shall also reimburse CONSULTANT for reasonable business-related expenses incurred as part of the consulting services, not to exceed _____ per instance without COMPANY's prior written authorization. Payment shall be made within thirty (30) days of receipt of an invoice of itemized Services and expenses and submission of appropriate vouchers and receipts as may be reasonably necessary to substantiate CONSULTANT's out-of-pocket expenses.

3. **Term and Termination.** This Agreement shall be effective upon full execution of this Agreement and continue for a period of one year. The Agreement may be extended by written agreement signed by the parties. Either party may terminate this Agreement with or without cause upon giving thirty (30) days prior written notice to the other party. Termination or expiration of this Agreement shall not affect any rights or obligations which have accrued prior thereto or in connection therewith.

4. **Confidential Information and Inventions.**

4a. With respect to any technical or business information of a proprietary or confidential nature which CONSULTANT may obtain from COMPANY under this Agreement or which is developed by CONSULTANT as a direct result of CONSULTANT's Services hereunder (all of such technical and business information being referred to hereinafter as "Company Information"), it is understood that until the Company Information in question has been disclosed by COMPANY to the public generally or until COMPANY grants CONSULTANT specific written approval to disclose Company Information, CONSULTANT will:

　　i)　treat Company Information as confidential;
　　ii)　not use any Company Information except as and to the extent necessary for the aforesaid consulting tasks; and
　　iii)　not disclose any Company Information to any third party without prior written approval from COMPANY.

4b. Consultant's obligations set forth in this Section 4 shall not apply with respect to any portion of the Company Information that:

  i) was in the public domain at the time it was communicated to CONSULTANT by COMPANY;
  ii) entered the public domain through no fault of CONSULTANT, subsequent to the time it was communicated to CONSULTANT by COMPANY;
  iii) was in CONSULTANT's possession free of any obligation of confidence at the time it was communicated to CONSULTANT by COMPANY;
  iv) was rightfully communicated to CONSULTANT free of any obligation of confidence subsequent to the time it was communicated to CONSULTANT by COMPANY;
  v) was developed by CONSULTANT independently of and without reference to any information communicated to CONSULTANT by COMPANY;
  vi) is required to be disclosed in response to a valid order by a court or other governmental body, or as otherwise required by law.

4c. Notwithstanding the above, prior to any subcontracting to third parties, such third party must be bound to the same obligations as under this Agreement regarding any Confidential Information prior to disclosure.

5. **Publications.** CONSULTANT shall not publish, nor submit for publication, any work resulting from the Services provided hereunder without prior written approval from COMPANY. Nothing in this agreement shall be construed as prohibiting or otherwise limiting CONSULTANT's ability to publish, or submit for publication, academic or scholarly works or works resulting from CONSULTANT's activities as a faculty member of _____, during or at any time after the term of this Agreement.

6. **Compliance.** In the performance of the Services hereunder, CONSULTANT shall comply with all applicable federal, state and local laws, regulations and guidelines. CONSULTANT shall also comply with COMPANY's polices when on COMPANY premises.

7. **No Restrictions.** CONSULTANT represents and warrants that the terms of this Agreement are not inconsistent with any other contractual or legal obligations CONSULTANT may have or with the policies of any institution or company with which CONSULTANT is associated.

8. **Independent Contractor.** CONSULTANT's status under this Agreement is that of an independent contractor. CONSULTANT shall not be deemed an employee, agent, partner or joint venturer of COMPANY for any purpose whatsoever, and CONSULTANT shall have no authority to bind or act on behalf of COMPANY. This Agreement shall not entitle CONSULTANT to participate in any benefit plan or program of COMPANY. CONSULTANT shall be responsible for, and agrees to comply with, obligations under federal and state tax laws for payment of income and, if applicable, self-employment tax.

9. **Assignment.** CONSULTANT may not assign this Agreement or any interest herein, or delegate any of its duties hereunder, to any third party without COMPANY's prior written consent, which consent is within COMPANY's sole discretion to grant or withhold. Any attempted assignment or delegation without such consent shall be null and void.

10. **Entire Agreement.** This Agreement contains the entire understanding of the parties with respect to the matters herein contained and supersedes all previous agreements and undertakings with respect thereto. This agreement may be modified only by written agreement signed by the parties.

This Agreement shall be governed by and construed in accordance with the laws of the State of _____ without regard to its conflicts of laws rules.

IN WITNESS WHEREOF, the parties hereto have executed this Agreement as of the day and year first written above.

TECHNO-WIDGETS, INC.　　　　**CONSULTANT**

By_____　　By: _____

Name_____　　Name_____

Title_____　　Title_____

Draw Up Specific Work Plans and Schedules

Following the practice of most large companies, I recommend drawing up a specific work plan or project description to describe the scope of a consulting engagement. This work plan or project description should then be attached to the standard agreement template (i.e., the "boilerplate") as an exhibit. The work plan should provide a detailed description of the anticipated work, deliverables, and a schedule or list of milestones. By treating the project plan as an exhibit, rather than as part of the body of the agreement, changes or new work plans can be drawn up and appended to the agreement without having to tinker with the boilerplate. This saves time and headaches, because the lawyers do not need to get involved in redrafting.

The client should control the work plan and refer to it periodically to assess the consultant's performance.

Stay in Contact

Good clients stay in contact with their consultants and do not treat consultants like a faucet—something to be turned on and off, and ignored at all other times. Consultants do their best work when they are consulted with for their expertise. To the extent appropriate, consultants should also be treated as part of the company team, even if only as a pinch-hitter, or as a member of the bullpen.

Pay on Time

Consultants, especially those who work for themselves, usually rely upon the timely receipt of consulting fees to make ends meet. Independent consultants do not usually have the luxury of a steady salary. However, if they are professional and conscientious, they will be right there with you when you need them, just like your own employees. Most start-ups would not think of paying their employees a few days late, or whenever the bookkeeper happens to come in, or only when cash flow allows. Respect payment schedules and pay consultants according to the terms of their consulting agreements.

How to Be a Bad Consulting Client

Be an Ivory Tower Academic

Inexperienced company founders, especially those from the halls of academia, may assume—naively, arrogantly, or both—that in a start-up, business management takes a back seat to science. Science, after all, is the hard part, isn't it? Business is a matter of putting together the appropriate documents, working things out with lawyers, presenting nice slides to investors, and opening up a bank account to deposit all the venture dollars that will surely come rolling in as soon as investors recognize the brilliance of the founders' technology. Thus, many academic founders treat the process of hiring a start-up business consultant as a perfunctory exercise. These kinds of academic founders can be recognized by their disregard for consultants' input, their lack of interest in "the business details," and their complaints about all the previous consultants and investors they have worked with who "didn't understand the technology" and were only interested in "stealing their ideas."

Be a Know-It-All Investor from an Unrelated Industry

My favorite example in the know-it-all investor category is the semi-retired garment industry magnate who is going to fund a new biotech start-up with a few of his friends and hire some consultant his tennis partner knows to write a business plan for $10,000. This kind of investor is always bragging about how he will "fund the whole thing out of my own pocket" if he has to. After all, having made umpteen millions selling designer suits and casual wear, what more is there to know? Besides, the academic scientist he is going to back is "a genius," has a lab full of Ph.D.s that "know the science," and does work "with all the big drug companies." This kind of investor is absolutely right. He does not really need a consultant. He just needs to find out for himself that getting a new drug to market in less than ten years is not the same thing as getting a new designer collection to retailers next season.

10.3   Finders

The financial industry has a long track record of creating respectable-sounding new titles for positions that have acquired a somewhat tarnished or down-scaled image. To shed their commission-hungry, out-for-themselves image, stockbrokers became "financial consultants" and now, in their latest incarnation, "wealth advisors." (Do their clients feel any wealthier?) In the same fashion, former stockbrokers, attorneys looking for some side income, and consultants with purported golden Rolodexes, formerly known simply as "finders" (i.e., money-finders) have morphed into "placement agents." Placement, as in private placement. Agent, as in (I liked this definition) "a representative of a business firm, esp. a traveling salesman; a canvasser; solicitor."[28] Yes, when you get right down to it, finders (or placement agents) are salespeople. Finders sell their contacts and networking abilities to start-ups and to other firms that need to raise capital. To investors, finders aim to sell investment opportunities.

Start-ups almost always need help raising money, and wherever there are people looking for money, there will be other people offering to help find it. This is the way the world works, and I make no bones about it. What does irk me, as a start-up entrepreneur and even as the manager of a seed-stage venture investment and development company, is the inefficiency of the fundraising process, of which finders are but a symptom. Inefficient markets create opportunities for middlemen. Middlemen in financial markets extract money from the system, and it is arguable whether their net effect is positive, negative, or zero-sum.

Start-ups have no money to begin with, and yet there are plenty of finders out there who will gladly make referrals and introductions to potential investors for an up-front fee, a monthly retainer, reimbursement of out-of-pocket expenses, and a nice commission. Highly fundable start-ups, with credible founders and experienced entrepreneurs or managers, do not need finders. Average start-ups, the kind that may or may not be able to raise money—depending upon timing, perseverance, and luck—would probably be better off recruiting useful board members and hiring high-quality

---

[28] *Webster's Encyclopedic Unabridged Dictionary of the English Language.* Portland House, 1989.

Working with Service Providers 143

service providers than paying for a finder. Low-quality start-ups, the kind that would basically be un-fundable under most circumstances, may have the greatest need for finders and the least ability to make productive use of them.

Before I continue, I should offer a *mia culpa*. I have been a finder. During my early years as a start-up consultant, I offered to be a finder and would include finder's terms in my consulting agreements. Those terms looked something like the following:

Exhibit 10
My Own Finder's Agreement

MEMORANDUM OF UNDERSTANDING

This **Memorandum of Understanding** ("Memorandum"), dated as of this first day of _____, by and between Convergent Management, Inc., a Delaware corporation, with principal offices at _____ ("CMI") and _____ ("COMPANY"), is entered into with reference to the following facts:

A. CMI is in the business of providing strategic business development, management consulting, technical consulting and fund-raising advisory services to start-up and development-stage biomedical technology companies.

B. COMPANY is engaged in the development of _____.

NOW, THEREFORE, in consideration of the foregoing premises and the covenants and agreements contained herein, the parties hereto agree as follows:

1. **Engagement**. COMPANY hereby engages CMI, and CMI hereby accepts such engagement by COMPANY, under the terms and conditions hereafter set forth.

2. CMI will assist COMPANY in identifying potential financial investors or corporate investors ("Target Companies"), arranging discussions and meetings with Target Companies, and facilitating successful closure of fund-raising transactions (collectively, the "Services"). CMI shall allocate its own time and resources in performing the Services as determined by CMI in its sole discretion.

3. **Compensation Payable for Successful Transactions**. If an investment transaction, partnering transaction or customer transaction is entered into by COMPANY with COMPANY's approval with one or more investors, strategic partners or customers introduced by CMI (the "Transaction"), COMPANY agrees to pay CMI, or its designee, a "Finder's Fee." For purposes hereof, a Finder's Fee shall be an amount equal to five percent (5.0%) of the aggregate cash consideration paid or payable to COMPANY in connection with the Transaction plus an amount equal to five percent (5.0%) of the fair market value, as determined in good faith by

Working with Service Providers

CMI and COMPANY, of the non-cash consideration of the Transaction, if any. If such aggregate consideration is increased by contingent or future payments, the portion of the Finder's Fee relating thereto shall be calculated by determining the present value, at an appropriate discount rate, of such contingent or future payments. Consideration paid into escrow and subject to forfeiture as a result of COMPANY's breach of representations, warranties or covenants shall be deemed to have been paid to COMPANY upon deposit in escrow. No fee payable to any other financial advisor by COMPANY shall reduce or otherwise affect the fees payable to CMI. COMPANY shall pay the Finder's Fee primarily in the form of equity in COMPANY, with equity of the same class of capital stock and at the same valuation as that issued to the investors or partners in the Transaction. Delivery of the Finder's Fee shall be made immediately following the Transaction, but in no event later than thirty (30) days thereafter. CMI may, in its sole discretion, request and receive up to 20% of its Finder's Fee in the form of cash, with the balance of the Finder's Fee paid in Equity. CMI shall have substantially the same rights in respect of the Equity as those granted the investors or partnering company.

For non-U.S. companies or U.S.-based subsidiaries of non-U.S. companies, CMI may, at its option, elect to receive its entire Finder's Fee in cash (U.S. dollars).

4. **Out-of-Pocket Expenses**. Regardless of outcome, it is understood that COMPANY will reimburse CMI for any reasonable out-of-pocket expenses incurred in connection with the Services. Such expenses may include, but not be limited to, telephone, fax and Internet charges, postage, courier, photocopies, parking and mileage. CMI will not incur any overnight travel charges outside of without prior authorization (written or e-mail) from COMPANY. CMI employs a computerized expense coding system for its telephone, fax, postage meter, and photocopying machine. Payment for expenses is due within 15 days of invoicing. CMI reserves the right to suspend all work, without penalty to CMI, if expense payments are not received in a timely fashion.

5. **Term**. The term of this Memorandum shall commence on the date hereof and shall terminate automatically on _____. Notwithstanding the preceding sentence, this Memorandum may be terminated by either party upon thirty (30) days written notice to the other party. Termination of this Memorandum shall not release either party from the obligation to make payment of all amounts payable herein. Any

provisions of this Memorandum which by their nature or the terms thereof extend beyond termination of hereof shall survive such termination, including without limitation the provisions of Paragraph 5 below.

6. **Non-Circumvention.** COMPANY agrees to pay CMI or its designee the Success Fee as described in Paragraph 3 hereof upon any Transaction occurring within one (1) year following the termination of this Memorandum. This non-circumvention protection shall remain in effect for one (1) year following any termination of this Memorandum.

7. **Independent Contractor.** This Memorandum does not make either party the employee, agent or legal representative of the other for any purpose whatsoever. Neither party is granted any right or authority to assume or to create any obligations or responsibilities, express or implied, on behalf of or in the name of the other party. In fulfilling its obligations pursuant to this Memorandum, each party shall be acting as an independent contractor. COMPANY agrees that CMI is entitled to rely upon all reports of COMPANY (and its affiliates) and information supplied to it by or on behalf of COMPANY (whether written or oral), and CMI shall not in any respect be responsible for the accuracy or completeness of any such report or information or have an obligation to verify the same.

8. **Indemnification.** Because CMI will be acting on behalf of COMPANY in connection with the Services, COMPANY agrees to indemnify CMI and hold it harmless to the fullest extent permitted by law against any losses, claims, damages or liabilities to which CMI may become subject in connection with this Engagement.

9. **Notices.** All notices, demands or other communications hereunder shall be in writing and shall be deemed given when delivered personally, mailed by certified mail, return receipt requested, sent by overnight courier service, or otherwise actually delivered to the address set forth above in the first paragraph by the name of each party hereto.

10. **Counterparts.** This Memorandum may be executed in one or more counterparts, each of which shall be deemed an original but all of which together shall constitute one and the same instrument.

11. **Amendments and Waivers.** This Memorandum may be amended only by a written instrument signed by the parties hereto. No waiver by any party of any term or provision of this Memorandum shall be deemed to have been made unless expressed in writing and signed by such party.

12. **Successors and Assigns.** This Memorandum shall be binding upon the parties hereto and all rights, covenants and agreements of the parties contained herein shall be binding upon and inure to the benefit of their respective successors and assigns.

13. **Further Assurances.** Each party hereto agrees to do all acts and to make, execute and deliver such written instruments as shall from time to time be reasonably required to carry out the terms and provisions of this Memorandum.

14. **Costs and Attorneys' Fees.** In the event that any action, suit, or other proceeding, including any and all appeals or petitions there from ("Action"), is instituted concerning or arising out of this Memorandum, the prevailing party shall recover all of such party's out-of-pocket costs and reasonable attorneys' fees incurred in each and every such Action.

IN WITNESS WHEREOF, the parties have agreed to the terms of this Memorandum as of the day and year first written above.

Convergent Management, Inc.   **Company**

By: _____   By: _____

William L. Robbins   Name: _____

President   Title: _____

Only once did I earn a finder's fee, and that was from a new venture capital firm that was raising its first fund and that planned to invest in highly specialized field in which I had many connections. Not once did I earn a fee from a start-up. Admittedly, I did not enter into many finder's agreements, but back then, when I was just getting started as a consultant, what did I know? If a start-up could not afford to pay me in cash but was willing to do a finder's agreement, why not? It seemed like a way to create some upside for myself, since I would be talking to potential investors anyway and, without a cash retainer, I did not have to commit any fixed amount of time to a finder client. As my thinking went, if I could find an investor for a client, that would be great. If not, no big deal. The truth is, if you are an inexperienced consultant and you do enough of these "no fixed time commitment" finder's agreements, you will find yourself spending all of your time chasing after investors for nothing. If you are a start-up founder, entrepreneur, or manager and hire a no-retainer, commission-only finder, you probably will get exactly what you pay for. And worse, if you do pay a retainer to a finder, odds are you will also get what you paid for—visible activity, but no investors.

Since I did not learn my lesson working as a finder, I paid additional tuition to learn from other finders. Having spent nearly $100,000 on a handful of paid finder engagements while trying to raise a $50 million fund, I had several totally useless experiences and one good one—which, nonetheless, did not bring in a single dollar of newly committed capital. The good experience resulted from working with a real professional; a person with excellent credentials, strong references, and a database full of *bona fide* prospects. The fact that my partners and I failed to raise $50 million had more to do with our lack of a conventional venture capital investment track record and bad timing than with our finder's capabilities.

More than finders, start-ups need board members, service providers, and helpful friends who are willing to help make introductions and referrals. Most of all, start-ups need founders, entrepreneurs, and senior executives who are willing to work hard, seek advice, improve their skills at fundraising, and persevere. No finder can make up for the lack of a helpful board, committed founders, effective senior managers, and a strong work ethic.

Finders may come into play to fill a very specific role, such as gaining access to certain classes of investors that are difficult to approach directly, and that are used to being solicited through intermediaries. For example, it has become an accepted (even necessary) practice for newer or smaller venture capital firms to retain placement agents to gain access to institutional investors.

For start-ups that wish to consider the services of a finder, I offer the following advice:

Do Your Due Diligence

Rely on trusted friends and colleagues, not word of mouth, or referrals of no consequence. Examine the finder's résumé and track record. Ask for a list of references and conduct interviews. References should include both clients and investors who might know the finder.

Involve Your Attorney and Board in the Agreement Review Process

Do not simply accept the finder's own agreement language. Either have it reviewed by counsel and your board, or have your attorney draft an agreement.

Set Milestones and Stick to Them

Do not fall into the trap of self-delusion. If you are not meeting potential investors, holding an expected number of meetings, or seeing concrete evidence of investor interest, it is time either to reevaluate your game plan or terminate the finder relationship.

Supervise the Finder Relationship Closely

Once a finder's agreement is signed, the engagement should not go on auto-pilot. Company founders, entrepreneurs, or senior executives cannot rely on the finder to do the heavy lifting. As intermediaries, finders need direction, they need to be supplied with fundraising materials, and they need to be debriefed on a regular basis.

11

Building the Start-Up Team

11.1 Building Teams on a Shoestring Budget

My goal in this chapter is to share with you some helpful information and advice about building start-up teams without the benefit of a multi-million-dollar budget.

If you can raise sufficient seed capital to recruit an experienced management team and hire enough staff to operate your company right from the get-go, more power to you. You have found early success where many others have failed. However, as with the vast majority of start-ups, you will probably have to build your business on a shoestring budget with a first-year bank account too small to pay yourself, no less to hire experienced managers and staff.

During my tenure in Start-Up Land, I have recruited and hired managers and staff for companies that were initially funded with a mere $100,000 or $200,000 of seed capital. For the type of investing I do, small seed rounds have been the norm, partly because the amount of capital at my disposal as a seed-stage investor has been relatively modest, and partly because my partners and I believe in starting companies low to the ground and building them organically with our own hands-on management. Partly by choice and partly by necessity, we ascribe to the start-up philosophy that says, more or less, "Build the business first, and then raise millions of dollars," instead of, "Raise millions of dollars, and then build the business."

How many times have you heard about well-funded start-ups that have hired stellar management teams and recruited a lab full of scientists, only to do a follow-on round of funding at a significant discount, be bought out at a fire sale, or go under ignominiously? These inauspicious scenarios share a common theme: too much money available to be spent on payroll rather than on value creation. Starting a company on a tight budget imposes a certain discipline that is beneficial to a company's judicious development, whereas ample start-up capital often results in too much money being spent on the wrong things at the wrong time. Since payroll is usually the number-one operating expense for start-ups, companies that have a lot of cash at their disposal run the risk of over-investing in expensive executives and managers who prove not to be critical to the start-up's early success. The result of this misallocation of resources is top-heaviness, pre-mature emphasis on management tasks as opposed to value creation, and an unsustainable payroll.

Building a start-up team on a shoestring makes every hiring decision critical, and, therefore, start-up entrepreneurs and investors should think very carefully about how they wish to develop the personnel assets of their companies.

11.2 The Core Start-Up Team

Whether you are an entrepreneur or an investor in a newly created company, all of the people on your start-up team should be individuals you know well and can trust implicitly. This is a tall order, and it will likely be more of an ideal than a reality. Doing start-ups is an intensely personal and highly interactive endeavor, and with all the challenges ahead of you, the last thing you need is a dud on your start-up team. If you have any experience with group projects in school, in your job, or perhaps in a volunteer organization, you are likely to have encountered a fundamental truth about all but the most carefully selected, highest-performing teams: 20 percent of the people usually end up doing 80 percent of the work. This is no earth-shattering discovery. The 80/20 rule applies in many situations. Think of the 80/20 rule of start-up teams as a corollary of the normal curve of founders (see Chapter 4). Most members of start-up teams will cluster toward the mean in terms of their ability to add value. There will also be a few high-performers and a few low-performers. Less frequently, you will find extraordinarily good performers and, unfortunately, extraordinarily bad performers.

My partners and I have been working together as a team since the late 1990s. By now, I probably know as much about their work habits and idiosyncrasies as I ever will, including what work they like to do best, what tasks turn them off, how they will react in particular situations, and what they will say in meetings. This is how well you should know the most important members of your start-up team. If you and your start-up team members are not very familiar with each other by the time of company formation, I can guarantee that you will be if you manage to stick together long enough. This point goes to the heart of what I am talking about. A start-up team can be a thing of abstract beauty and can accomplish great things when its members get along, respect each other, and make meaningful contributions to the full extent of each individual's capabilities. A start-up team can also hasten the demise of a company if its members fail to gel, fail to communicate with each other effectively, and fail to carry their fair (but not necessarily equal) share of the workload.

The key individuals who come together to create and lead a new start-up company make up what I refer to as the "core start-up team," or simply, the "core team." Members of the core team would typically include three to five people who conceive the company and without whom the company could not get off the ground. In a technology-oriented start-up, the core team would include:

- The scientific or technical founder(s)
- The seed investor(s)
- A dependable, "always there," hands-on manager
- A corporate attorney well liked and equally trusted by all sides

All members of the core team, with the possible exception of the attorney, should posses certain attributes. First, each core team member needs to be able to *afford* to do a start-up. I mean this quite literally. Start-ups consume time and money like a newborn infant consumes baby formula, and like a newborn, the start-up won't be going away anytime soon. Start-ups are there twenty-four hours a day, seven days a week, good days and bad, and they are anything but a nine-to-five job. So, returning to my point, each member of the start-up team should have either an independent and reliable source of income (a real job), be financially independent (which usually means having successfully cashed out of some previous deal or deals along the way), or be able to get by with low or no pay either by having a low-overhead lifestyle and/or by being able to land paid consulting gigs to cover living expenses.

Furthermore, all members of the core team should have a proven aptitude for the ascetic life of the start-up. This is not to say that all the members of the core team should crave the simple life, willingly renouncing all creature comforts. No. I would much prefer to work with people that value the good things success can bring, but they should not expect to be coddled, nor should they be "high-maintenance." In my own experience, individuals with certain backgrounds are not well suited for life in Start-Up Land. First among these individuals is the corporate careerist--the middle manager with ten or more years of big company experience who finds himself or herself "in the market" for a position with a start-up company due to a layoff or some other mid-career change of plans. More often than not, corporate careerists have become too accustomed to the vast and omnipresent infrastructure of their corporate employers to function effectively in the Spartan environment of the typical under-funded start-up company.

Please do not get me wrong. Corporate careerists are not bad people, and they may make great hires for young companies that are past the start-up stage and in need of adult supervision, but their survival instincts are adapted to the corporate world and not to Start-Up Land. Corporate careerists are reared within a structured, hierarchical society of entry-level, middle management, and senior executives with distinct titles and specific responsibilities. Corporate careerists have honed their skills at politicking, consensus building, avoiding conflict, and standing out just enough to be noticed by their superiors without causing friction among their peers. Corporate careerists are used to having secretaries, support staffs, in-house service departments, departmental travel accounts, airport limos, in-house dry cleaning, and an impressive array of menu choices at the company cafeteria (at subsidized prices). Today's large corporations have been configured as great mother ships from which employees need never leave, during normal working hours, except, perhaps, for family emergencies. Large corporations have on-site child care, on-site fitness facilities, on-site banking, comprehensive benefits programs, and a global footprint that make it possible to go from the U.S. headquarters to a European research site to an Asian production facility without ever leaving the company doorstep. So, tell me, given everything you know or have been told about what it is like to work in a start-up with dingy offices, hand-me-down furniture, constant cash concerns, no administrative support, and the need to get help from the outside for just about every business necessity (photocopies? airline reservations? health insurance?), would you expect a corporate careerist to parachute into your start-up company and hit the ground running? I don't think so. I would think very carefully about having a corporate careerist as a key member of my core start-up team. Some start-up entrepreneurs or early investors may think having one or more people on the core team with strong corporate credentials and recent *Fortune 500* management experience would be a big plus. Well, I think it's a recipe for problems. Time and again, I have seen corporate careerists perform suboptimally in start-up situations because they have not got the genes for it. They are like gilled sea creatures suddenly thrown up on dry land. Some adapt, a few thrive, but most will perish.

Despite everything I have said about the non-suitability of corporate careerists as members of the core start-up team, there is another breed of ex-corporate denizen that makes an ideal core team member: the corporate refugee. Corporate refugees, as distinct from corporate careerists, have escaped the corporate world in search of a better life. Corporate refugees may have years of corporate experience to their credit, but through a process of self-actualization, they have realized that corporate life does not suit them well. Corporate refugees find the corporate world to be too confining, too all-consuming. The genotypic and phenotypic makeup of the corporate refugee makes him or her unsuitable for corporate life. Would-be corporate refugees abhor rigid hierarchy, bridle at authority, are not threatened by innovation, and typically end up resenting the all-encompassing embrace of their employers. Simply put, corporate refugees are well suited for life in Start-Up Land, as if by natural selection.

I am a corporate refugee. My partners, for the most part, are corporate refugees. Many of our fellow start-up team members and early hires are corporate refugees. What unites us all is a common genetic makeup that renders us acutely susceptible to the insults of corporate life, yet well adapted to the rigors of survival in Start-Up Land. Thus, when forming core start-up teams, it only stands to reason that we would look for more of our kind.

What other characteristics should you look for in core team members? One desirable characteristic is a multidisciplinary attitude. Specialists tend not to be well suited for the fluid environment of the start-up. Specialists tend to get hung up in their own narrowly focused thinking, and in technicalities. Take, for example, accountants. Do not put an accountant on your core start-up team unless you want every problem reduced to its absolute cost and every decision based on how little you can spend. I will be the first to recommend involving a good accountant in setting up your start-up's books and financial records; in setting up and administering payroll, benefits, and retirement plans; and in setting up purchasing systems; but accountants are not trained to think outside the box. To the contrary, they are trained to see the sides of the box and to recognize what is inside and what is outside the box, but they are not in the business of building boxes, nor will they tell you which box you should build, or how to build it. Certainly, if you are starting a financially oriented business of some sort, it may make perfect sense to include an accountant on your core start-up team. But when it comes to technology-oriented start-ups, I prefer to hire accountants for specific tasks, and not have them core team members.

All members of your core team (again, the attorney is an exception) should be multi-enabled. That is, aside from specific areas of professional expertise, each core team member should bring other talents and skills, as well as an unquestionable willingness to use them when needed. In the start-ups my partners and I run, we have scientific founders who, in addition to being great scientists, are excellent communicators who are wizards with slide presentations and a laser pointer. We have a business development expert who is an excellent writer. A business strategist who is an excellent research manager. A technology transfer expert who excels at people skills. And several engineers who can get anything done with little or no outside support. The last thing you want on your core team is a person who will do "A" proficiently but is useless for, or gets in the way of, doing "B," "C," and "D."

When forming a core team, be skeptical. Move with caution. Get to know prospective team members over a period of time and in a variety of situations. Remember, these are people who may own stock in your company, sit on your board, speak for your company, make important hiring decisions, and spend your money. Do not rush to invite someone to join your core team simply because he or she has great credentials, is enthusiastic, or comes well recommended. Think about all the desirable and undesirable attributes I have mentioned. Consider the person's background, work history, ability to contribute beyond a narrow area of expertise, and ability to contribute on multiple levels.

Also, consider this: A core team member need not be permanent, need not be an equal partner, and need not be a company insider. You can try people out on a voluntary or consulting basis. You can hire a service provider to handle certain well-defined tasks or areas of responsibility without giving up any equity or sharing influence and decision-making authority unnecessarily.

The best place to look for core start-up team members is your own circle of close business and academic colleagues and personal acquaintances. These should be people with whom you have worked before, who are reliable, who consistently produce work of good quality, and who you can get along with under most any situation, no matter how stressful or challenging.

11.3   Critical Early Employees

The critical early employees in a technology-oriented start-up company are the people who are going to do the work that will ensure your early success. Critical early employees at new start-ups are usually one-of-a-kind sorts of people who have excellent scientific or technical capabilities, a highly positive, can-do attitude, a special aptitude for multitasking, a sense of urgency, and an irrepressible drive to solve problems and make things work. Have I left anything out? Oh, yes. Critical early employees are motivated more by the opportunity to work on intellectual challenges than by the opportunity to get rich quickly (after all, we are talking about cash-strapped start-ups, not amply funded research operations), and they think and act more like owners than employees. A few more things: Critical early employees do high-quality work, are not deterred by initial failures, and while they like things done right, they will tolerate a certain degree of messiness in the interest of making progress. I sing the praises of early employees who possess these desirable characteristics, because to have such people on your team is a real pleasure. I can think fondly of one or two such individuals in just about every successful (or still promising) start-up company with which I have been involved. The inability of a once-promising new start-up to make early progress toward its technical or scientific objectives can often be attributed to management's failure to make the critical early hire. I believe so strongly in the importance of the critical early hire that I consider it foolhardy to start a company before knowing who the critical early hires will be and whether they will sign on the dotted line once initial funding becomes available.

Company founders and their investors must succeed at bringing on board critical early employees to accomplish some vital steps in the early life of a technology-oriented start-up. Critical early employees can be expected to:

- Plan, build out, equip, and stock the company's first laboratory
- Design and conduct important early proof of principle experiments, feasibility projects, or prototyping efforts, often on their own and usually by begging, borrowing, and procuring at attractive rates (preferably for free) whatever supplies, reagents, equipment time, or other resources are needed to get the job done
- Write initial grant applications to help secure federal, state, or private research and development funding
- Generate and sometimes present scientific or technical data that can be incorporated into business plans and presentations
- Speak credibly for the company on technical or scientific matters at meetings with potential investors or corporate partners
- Help recruit other talented individuals to the organization by virtue of their obvious scientific or technical competence, their positive energy, and their enthusiasm for the company's mission

Successful early employees, like highly fundable founders, are outliers on the normal curve. Compared to the universe of potentially qualified new employees, the critical early employee who stands head and shoulders above the rest may be somewhat of a misfit in the world at large. The best of critical early employees have so much productive energy, so many ideas (good ones, impractical ones, crazy ones), and sometimes, such a childlike desire to see things work out that, to the outsider—or to the traditional, buttoned-down, and authority-conscious types who rule the roost in corporate research and development departments or buttoned-down academic departments—they may seem "a little out there" or "too intense" or "too uncontrollable." I like the last disparaging comment the most, because, as I have learned the hard way, if there is anything a start-up founder, manager, or investor can do to get in the way of an effective early hire, it is to try to "contain" the early hire's energy, "channel" his or her enthusiasm, and "control" his or her efforts. This is a bad idea. There have been times when a wild-eyed early hire would drive me nuts with his or her seemingly unfocused behavior, and I have felt compelled to impose my own sense of order on a seemingly unruly situation. Had I persisted or succeeded in doing so, it would have been a disservice to the individual, a detriment to the company, and a blemish on my own reputation as a manager. To attempt to channel a critical new hire's enthusiasm and control his or her seemingly scattered efforts is to negate precisely those positive attributes you should seek in a critical new hire in the first place. Start-ups are messy. The creative process is messy. The manner in which really bright and effective people operate may be messy. So, deal with it, or consider a more neat and tidy profession than doing start-ups.

How do you find critical early employees? For a company that gets its start as a spin-out from an academic lab, look no further than the faculty member who runs the lab. Senior faculty members are a great source of referrals and recommendations for current or former Ph.D.s, post-docs, and up-and-coming colleagues who may be interested in exploring Start-Up Land. If your company-to-be has academic faculty members as founders, they can add tremendous value by helping to identify and recruit talented young scientists or engineers for whom they may have served as a Ph.D. advisor or mentor. I and my partners have been able to recruit and hire some wonderfully talented, energetic, and highly motivated early employees by asking our academic co-founders who they would recommend among their cadre of former students and post-docs. These former students and post-docs may be found making a name for themselves as junior faculty members or research fellows at other academic institutions or as entry-level bench scientists or engineers at large companies.

Before you, as a start-up entrepreneur or investor, consider placing employment advertisements in scientific and trade journals or posting job openings on the Web or contracting with a recruiting firm, start with your most reliable and likely sources: the people you know. Thus, in addition to seeking input from your scientific or technical founders, you may wish to spread the word around other start-ups you know of in your immediate geographic area (unless you wish to keep your new company or the specifics about the position(s) you wish to fill under wraps). If you want to play things close to the vest, at the very least, chat with some other company founders you can trust who may have contacts in your field of interest. Ask your corporate counsel about other companies and individuals with whom he or she has worked and whether he or she may help you make some connections to potential early employment candidates for your own start-up.

Academic departmental mixers or academic industry network events can also be a good way to put some feelers out about start-up positions you may wish to fill, assuming you are looking for people who may be approaching completion of a Ph.D. program or post-doctoral fellowship. These sorts of people are usually eager to learn about job openings either for themselves or their friends. Keep in mind that this method of on-campus recruitment is only appropriate if you are looking for bench scientists or, perhaps, individuals with enough maturity to help get a project off the ground in consultation with more experienced scientists or managers (such as faculty members who are company co-founders). This sort of arrangement can work out well, provided that the newly hired Ph.D. or post-doc and the academic founder do not revert to an unhealthy professor/student relationship when a more business-like supervisor/employee interaction is needed.

Following are some other factors to consider when recruiting critical early employees:

Location of the Search

Start your search locally, and work outward geographically. If your start-up is closely affiliated with an academic center, a medical center, or large corporate employer in your area, the natural place to look is close to home. Otherwise, expect a longer search process and higher recruitment costs.

Personal Situation and Marital Status

In case you are not familiar with employment law, it is a no-no to inquire about a job applicant's personal life or marital status during a job interview.

So, don't ask. But, if you need to ask, perhaps you do not know the prospective employee well enough in the first place. To put it bluntly, critical early employees are not the kind of people you hire off the street or through responses to advertisements and Web postings. Critical early employees should be people you, your scientific/technical founders, or your investors have worked with before, or people who come highly recommended through sources close to you that you can trust without reservation. Along with this level of foreknowledge or trust comes the expectation that a critical early employee's marital status, plans for marriage, living arrangements, family situation, and so on are not an issue. Preferably, they should be a plus. By this, I mean it is preferable to hire people whose personal situation is stable and not heading into a period of uncertainty that would negatively impact the prospective employee's ability to concentrate on his or her job. Doing start-ups can be a personal rollercoaster ride. The last thing you need is a critical early employee riding a rollercoaster at work and another one at home.

Stage of Career and Expectations

Critical early employees will most certainly have career aspirations that may or may not be in conflict with a start-up's needs. Until now, we have focused our attention on younger employees of an age typical for a new Ph.D. or post-doc; someone in his or her mid-to-late twenties to early thirties. As with questions about marital status, you must not ask questions about an applicant's age, but good candidates for critical positions in start-up companies tend to be early career types who have the drive, energy, up-to-date technical training, and ability to tolerate a high degree of financial and career risk. Start-ups are not for people who need a secure income, regular work hours, and the stability of a large employer. How many scientific or technically oriented go-getters do you know who own a home, pay a mortgage, have a few kids, take long vacations, golf on weekends, and relish the opportunity to lay it all on the line for the sake of some unproven start-up company with no lab, no revenue, no employees, and an enormous amount of promise? See what I mean? The ideal scientist or technical professional for a critical early position in a start-up company is someone who is at the right stage of his or her career to take risks. The best candidates for critical new positions in start-ups see a bigger financial and career downside in *not* taking a risk early in their careers, when there is still ample time to rebound from a stumble. When considering a start-up position, the best candidates focus their attention on the upsides rather than the downsides. They are looking for opportunities to learn, develop new skills, work alongside smart people, and improve their future employability. They may also be eager to maintain or resume a valued relationship with a favorite Ph.D. advisor or post-doctoral mentor. These reasons are usually mixed in with a desire to live in a town or near an academic institution that is conducive to a preferred lifestyle (i.e., intellectual, outdoorsy, etc.).

It is essential when considering the profile of the ideal early employee to think about the prospective employee's career goals and expectations. What is the prospective employee really looking for, aside from a paycheck and a chance to build equity? How closely does the opportunity you offer match his or her career objectives, lifestyle preferences, personal situation, and other needs? After all, you want your critical early employees to love what they will be doing and to have the same kind of intellectual curiosity and sincere enthusiasm for new learning that previously propelled them through Ph.D. programs or post-doctoral fellowships at the most demanding academic institutions, or through entry-level scientific or technical positions at the most well-respected large companies and the hottest small ones.

Sometimes, you will find an ideal early employee who does not come fresh from academia or who has been "out in the real world" for five, ten, or more years. What these (usually) older, more experienced people bring to the start-up is industry knowledge, positional wisdom (about their role and the roles of others in commercial organizations), and the maturity and self-confidence to manage not only themselves and projects, but also other people. In fact, there is one type of critical position in a start-up that should only be filled by someone with five or more years of industry experience, and that is the position of scientific or technical manager. When you include management ability in the hiring specifications, new Ph.D.s or post-docs usually do not have enough commercial and supervisory experience to manage other people, nor to manage projects that require the cooperation of a team. This is when it is preferable to hire someone who has "been there" before. This may be the dependable scientist who you could always rely upon at your previous start-up, or the hard-working, never-complaining engineer from your last employer who always came through with the goods even when funding was short, working conditions were oppressive, or the boss was insufferable.

Thus, the highly motivated, highly recommended new Ph.D. or post-doc, or dependable veteran of previous start-ups, is the kind of person I would want helping me to get the critical work going at my own start-up company.

11.4   Methods of Recruitment

The "Personal Knowledge and Referral Method"

As we have discussed, the preferred method for recruiting critical early employees is to contact people known to you or to other trusted sources from who you may request referrals and introductions. But this method goes only so far and will yield a finite number of prospects from a limited pool. The "personal knowledge and referral method" is the right way to go to get your company off the ground, but you will need to cast a bigger net to transform your company from a close-knit start-up with a hand-picked team to a going concern with a full complement of productive employees.

Job Postings and Advertisements

I have found that job postings and advertisements produce satisfactory results for entry-level positions or other jobs that require a bachelor's of science degree or, at most, a master's degree in fields such as molecular biology or chemistry. Job postings and advertisements should be very specific about the job description as well as the preferred level of education, job-related skills, and work experience. Following is an example:

Exhibit 11
Job Posting for Research Technician–Biology

Position Type: Full-Time
Title: Research Technician–Biology
Location: Labville, CA 90000

The research technician–biology will maintain a frog colony and perform surgeries on *Xenopus laevis* frogs to isolate and process oocytes for RNA injection. In addition, this individual will carry out mRNA injection into oocytes and be responsible for preparing the various solutions required for maintaining oocyte quality and health. Familiarity with sterile techniques and general laboratory procedures including DNA isolation, PCR, cloning, and cell culture is desirable. Responsibilities will also include the accurate and orderly documentation of daily activities in compliance with standard operating procedures. The candidate should have outstanding interpersonal skills and be a team player. The ideal candidate must have a B.S. degree in biology or a related discipline and zero to one year of academic or industry laboratory experience. Prior animal handling experience will be considered a plus.

Job postings work well for start-ups located within reasonable commuting distance of university campuses or in areas with a significant concentration of employers in relevant industries. Generally, what you should be looking for are well-educated and recent college or university graduates, because they tend to be highly motivated to enter the work force, eager for training and work experience, and less concerned about compensation, benefits, and job security issues. This is not to say you should take advantage of naïve, entry-level employees. Quite to the contrary, I am emphatic about offering qualified applicants for entry-level scientific, technical, or administrative positions a high level of opportunity, but I find that the better entry-level prospects are more motivated by the chance to work side by side with top-notch scientists and engineers and to receive mentoring from widely respected academic founders or highly experienced managers than they are by a few extra dollars of compensation or by the availability of a lavish benefits plan.

For start-ups, I only recommend doing job postings and advertisements within local job markets (approximately a twenty-five-mile radius), because your objective should be to find qualified candidates while avoiding issues such as travel expense reimbursement (for interviews), relocation costs, lack of familiarity with the area, lack of established living and personal arrangements (which could be a big distraction for a new employee, especially a recent college graduate), and, quite frankly, lack of job alternatives, should things not work.

Start-ups I have managed have placed postings and advertisements for open positions on company Web sites, Web sites and bulletin boards of local industry networking organizations, university and college placement office or club Web sites[29], on the career pages of life science and high technology industry Web portals[30], and through for-profit career portals.[31] Scientific publications such as *Nature*, *Science*, and *Chemical and Engineering News* also provide job posting resources for start-ups, although the advertisements you find in the end pages of these print publications are usually for positions requiring a higher degree of education and experience.

Contingency Recruiting Firms ("Headhunters")

So far, in our search for start-up employees, we have discussed the personal knowledge and referral method and the job posting and advertising method. The next step up in the escalating campaign to recruit and hire new employees for start-ups is the contingency recruitment firm, or "headhunter." Based upon my own mixed experiences with the contingency recruitment method, I would say the term headhunter is somewhat of a misnomer. Sometimes, contingency firms (particularly those of lesser quality) can seem like "bounty hunters," because what they are really after is not the uniquely qualified individual (the "head"), but rather the placement fee (the "bounty"). Recruiting firms come in two varieties: those that charge a fee contingent upon the successful placement of a recruit and those that charge a retainer fee. Contingency recruiting firms are a useful resource for employers who seek to fill scientific or technical positions that require from three to ten or more years of experience within a specific field or discipline, and usually within specific industries, types of companies, and job

---

[29] For example, the Caltech Biotech Club, at www.biotech.caltech.edu
[30] For example, www.biospace.com
[31] For example, www.monster.com

classifications. Contingency firms maintain large databases of potential job candidates who posses a certain baseline level of qualifications for a particular type of job assignment. In a typical scenario, an account manager from a contingency firm will discuss the employer's proposed job description(s) along with a set of criteria for prospective candidates including academic background, technical skills, employment history, title, and compensation. The account manager will then screen his or her company database for "hits," which in this case means names and résumés (or *curricula vitae* for scientists). The account manager may also conduct a process of directed searching and cold calling to turn up names of other qualified candidates. Once a group of hits has been identified, the account manager will submit the most promising résumés or *curricula vitae* to the employer (i.e., the client), who will then review the submissions and notify the account manager of those prospective candidates the employer may wish to interview. Thus begins an iterative winnowing process by which the account manager submits candidates, the employer reviews the candidates and selects a subset to interview, a smaller group proves to be both employable and available, and, eventually, a job offer is prepared and one qualified candidate accepts the position. At this point, the contingency firm's account manager says, "bingo," and collects a placement fee for his or her firm and a commission for himself or herself.

The contingency fee is generally a percentage of the new hire's first-year cash compensation, but by definition this fee is only paid if the search results in a successful hire. There are usually contractual terms to define what constitutes a successful hire (i.e., how many months the new employee must remain on the job) and what new fees will be charged, or remedies offered, if a new employee leaves his or her new position or is let go prior to some minimum cutoff date.

Because contingency firms only get paid for successful placements (although they may be paid up front or monthly for out-of-pocket expenses such as may be incurred for Web postings, placement ads, administrative costs, etc.), their business tends to be volume-oriented, and their primary motivation is to "make the placement." There is nothing wrong with this approach unless the contingency firm develops a reputation for placing warm bodies to collect placement fees rather than long-term employees to establish a reputation for quality service. Thus, when considering contingency firms for hire, the start-up founder or entrepreneur must pay close attention to the reputation of the firm, its track record for making successful, long-term placements, and its roster of satisfied clients. Perhaps the best indicator of a contingency firm's track record is the length of its list of repeat clients.

Retained Executive Search Firms

Highest in the hierarchy of employment firms for hire is the retained executive search firm, which, as its name indicates, receives its compensation in the form of a retainer fee. The retainer fee is typically paid in increments, on a fixed-timing basis (one-third on execution of agreement, one-third 30 days later, and one-third 60 to 90 days thereafter). Unless a retained search firm is paid on the basis of performance milestones, which is rare, search fees may actually be paid out prior to successful completion of a search. In other words, by paying search fees on a fixed-timing basis, the client runs the risk of having to pay a full retainer before the vacant position has been filled. By identifying and retaining a search firm that is accountable to performance milestones, the client can mitigate exposure to financial risk.

Retained search firms will typically limit the scope of their business to executive-level employees ranging from the director level on the low end to chief executives on the high end. From a practical standpoint, retained search firms in the life science and high technology industries tend to accept searches for executive positions receiving a minimum of $150,000 per year in base salary. This salary level is determined by the basic economics of the retained search business, since fees are usually calculated as a percentage of the new hire's first-year cash compensation, inclusive of bonus. Retained search firms conduct searches that are more narrow and personalized than searches conducted by contingency firms. Retained searches tend to be more time-consuming, and more demanding in terms of search criteria, initial screening, due diligence, and the level of one-on-one interaction with the client. Thus, the retained search professional tends to operate as a high-end organizational strategy consultant or management advisor rather than as an account manager whose involvement with the client tends to be more superficial and rarely requires in-depth interaction with senior management.

The more experienced retained search professionals are usually career veterans who have worked at employers within their target industry before entering the search field or have spent many years in the human resource, organizational, or general management consulting areas. Experienced retained search professionals posses a detailed knowledge of industry trends, hiring practices, salary levels, and compensation structures, as well as a broad knowledge of important employment factors such as regional housing prices, the quality of local public schools, and relocation costs. Experienced retained search specialists should also be comfortable interacting with senior management and boards of directors, and they should be expert in the language and terms of employment agreements.

The total fee for a retained search can easily exceed $60,000, and it would not be unusual for total fees to exceed $100,000 on a search for a senior executive with a base salary in the neighborhood of $250,000, which is the going rate—not including bonuses and equity-based compensation—for a start-up CEO in a start-up funded by venture capitalists. A sample of a performance-base retained search agreement, the kind I recommend, can be found in Appendix 14.7.

Hiring a retained search firm to conduct an executive search for a brand new start-up does not make sense in most cases, but not just for the obvious reason—high cost. Before the cost of a retained search, the start-up entrepreneur, founder, or investor must consider whether hiring the type of executive that is the normal bread and butter for retained search firms would even be feasible, given most new start-ups' less-than-robust financial position, immature business plan, and lack of infrastructure. In my opinion, most brand new start-ups need the kind of full-salaried CEO that retained search firms specialize in about as much as they need a company jet. Unless your start-up has closed a *bona fide* Series-A financing of at least $3 million, or was founded by scientists or entrepreneurs with a proven track record of founding successful new ventures, my advice is not to engage a retained search firm until your company is on a more stable footing. Instead, focus on hiring the best employees you can find for critical lab positions and find an experienced and dependable scientific or technical manager who can oversee early research and development efforts. Save the retained executive search until your start-up has the funding and infrastructure in place to make the recruiting and hiring of experienced executives a realistic proposition.

11.5 Compensation and Benefits

I could devote an entire book to the topic of compensation and benefits for start-ups, and perhaps I will someday. Even devoting a full chapter to this topic would be insufficient to cover the basics and intricacies of base compensation, bonus arrangements, stock options, insurance coverage, and retirement savings plans. Thus, in the interest of space and practicality, I will use this section to mention just a few of the many "good to know" points and avoidable "gotchas" that any start-up founder, entrepreneur, or early investor should bear in mind when it comes to the compensation and retention of employees.

Salary Levels

If you or your seed investors have enough employment experience and prior start-up experience to be intimately familiar with job descriptions and prevailing pay levels within the industry in which you operate, and have access to colleagues and advisors with whom you can consult on matters of compensation, there is little need to get too fancy when it comes to creating and proposing basic compensation packages for potential employees. However, every start-up company reaches a point where determining salaries simply by "knowing the market" will no longer cut it and, indeed, is a bad idea. Today's employees have access to a wealth of information about compensation, either from their friends, from publications, or most notably, from the Internet. Web sites such as www.salary.com are a tantalizing source of statistics about pay levels within particular industries and job classifications, and employees at start-ups have every right to use this information and to request an explanation from management about how salary levels in their companies are determined. When such requests arise—typically once the staff gets large enough to include more than just the "original" team (my rule of thumb is about ten to twelve employees)—answering by saying, "We just know what the salary levels should be," rings hollow. This is the time when I would resort to purchasing an independent salary survey. These surveys can be bought "one off" from a syndicated source, but this is not very helpful, because these published surveys offer just a snapshot in time and tend to pool data from a large number of employers of different sizes and stages of development, from different geographic regions, and from dissimilar industry sectors. You can pay anywhere from hundreds to thousands of dollars to receive these published surveys.

Instead of purchasing a "one-off" survey, I would recommend subscribing to a reputable and comprehensive annual survey such as the Radford Survey (www.radford.com). The Radford Survey enables even the smallest start-up to subscribe at an affordable rate to a comprehensive, industry-specific survey of compensation. These surveys collect and organize data by industry sector, size of employer, geographic region, job title, and other factors. Thus, the data can be normalized for the purpose of comparison, providing the subscriber with objective, statistically significant, and up-to-date information about compensation levels for a wide range of positions, from lab tech to CEO. Plus, by subscribing to Radford, the employer can actually participate in the survey, thus ensuring that the employer's own data are incorporated into future survey results. The reason I advocate subscribing to an independent, widely recognized compensation survey is that doing so reduces subjectivity in the setting of company compensation levels and arms the start-up employer with hard data to provide to discuss with employees. The sort of publicly available data employees may find on the Web or in publications is poorly controlled for differences between employers and differences between job titles and responsibilities at different companies, and in all likelihood, these publicly available salary surveys are biased by all the factors your college statistics professor warned you about. There comes a time in every start-up that informality in human resource management succumbs to the realities of managing employees in growing organizations. When your company passes the ten- to twelve-employee threshold, it is probably time to subscribe to an independent salary survey.

Stock Options

If your start-up puts out a press release announcing the closing of a successful fundraising round of any significance, it will not be long before purveyors of stock option recordkeeping software start calling. Save your money. Until you have enough employees to require the hiring of a full-time human resource manager, administration of stock options is not something you should worry about too much. If you have a good corporate attorney and are competent with a Microsoft Excel® spreadsheet, that's all you need to set up and administer a stock option plan. What we are concerned about specifically in this section is not how to create a stock option plan (your attorney will provide the requisite documents) or how to implement it (assuming you have investors who are savvy about how to use stock options), but how to establish stock option-based compensation levels that make sense for an early start-up company and will not come back to haunt you when it comes time to hire more employees or highly compensated executives, or to raise another round of financing.

Too often, lacking experience or adult supervision, start-ups will treat stock options like Monopoly® money rather than as a unit of compensation representing a future claim on the company's ownership. If new entrepreneurs and founders realized that the stock option awards they blithely give away by the fist full (whether properly documented, verbally promised, or somewhere in between) will dilute the company's equity, create future owners that the entrepreneur or founder may regret one day, and establish precedents that could make future decisions about compensation very expensive, very painful, or both, then stock options would be treated with the care and prudence they deserve.

Leaving all the theories, opinions, and arguments about stock options to the academics, compensation consultants, and armchair policy wonks, I will make just a few points:

- Options have real value and real cost, but no two people agree as to exactly what these are, so don't get all worked up about it.
- Since the bursting of the dot-com bubble, stock options in start-ups have lost a lot of their fabled allure. Today's start-up employees are not wowed by offers of stock options, and they tend to put much more weight on cash-based compensation.
- Excessive generosity with stock options may make you popular with the troops, but it will eventually make you look foolish.
- As with salary levels, stock option award levels for employees should be based on objective, third-party data for comparable companies of similar size, stage of development, industry sector, geographic region, and so forth.

- The granting of stock options has come under increasing scrutiny by federal regulators, and new regulations require more rigorous procedures and documentation for issuing new options. Consult with an attorney knowledgeable in the regulation of stock options before making any commitments in this area.

Relocation Arrangements

Hiring critical early employees or, at later stages, managers and executives may entail relocation expenses. Limiting ourselves to start-up situations, offering new employees assistance with the purchasing of a new home, the sale of an old home, or anything other than temporary living arrangements should be out of the question. What I have done, typically, is to offer reimbursement for certain well-defined moving expenses within a certain period of time. Assistance with month-to-month housing leases, furniture rentals, fees for moving companies, costs for hook-up of basic utilities, and perhaps a few round-trip airline tickets that may be needed to wrap up out-of-town personal affairs is perfectly reasonable, provided that these cost items are written into the employee's offer letter and documented with receipts.

Severance Packages

In my opinion, severance packages for start-up employees should be resisted and then only agreed to for more experienced new hires who are taking a significant financial or career risk by accepting your job offer. This criterion would limit the offering of severance packages to employees who are relocating over a great distance or walking away from a well-compensated job at a stable employer. Having entered into a number of such agreements, some of which have resulted in the invocation of a severance provision, I would say the following:

- Two months of full severance pay will not be enough for more experienced, senior-level managers. Most will ask for a year and some will settle for six months. Alas, for a start-up, six months is a long time to pay severance--probably too long. If highly compensated employees must be let go to preserve cash, having to pay out a full salary for another six months limits the start-up's financial flexibility for half a year. Paying severance for one executive's salary may be equal to the cost of salaries two or three more junior employees, and in many cases, these junior employees may be more important for generating cash flow or making tangible progress on a value-enhancing project than one senior executive.

- If a prospective employee who would ordinarily be entitled to some minimum level of severance gets hung up on negotiation of the terms and duration of severance, step back from the negotiations and ask yourself and the potential new hire whether the job opportunity being offered is truly right for the prospect and the company. Odds are, the potential new hire who gets hung up on the terms of a severance package is either insurmountably uncomfortable about the degree of risk the new position entails or has too much firsthand experience with severance pay. Either case raises a great big red flag, and the employer would be making a potentially costly mistake by yielding ground.
- My conclusion: The more time-consuming the negotiations over severance pay, the more risky the new hire.

Bonus Arrangements

Bonus arrangements for new employees are a dangerous place to tread for start-ups. There is enough uncertainty to a start-up without having to hypothesize how many ways a new vice president of research or vice president of business development can earn a bonus. Having negotiated various sorts of bonus arrangements for incoming executives in start-ups, I can with conviction that prospective employees who are looking for bonuses do not belong at start-up companies. At start-ups, employees should be in it for the long haul or they should be out. This does not mean every new employee should expect to hang around forever. But it does mean every new employee should be attracted by the inherent opportunity of the venture and not by the chance to score a $20,000 bonus. Start-ups are about team effort and going the extra mile. Negotiating individual bonuses for certain employees in start-ups not only goes against this principle, but it also sets up the company to pay out incremental compensation it usually cannot afford to spend.

- My conclusion: Do not dicker over bonus arrangements in start-up situations. If the job is worth more, acknowledge this fact with a higher salary or some other non-contingent compensation. But do not set yourself up for contingent bonuses you may find yourself unhappy, or unable, to pay. If a prospective employee wants to negotiate a bonus package, find out why. Odds are that his or her compensation requirements or expectations for the amount of time he or she expects to stay on board are inconsistent with the long-term needs of the company and with the principle of team effort.

Benefits Packages and Retirement Plans

As a rule of thumb, it is neither necessary nor cost-effective for a start-up to offer company-sponsored insurance coverage or a retirement savings plan until the company adds its tenth full-time employee. However, I believe the company has a duty to look after the welfare of its employees, especially given the higher-than-normal level of risk the employees typically assume by joining a start-up. Therefore, it has been my practice to reimburse new employees for at least part of their individual health insurance premiums until such time that it makes sense to offer a company-sponsored health insurance plan. Start-up founders or executives should consult with an accountant about the proper treatment of individual health care insurance premiums paid for or reimbursed by the company, as these payments may be considered as taxable income for the employee and may be subject to the payment of additional payroll taxes by the employer. Whatever the tax treatment, I believe it is good business for start-ups to help their early employees cover costs that would otherwise be covered by larger, more stable employers. Once the start-up does reach a head count of approximately ten employees, the advantages of offering company-sponsored benefits start to outweigh the added cost, because administering a company plan becomes easier than trying to keep track of separate reimbursements to individuals or separate payments the individuals' own insurance carriers. Offering company-sponsored benefits eventually becomes a necessity to remain competitive with other companies in the employment market, and employees can be more productive if their basic insurance and retirement needs are taken care of by their employer. With that said, it is not necessary to offer a full-blown cafeteria-style benefits program or a comprehensive retirement savings plan all at once. These benefits can be phased in over months or even years, depending upon the company's growth and financial condition. Company founders, entrepreneurs, and investors should pay close attention to the costs involved in offering various kinds of insurance coverage (health, dental, vision, life, disability) and retirement savings options (such as company contributions), because once a company offers a particular benefit, it can be difficult to cut back the benefit in times of financial stress without hurting employee morale and causing valued team members to start circulating their résumés.

Employment Attorneys and Human Resource Advisors

Start-up founders, entrepreneurs, and investors who work closely with start-ups should make it a habit to consult with attorneys experienced in employment law and to retain a good human resource advisor to help contend with complicated employment situations such as layoffs and terminations for cause. Another area where specialized advice is necessary is immigration law, since hiring scientists and engineers from countries such as China and India is now common, and employers can easily run afoul of ever-changing regulations concerning the hiring of non-residents

Good Hiring Practices and Recordkeeping

One of the most important lessons I have learned in the course of staffing numerous start-up companies is that setting up good hiring processes and procedures and establishing standardized employment practices—including creating and maintaining personnel files that are fully in compliance with federal and state regulations—makes human resource management easier, less time-consuming, and above all, safer and less confusing when problems arise. The time to have good personnel files is before problems arise, not afterward.

For a sample of a job offer letter that touches upon many of the issues we have discussed in this chapter, please refer to Appendix 14.9.

Chapter 11 Addendum: IRS Definition of an "Employee"

Start-ups can get themselves into trouble with state and federal taxing authorities and with workers compensation insurance providers by improperly classifying members of the start-up team as independent contractors rather than as employees. Start-ups and many other employers are tempted to treat team members as independent contractors rather than employees to avoid the cost of payroll taxes, workers compensation insurance, and other benefits, as well as the extra costs of payroll services (such as ADP) and the bookkeeping required to administer payroll. Tax authorities and workers compensation insurance providers are always on the lookout for lost revenue.

Start-up entrepreneurs, investors, and executives with hiring authority are advised to consult with their accountants, attorneys, or human resource advisors about how to properly classify people hired and paid by the company to perform work on the company's behalf. Penalties for not following the rules can be stiff.

Employee or Independent Contractor? [32]

Whether someone who works for you is an employee or an independent contractor is an important question. The answer determines your liability to pay and withhold federal income tax, Social Security and Medicare taxes, and federal unemployment tax.

In general, someone who performs services for you is your employee if you can control what will be done and how it will be done.

The courts have considered many facts in deciding whether a worker is an independent contractor or an employee. These facts fall into three main categories:

- **Behavioral Control:** Facts that show whether the business has a right to direct and control. These include:

---

[32] This material is quoted verbatim from the official IRS Web site. For more information, go to www.irs.gov and search for "independent contractor."

Building the Start-Up Team

  - o Instructions: An employee is generally told:
    1. When, where, and how to work
    2. What tools or equipment to use
    3. What workers to hire or to assist with the work
    4. Where to purchase supplies and services
    5. What work must be performed by a specified individual
    6. What order or sequence to follow
  - o Training: An employee may be trained to perform services in a particular manner.

- **Financial Control:** Facts that show whether the business has a right to control the business aspects of the worker's job include:
  - o The extent to which the worker has un-reimbursed expenses
  - o The extent of the worker's investment
  - o The extent to which the worker makes services available to the relevant market
  - o How the business pays the worker
  - o The extent to which the worker can realize a profit or loss

- **Type of Relationship:** Facts that show the type of relationship include:
  - o Written contracts describing the relationship the parties intended to create
  - o Whether the worker is provided with employee-type benefits
  - o The permanency of the relationship
  - o How integral the services are to the principal activity

For a worker who is considered your employee, you are responsible for:

- Withholding federal income tax
- Withholding and paying the employer Social Security and Medicare tax
- Paying federal unemployment tax (FUTA)
- Issuing Form W-2, Wage and Tax Statement, annually

- Reporting wages on Form 941, Employer's Quarterly Federal Tax Return

For a worker who is considered an independent contractor, you may be responsible for issuing Form 1099-MISC, Miscellaneous Income, to report compensation paid.

12

Building Boards of Directors and Scientific Advisory Boards

12.1 Criteria for Forming Boards and Selecting Directors

Choosing people to join a start-up's board of directors (BOD) or scientific advisory board (SAB) should not be a popularity contest, nor an effort to see how many ex-big company CEOs and Nobel Prize winners can be squeezed into a press release. When it comes to BODs, there are really only two kinds to concern ourselves with: useful ones and not-useful ones. As for SABs, there are three kinds: useful ones, not-useful ones, and ones packed with scientific luminaries who look great in fundraising materials, if that's your primary goal.

Start-up companies need BOD members who have sufficient time to devote to important business issues and enough relevant experience to render sound advice. Are credentials important? Of course they are. Absent any other indicators of worthiness, it is almost always preferable to appoint people to your board who have worked at recognizable companies and held positions of authority. These are factors that signal to potential investors, employees, corporate partners, and service providers that you—as a founder, entrepreneur, or seed investor in a company—know the right kinds of people, have the right kinds of connections, and offer an opportunity exciting enough to attract noteworthy people to your BOD. However, no board candidate, no matter how impressive his or her credentials or how lofty his or her latest job title, should be considered purely on the basis of his or her résumé. What really matters is the board candidate's breadth of relevant experience, wisdom, evenness of temper, and openness of mind. Board members are people whose counsel you will need in times of great opportunity and in times of distress. You will need board members for approval of routine matters and authorization of drastic actions. You may need to reach your company's directors at odd hours, or under awkward circumstances of the kind you might otherwise prefer to keep to yourself. Thus, as you consider people who you may wish to invite to join your BOD, ask yourself: Is he or she the kind of person I could speak to candidly and under any circumstances? Has he or she held positions of importance or borne important individual or organizational responsibilities without being self-important? Will the candidate be available when needed without making you feel like you are two feet tall when you need to interrupt his or her vacation to get advice on a critical matter? If your answer to any of these questions is "No," I recommend finding another candidate, because running a start-up is difficult enough without the headache of self-important or less-than-helpful directors. Equally important to avoid is the board candidate who reveals a tendency to be excessively opinionated, inflexible, or slow on the uptake.

12.2 How Not to Form a Board

Having consulted for companies with "board problems," I believe start-ups find themselves saddled with difficult, ineffective, and sometimes mean-spirited boards for one or more of the following reasons (one usually begets another):

- Board members are selected for their résumés and not their character.
- Board members get selected because they are friends of other board members or of investors, and not because they will add real value to the company.
- Start-ups do not pay enough attention to the personalities of their investors (who may demand board seats as a condition of funding) before accepting their investors' money.
- Start-ups pay too much attention to what the board "looks like" to outsiders, and not enough attention to what the board "feels like" to insiders.
- Too few people are involved in determining the composition of the board.

- The founder(s) or initial investor(s) do not invite input from reputable advisors such as other companies' senior management, board members at other companies, attorneys, and successful private investors.
- The founders or initial investors think only they know what's right for the company.
- The founders have no intention of giving up control, or they place other concerns or goals ahead of the organic growth of the company.
- The founders or initial investors lack the business experience or connections to know where or how to find good board members (as may happen with academic start-ups).

The best way to avoid making mistakes with the selection of board members is not to assume that you have all the answers, and to consult with other people and companies that seem to have done a good job of building effective boards of directors. Also, there should be no rush to form a BOD. Inexperienced company founders and investors assume they must form a full board of directors as soon as they form a company. Not only is this not the case, but doing so can set the stage for board problems that are difficult to resolve. The time to get to know board members and their styles of thinking is before inviting them to join the board, not during a start-up's first few board meetings. If your first few board meetings leave you with a queasy feeling about one or more of your board members, that queasiness is probably justified.

12.3 Advice on Board Size for Start-ups

Most start-ups begin as very small operations with few (if any) employees. At this early stage, especially if no outside investors are involved, there may be no issued stock, no stock options, no payroll, and no benefits plan; indeed, there may be few matters that require the input of outside directors. Rather than complicate life by trying to figure out what outsiders to invite on the board, limit the start-up board to a few competent insiders and go slowly with corporate matters that require board decisions. If you are a company founder or entrepreneur, the first professional investors you bring on board will have their own ideas about what your company's board should look like, so you are better off going into the initial fundraising process without having appointed a full board. Otherwise, one of the first things potential investors will focus on, assuming they have any interest in your company, is the composition of your board. Unless the people on your board are of unquestionable stature, odds are that they will appear as a net negative for investors or, at the very least, investors will assume they will need to reconstitute your board. So, why not just assume from the start that potential investors would prefer a clean slate when it comes to board membership instead of giving potential investors targets to shoot at?

Thus, I advise start-up founders and entrepreneurs not to rush into forming a board of directors until the circumstances of the company demand a full-fledged board. In my experience, professional investors would view a small start-up board as a net positive. A small start-up board suggests to the investor that the founders/entrepreneurs have spent more time focusing on important operational issues than on worrying about such niceties as the board of directors.

While I do not advocate building a board of back-slapping good buddies, I do think board harmony is important. Board members should feed off of each other's good ideas and constructively criticize ideas of lesser merit. But board meetings should not be places for heated arguments and shouting matches. Board meetings should be relatively orderly affairs that follow a predetermined agenda and take advantage of each board member's unique expertise, and of positive group dynamics.

12.4 Using Boards Productively

Almost all the advice I can convey about working with board members and using board meetings productively boils down to effective communication. Following are some suggestions:

Raise Critical Issues Before, Not During, Board Meetings

Board meetings are not the time to spring surprises on board members or float trial balloons about contentious issues. The time to raise critical issues is during the weeks *before* board meetings, when management has the opportunity to control the delivery of bad news, the discussion of sensitive issues, or the announcement of unpleasant surprises. Boards of directors tend not to handle new information well when the information is delivered unexpectedly during a board meeting. The point to be made is not that board members cannot handle surprises, but that board members prefer to have time to digest important new information, so they can render well-informed opinions and recommendations.

Discussing important or controversial issues ahead of time with key board members, either by telephone or in person, demonstrates to individual board members that you value their thoughtful consideration of company matters and that you, as a founder or senior manager, are considerate and respectful. Airing touchy issues that may provoke strong reactions from board members is almost always better done one on one and in advance, rather than in the unpredictable environment of a board meeting. Discussing sensitive issues in advance of board meetings allows time for diplomacy, damage control, and consensus building. Also, controversial issues and sensitive situations have a way of working themselves out over time as new information becomes available, or as cooler heads prevail.

Communicate with Board Members Frequently and Informally

The best way for a start-up CEO to keep himself or herself out of hot water with the board is to communicate frequently and informally with individual board members and with the board as a whole. E-mail is an invaluable tool for maintaining an open channel of communication with board members, but it must not be used as a replacement for personal interaction. E-mail can be used for routine notices, scheduling, providing non-critical updates, and confirming plans or decisions. E-mail should not be used to deliver unexpected negative news, or information of a personal or emotionally charged nature, nor should e-mail be used as "safe cover" when a phone call or face-to-face meeting would be better. If you are a CEO, a company founder, or an investor, it is almost always easier to discuss and defuse emotionally charged or controversial board issues once the habit of frequent and informal information exchange among board members has been established. Limiting communication with the board to the short period of time immediately before, during, and after board meetings makes the airing of sensitive issues or unexpected negative issues more difficult, precisely because board members will come to expect that any communication that is "out of the ordinary" must signal problems. On the other hand, the sharing of too many day-to-day operating matters with board members by the CEO or company founder may invite micromanagement by board members or create the perception that the managers in charge cannot make their own decisions.

Effective communication with board members is really an art, considering the wide variety of issues and personalities that must be taken into account. Each board member will have his or her own preferred means of communication—written or spoken, brief or detailed, just the facts or all the details—and the astute CEO, founder, or investor will choose the best method of delivery based upon the type of information, the context, and the communication style of the receiver.

A good rule to live by when considering whether a particular issue or piece of news should be shared with the board between board meetings is to ask yourself, as the deliverer, whether the withholding of information would be detrimental to the company (due to your failure to seek the board's input), to the board's perception of your judgment and candor, or to the board members themselves (if, for example, you were to withhold information that could put a board member in an awkward or embarrassing position).

Deliver Bad News Promptly

Bad news does not age well, and it should always be delivered with due consideration to its urgency, its potential to harm the company, and the ability of board members to take appropriate and timely action. When in doubt, get it out.

Present Solutions, Not Problems

Board meetings are not meant to be dumping grounds for management's problems. Board meetings should be forums for proposing *solutions* to problems. Thus, it is the role of management to identify problems (preferably in advance) and to seek feedback at board meetings on ways to address them. The same can be said for presenting opportunities. To consume valuable board meeting time recounting past victories may make for pleasant conversation, but it does not accomplish much. Instead,

Building Boards of Directors and Scientific Advisory Boards 185

management should use board meetings to set objectives and plot strategies for future victories.

12.5 The Value of Scientific Advisory Boards

Scientific advisory boards may be partly practical, and partly symbolic. In a practical sense, SABs can provide the kind of dispassionate, third-party advice and feedback on scientific or technical matters that cannot be expected from a company's internal managers. The same can be said for paid consultants, who may find it difficult to render opinions that are entirely impartial. Because SAB members typically hold secure academic faculty positions or well-compensated corporate management roles, they have less reason to be concerned that their comments about a start-up company's science or technology will put their scientific advisory roles (or SAB compensation). The carefully recruited SAB can serve a variety of useful purposes, including:

- Conferring scientific credibility on a new start-up
- Acting as a sounding board for scientific or technical matters
- Providing access to the higher echelons of academia, corporate organizations, granting agencies, professional societies, and so on
- Personally intervening to influence key decision-makers
- Being a reference for potential investors or corporate partners
- Helping to attract and recruit senior executives and scientists
- Making referrals to experts and authorities in specific scientific disciplines, fields of research, or clinical practices (for physicians)
- Publishing or speaking about research or technical developments relevant to the company
- Attracting positive publicity and notoriety

Exhibit 12, which follows, is a reproduction of an actual press release from Neurion Pharmaceuticals Inc. It illustrates the kind of positive luster a highly respected scientific advisory board member can add to a start-up company's reputation.

Exhibit 12
Press Release About Scientific Advisory Board Member

Press Release   **For Immediate Release**

Contact: William L. Robbins, Chairman, President, and CEO

Neurion Pharmaceuticals Inc. Scientific Advisor Robert H. Grubbs Wins 2005 Nobel Prize in Chemistry

PASADENA, CA—(BUSINESS WIRE)—October 10, 2005—Neurion Pharmaceuticals Inc., an ion channel drug discovery company, announced today its congratulations to Dr. Robert H. Grubbs, professor of chemistry at the California Institute of Technology (Caltech) and winner of the 2005 Nobel Prize in chemistry. Dr. Grubbs is one of the original members of Neurion's scientific advisory board (SAB) and one of three Neurion SAB members drawn from the Caltech faculty.

According to the official statement by the Royal Swedish Academy of Sciences in Stockholm, Dr. Grubbs and two other winners will share this year's prize in chemistry "for the development of the metathesis method in organic synthesis." Metathesis is an organic reaction that makes many scientifically and commercially important chemical processes more efficient, and enables the production of "custom-built" molecules with novel properties.

Dr. Dennis Dougherty, George Grant Hoag Professor of Chemistry at Caltech and scientific co-founder of Neurion, said of his long-time colleague and office neighbor, "We are tremendously proud of Bob. It has been an honor to be associated with him all these years at Caltech and to receive his counsel as a fellow member of Neurion's SAB."

Grubb's work is now applied routinely in fields as diverse as pharmaceuticals, plastics, and sporting goods materials. Discoveries from his lab are the basis of several life science start-up companies in Pasadena. He is widely regarded as a friend, trusted advisor, and role model for Caltech entrepreneurs in the life sciences and chemistry.

About Neurion

Neurion Pharmaceuticals Inc. (www.neurionpharma.com) is a privately held, early-stage pharmaceutical company whose mission is to discover and develop safer and more effective pharmaceuticals that target ion channels. The company uses its proprietary drug discovery and lead optimization platforms to understand the structural basis of ligand interactions with ion channels, and to design better drugs by exploiting this knowledge.

Having a Nobel laureate on a company's SAB is a wonderful thing and an honor, but recruiting scientific luminaries to an advisory board primarily for their star appeal is a questionable practice. A star-packed SAB may be impressive on paper, but having a roster of scientific advisors that reads like a who's-who of science only says the company has a lot of connections and, probably, that it can afford to throw around a lot of stock options and consulting fees (called *honoraria* when paid to eminent scientists and clinicians, who respond to a higher calling than mere financial gain). Of course, what's the point of having a SAB if none of its members are recognizable? All I recommend is that other factors be taken into account when considering potential SAB members. These factors should include:

- Will the candidate be responsive, or will he or she be so busy with his or her ordinary duties, meetings, conferences, and travel schedule as to be chronically unavailable?
- Will the candidate be "conflicted out" of any significant involvement with a start-up because of his or her prior or simultaneous commitments to other companies' scientific or commercial pursuits (including, potentially, the candidate's own scientific or commercial pursuits)?
- Could the candidate be trusted to speak candidly and knowledgeably about a start-up's science or business while still "saying the right things" and not being so scientifically pure or lofty as to create doubt or uncertainty about a company's science or business plan? Sometimes, eminent scientists who spend most of their waking hours on intellectual pursuits cannot be bothered with mundane business matters. Even unintentionally, this personality type may turn off investors, media representatives, or other business contacts by seeming uninterested in company matters or by speaking with impeccable academic objectivity about a company's prospects when a bit of marketing license would be more helpful.

One final point to make about forming SABs for start-ups echoes the same point made about forming BODs: What's the rush? Just because a new start-up has been founded does not mean it must immediately form a formal scientific advisory board, fully stocked with scientific, technical, or medical prize winners, society presidents, holders of chaired professorships at fine universities, and former chief scientists of major corporations. Recruiting a high-quality SAB takes a lot of founder time and senior management attention. There is also a cost—in terms of stock options to be awarded or consulting fees)—to be paid, as well as legal fees that might be incurred to draft agreements (if they are to be done properly). Furthermore, a company may not know for sure at its founding which scientific areas will be of most importance to its future development and, therefore, what types of scientific expertise should be represented on the SAB. Indeed, a start-up company's scientific focus is likely to change over time, meaning different expertise may be needed at different times. Thus, thought should be given to whether potential scientific advisors should be generalists or specialists, and whether their expertise is likely to remain relevant over an extended period or be of only short-term relevance. In the later case, it may be preferable to retain a scientific advisor purely as a project consultant rather than as a full-fledged SAB member. If a scientific consultant proves to be highly useful, he or she may be invited to join the scientific advisory board at a later time. This arrangement adds the benefit of getting to know a potential SAB member before making a long-term commitment.

Readers may refer to Appendix 14.8 for an example of a letter of invitation for an SAB member.

13

Corporate Partnering

In my more than twenty years of work in business development, strategic partnering, and fundraising, I have had some decent successes, some dismal failures, and more deals that went nowhere than I care to remember. But my experiences were real, mostly valuable, and gave me a storehouse of anecdotes and lessons learned.

13.1 The Conventional Thinking About Corporate Partnering

Getting in bed with corporate partners has typically been viewed with some skepticism by venture capital investors. According to conventional wisdom, pursuing corporate investors or corporate-funded collaborations as a financing and business strategy puts the start-up at risk of becoming a corporate vassal, and risks scaring off other investors or potential partners. Certainly, some of this concern about corporate investors and partners have been—and still are—justified. Large corporations may have short-term or long-term goals that are at odds with the ultimate business objectives of the start-up. Large corporations have a well-deserved reputation for being ponderous, bureaucratic organizations that can tie up small, entrepreneurial companies in protracted and fruitless discussions and negotiations. Corporate investors also have a track record of investing at inflated valuations because, as the thinking goes, they are more interested in gaining strategic advantages than in negotiating the lowest possible valuations for their investment dollar. All these points are true, to a point. But they also reflect an inherent friction between financially motivated venture capital investors and strategically motivated corporate investors (or their colleagues in corporate research and development). After all, it is the venture capitalist's nature to get into a deal at the lowest possible valuation and get out at the highest possible valuation. To a venture capital investor, the presence of a corporate investor in the start-up board room, or of a corporate research and development collaborator in the start-up lab, can be cause for concern and potential conflict.

In this chapter, we will look at both the downsides and the upsides of corporate investment and corporate partnering for start-ups. However, in my opinion, one particularly important factor in the current investment environment for start-ups tips the scales in favor of corporate funding and partnering. That important factor is the seed-stage funding gap. It is an undeniable truth that, as mainstream venture capital firms have vacated the seed-stage investing space, corporate investors and corporate research and development collaborators can help fill the void.

13.2 The Downsides of Corporate Partnering

Bureaucracy, Risk Aversion, Delay, and Indecision (Need I Say More?)

More than anything else, doing business with large corporations takes patience. If you want quick purchase decisions, go into retail. Big companies take an inordinate amount of time to make decisions involving the spending of money. In my own experience, the selling cycle at large companies for a deal of any size worth thinking about has expanded over the last decade to the point where nothing conclusive happens in less than nine months to a year. For entrepreneurs used to making quick decisions without a lot of input from others, trying to close an important business or investment deal with a corporate partner or investor can be frustrating and demoralizing. It can also challenge the staying power of start-ups with constrained resources and dwindling bank accounts.

Why do big companies take so long to make decisions? Part of the reason is sheer size. Companies in some global industries such as pharmaceuticals, telecommunications and chemicals have gotten so big over the past twenty-five years that they exist as entities unto themselves and, but for the need for new revenue and occasional fresh air, could sustain their own internal momentum indefinitely with staff meetings, management reviews, strategic planning sessions, training seminars, company off-sites, reorganizations, rightsizings, and downsizings. To make matters worse, managers at companies in today's consolidating industries (that would included just about all companies that compete globally) are caught up in a seemingly endless cycle of change—preparing for it, suffering through it, or trying to forestall it. A significant number of managers at major companies are so preoccupied with the fallout of mergers, acquisitions, and reorganizations that trying to do business development with them is like trying to get the attention of a deck hand on the Titanic.

Another challenge start-ups face in pursuing corporate funding or strategic partnerships is that big companies are inherently risk-averse. Every decision of consequence (and some of no consequence) must be run up the management flagpole, and, half the time, no one is there to give a salute, because the "senior director of this" or the "vice president of that" is attending yet another company off-site and will not be able to render an opinion on your start-up company's painstakingly prepared proposal until, well, a week from next month.

Adding to the start-up company's difficulties in getting the nod of approval from the powers that be in large corporations is the troubling scarcity of corporate managers with decision-making authority or decision-influencing ability who are able to act independently or with anything resembling (dare I say?) entrepreneurial spirit. The trick for start-ups that want to do business with big companies is to find and latch onto the respected elders, up-and-comers, and savvy survivors in big companies who still have that rare ability to *make things happen*. To my mind, this is the only universally effective and reliable means of penetrating, navigating, and successfully circumventing corporate bureaucracy and arriving at definitive decisions (with luck, of the "yes" variety, although a "no" delivered without undue delay can be just as helpful to a start-up with precious little time to burn).

Over-Committing Limited Start-Up Resources to Corporate Objectives

Another reason that start-ups should carefully consider their goals and limitations before embarking upon a campaign of corporate fundraising or partnering is the natural tendency to over-commit resources to serve the corporate investor's or partner's objectives rather than the start-up's, or its shareholders' objectives. Many a start-up has unwittingly fallen prey to the siren song of corporate funding, only to be led astray by corporate priorities that are at odds with the start-up's business plan, its investors' expectations, or its employees' aspirations. This unhappy situation can arise when a start-up finds itself gradually committing more and more time and resources to please a corporate suitor in the hopes of achieving some future financial gain, be it in the form of an equity investment, a fee-for-service contract, or revenue from product sales or licensing fees. These potential gains are certainly worth pursuing for the right reasons, but sometimes they come at too high a cost. When might this be so? One indicator is when a start-up whose business plan calls for the development of a new technology or product subjugates its own priorities, redirects its research and development resources, and sacrifices its internal deadlines to pursue short-term service revenues. Start-up entrepreneurs and seed-stage investors need to remain vigilant to the risks of misdirecting company resources because of some perceived financial benefit that turns out to be short-lived, illusory, or counter to the start-up's own strategic mission.

I have experienced this personally on more than one occasion. Once, a start-up in which I was involved invested in some expensive equipment and several months of time-consuming training for equipment operators in the misguided expectation that owning such equipment would all but guarantee the winning of new business from clients engaged in clinical trials for certain types of implantable medical devices. These clients required access to this specialized equipment and gave encouraging signals that my employer's acquisition of the equipment would be rewarded with new contracts. Unfortunately, these clinical trials proved to be highly speculative, were frequently discontinued, and were closely tied to certain academic investigators. Consequently, the expensive new equipment that my employer purchased sat idle for months on end, and the technicians trained to operate it felt, rightfully, that their time could have been spent more productively doing other work. The promise of significant and sustained new business was never fulfilled, and management (myself included) took a credibility hit for buying into a false premise and over-committing scarce resources.

The moral of this story is that a start-up must not allow itself to stray from its chosen path simply to please a potential corporate investor or strategic partner. There are times when this may be a reasonable thing to do, but only if the advantage to be gained would be substantial and sustainable.

Mainstream venture capital investors take a particularly dim view of start-ups that split their effort between the pursuit of internal development goals and the pursuit of service contracts and fee-for-service arrangements.

Another risky behavior for start-ups is engaging in too many "feasibility studies," "proof-of-principle evaluations" or "pilot projects" for potential corporate investors or partners. Start-ups often engage in these activities in the hope of clinching a corporate investment or funded collaboration, but more often than not, the study or project will be completed at some cost to the start-up and the corporation will lose interest, change priorities, or fail to approve a follow-on budget. This is why I make it a point in my discussions with potential corporate partners to avoid the terms "feasibility study" and "proof of principle" altogether when preparing proposals or negotiating initial business deals. Often, it is better to decline such "opportunities" to prove oneself than to engage in a short-lived and (usually) under-funded "technology evaluations" that may prove in the end to be little more than a stalling maneuver for the prospective corporate investor or partner. Once a start-up has proven that its technology is beyond the concept stage, its management should not fall for beguiling requests from big companies for a quick "feasibility study." or "proof of principle evaluation or "pilot project."

Relying Too Heavily on a Single Partner

Of course, for small start-ups, getting in bed with a corporate partner also carries with it the risk of getting squashed when the partner rolls over. This is invariably a risk when a start-up comes to rely upon a large partner too heavily for revenue or equity funding. To be sure, things may start out well at the beginning of a corporate partnering or investment relationship. Cash flows in at contract signing, wine flows out at the celebratory dinner, and all participants in the deal get the warm fuzzies. The business relationship advances. Everything is hunky dory. But corporate priorities change for reasons that have absolutely nothing to do with the start-up and are totally outside of its control. The corporate partner's or investor's managers may get promoted or reorganized out of their previous assignments. Corporate partnering budgets may get slashed to fund acquisitions. And when the corporate partner changes its tune and the start-up does not have another dance partner warmed up and ready to swing, the sock-hop is over and the start-up may get left in the lurch. As a start-up founder, entrepreneur, manager or investor, if you can help it, do not get yourself or your company in this position. As soon as your start-up signs a contract with one big partner, start lining up the next partner. It is usually just a matter of time before at least one of your major partners is going to lose interest in your company for one reason or another, so do your best always to keep your dance card filled.

Selling the Farm Before the Crop Comes In

Another fear that venture capitalists have about a portfolio company getting too closely involved with a corporate partner is that the portfolio company will license out or sell its "crown jewel" technology assets too early in the commercialization cycle, thereby undervaluing the asset, or cutting off future avenues of growth. This is a legitimate concern. Determining the optimal time to license out or sell a valuable piece of technology takes a finely tuned ability to sense when a technology's value is at its peak.

Granting Exclusivity without Adequate Protections

Another potential downside to corporate partnering is granting exclusivity (sometimes referred to by experienced start-up executives as the "E word") without adequate protections and controls, and without recourse in the event of non-performance by the corporate partner. This can happen, for example, when a technology-oriented start-up company that lacks marketing muscle teams up with a larger company that has strength in marketing and enters into an exclusive arrangement to co-market or distribute the start-up's products or services. In this situation, the larger company is usually motivated by the opportunity to gain a technological advantage over its competition. The larger company seeks to achieve this by associating itself with a cutting-edge start-up and positioning itself to be the exclusive provider of some "hot" new technology that is not offered by the competition. The risks of granting exclusivity are manifold, especially for a small start-up that gives away control of its key technology or key markets without also negotiating terms that penalize the larger partner or entitle the start-up to regain control of the technology in the event of non-performance by the larger partner. The risks of exclusivity vary according to circumstances.

What entices a start-up to enter into an exclusive agreement with a corporate partner? One enticement is vanity, pure and simple. It can be a real "head rush" for the management of a start-up company to learn that a potential corporate partner thinks highly enough of the start-up's technology to want some sort of exclusive rights to it. Inexperienced founders, entrepreneurs and seed investors may be tempted to enter into exclusive agreements too hastily because of "pride of recognition." To work in relative obscurity for many months or years and suddenly to find one's technology sought after on an exclusive basis by a well-known corporate partner can be a real ego booster, and in such circumstances, a start-up's overeager management or impatient investors may be inclined to grasp at an exclusive deal without appropriate attention to the downsides.

Another reason start-ups will consider exclusive deals with undue haste is desperation. Chronically in need of cash, many start-ups may be drawn into an exclusive deal by the prospect of an up-front cash payment, the promise of steady cash flow, ready access to otherwise unaffordable resources, or the gain of much-needed credibility by virtue of association with a well-known corporate partner.

Still another reason start-ups may naively entertain an exclusive relationship with a corporate partner is concern about being left standing on the sidelines while competing start-ups team up with the most desirable corporate partners. The concern here is that the start-up will play the exclusivity game for the wrong reasons. Rather than considering what is best for the development and commercialization of its own technology, the start-up may lose sight of its own objectives and respond in lock-step fashion to what its competitors are doing. Also, start-ups may put too much weight on the value of a corporate partner's name, sales force, or distribution outlets while unwisely ignoring the corporate partner's motivations for demanding exclusivity in the first place. Does the corporate partner intend to commercialize the start-up's technology, or simply to keep the technology off the market, thereby avoiding competition with the corporate partner's own technology or products? Is the corporate partner's real agenda to keep a start-up out of a competitor's hands rather than to bring the start-up's technology to market in a way that maximizes value for the start-up? These are questions that start-up founders, executives, and investors should ask themselves before agreeing to discuss the "E word" with a potential corporate partner.

Despite the risks, there are cases when an exclusive agreement with a corporate partner makes sense. Sometimes, the question of whether to do an exclusive deal comes down to how much the corporate partner is willing to pay. If the amount of cash or valuable stock being offered by a prospective corporate partner is too good to ignore and helps the start-up and its investors achieve important strategic or financial objectives, to reject exclusivity out of hand would be short-sighted. If granting exclusivity brings access to development or marketing resources that would otherwise be unattainable, either within a desirable period of time or within a feasible budget, negotiating an exclusive deal might be a sound business strategy.

Downside Protections for Corporate Partnering Deals

While I am biased against doing exclusive deals early in a start-up company's lifecycle, there are ways to protect the start-up and its investors from some of the risks I have described. Following are some ideas about protective terms that start-ups can include in their negotiations, but (here comes the legal disclaimer) you should consult an attorney who is experienced in corporate partnering deals about the specific protections that might make sense in your particular case.

Get Paid Up Front

A rule to live by is to get paid at the beginning of a business relationship, and not to base payments that you require to fund initial project, staffing, or overhead costs on contingencies. One of the time-honored "gotchas" that experienced start-up entrepreneurs and seed-stage investors will recall with a wry smile is the deals they signed that failed to provide for run-up costs or ongoing resources to support a corporate collaboration. You should avoid falling into the trap of pricing a corporate-funded collaboration on direct, variable costs (time and materials) without also accounting for indirect overhead costs, and opportunity costs of foregone business. Another "gotcha" is the contingent payment ("If you complete certain milestones by date X, the corporate partner will make payment"). In corporate collaborations, particularly of the exclusive variety, there are too many unforeseen circumstances under which contingent payments do not work out as planned, and as an entrepreneur or investor, you do not want your company to end up in the hole thanks to a poorly negotiated payment schedule.

Get Paid for Risk

Generally, exclusive partnering deals entail a higher degree of risk than non-exclusive deals. As the entrepreneur or investor, you should be fairly compensated for this risk. The kind of risk I am talking about is that of putting many, or all, of your eggs in one basket. Depending upon the scope of exclusivity that you grant, you could be putting your company's future in someone else's hands, and this fact should be reflected in the price you are paid as well as in the timing of payments you receive, starting with that all-important up-front payment. Another increased risk in an exclusive deal is related to opportunity cost. Once you tie the knot exclusively with one partner, what are the odds that you will give up future business from your newly exclusive partner's closest competitors? How much would this lost business be worth? Factor this into your deal pricing.

Build in Performance Guaranties

Exclusive partnering agreements specify that paying partner will deliver certain results in return for the right to some form of exclusivity. The partner may be expected to provide a specified level of financing or in-kind support, to complete development of a product incorporating the start-up's technology, to achieve a specified level of product sales, or to enter certain new markets. These and other aspects of the partner's anticipated performance should be benchmarked in the partnering agreement, and certain guaranties should be built into the agreement to put some "teeth" into the terms. In other words, it should be clear in the agreement that a partner's non-performance has real consequences and, preferably, that these consequences will be painful. What types of guaranties might be written into an exclusive agreement? Here are a few:

- Completion guaranties
- Date guaranties
- Minimum product attributes (cost, speed, lifetime, etc.)

- Minimum unit sales levels
- Minimum revenues
- Minimum number of new customers
- Minimum number of new markets entered
- Guaranteed support levels (research and development resources, staffing levels, etc.)

Clawbacks

Exclusivity implies giving up a piece of something completely, at least for some period of time. Exclusivity is all or none. Even non-exclusive partnering deals can require a start-up to relinquish certain rights or flexibility. But, under certain circumstances, what has been given up can be taken back. This is the essence of a "clawback provision" in a business deal. Suppose you, as a start-up entrepreneur or executive, grant exclusivity to a large corporate partner for sales of your product in certain markets. For example, let us assume you have given up the markets in Western Europe (on a country-by-country basis) but have kept rights to the Americas (North and South). Now, suppose your partner was to meet certain marketing and sales milestones within the Western European region within a specified period of time, but fails to do so. With a clawback provision, the company that granted the original exclusivity could, for the sake of argument,, regain rights to, say, France, Spain and Italy. Another clawback might involve the return of certain hard assets or equity that changed hands at the commencement of an exclusive deal. Perhaps a larger corporate partner makes an equity investment in a start-up in return for exclusive access to technology, and then fails to live up to its end of the bargain. In this case, the start-up may be able to claw back some of its equity. The net effect for the start-up is to regain some of the control it may have initially surrendered as part of a deal gone sour.

Escape Clauses

The ultimate "out" of a bad deal is the escape clause. It means what it says. If Partner A fails to perform, Partner B gets to walk away with all of its marbles. The intent of an escape clause is to provide a sort of ultimate remedy within the bounds of a previously negotiated agreement. Escape clauses might involve partial or total forfeiture of exclusive rights, or punitive payments to compensate a wronged partner once and for all for opportunities forgone, or some other variant. But an escape clause can work both ways—against either the grantor or the grantee of exclusivity. I have talked mostly about downside protections for the grantor, but the grantee should also have recourse if things do not go as planned. For example, if the exclusive technology turns out not to perform as promised, the licensee may wish to return rights to the licensor and walk away from the deal.

13.3   The Upsides of Corporate Partnering

By some accounts, corporate partnering is more fun and interesting than chasing investors and raising money. For most start-ups, fundraising among the usual sources—angel investors and venture capitalists—is just a ceremonial dance with a foreordained outcome. "It's too early for us." "Keep us posted." "We'll get back to you." And for this, start-up founders and entrepreneurs will spend countless hours honing their PowerPoint presentations, trudging through airports, and cooling their heels in investors' conference rooms while waiting for the general partners to arrive (late, as usual). This is not anyone's idea of a good time, and it certainly is not intellectually stimulating.

Successful corporate partnering is particularly valuable for the following reasons

Corporate Partners Can Provide Direction

Most start-ups do not really know what they want to be when they grow up. In fact, three or four years after their founding, many start-ups look nothing like what they originally set out to be. Why? Because founding technologies fail to deliver, new investors and new management decide to change direction, and serendipity happens. One thing corporate partners can provide that start-ups often lack is a definite direction. Corporate partners usually engage start-ups in collaborations to help solve specific problems or evaluate new technologies or products. For start-ups, a big company's research objective, or the solution to a big company's scientific problem, can represent something concrete to pursue. Corporate partners can help a start-up focus its limited resources on achieving particular milestones within a specific timeframe and a specific budget. Corporate partners can provide not only a target to shoot for, in the form of a contract with defined inputs, work plans, schedules, and deliverables, but also a management framework that gives structure to a project.

If a start-up does not know exactly where it wants to go with its technology, a corporate partner can help set a path forward.

Corporate Partners Confer Credibility

Announcing a new contract with a well-known corporate partner or presenting non-confidential research results from collaboration with a top-tier company can confer instant credibility on a start-up that wants to make a name for itself. Landing a contract with a Fortune 500 company is valuable not just for name recognition, but for the experience. Large companies typically subject start-ups to extensive due diligence before executing business agreements of significant dollar value or duration, and going through the corporate due diligence process can help a start-up get its own house in order. Also, leading companies in an industry tend to perk up their ears and pay attention when a little-known start-up lands a partnering deal with a major competitor. Sometimes, just by announcing a partnering deal with Major Company A, a start-up may suddenly receive inquiries from Major Companies B, C, and D.

Corporate Partnering Provides Much-Needed Cash Flow

Corporate partners represent an important potential source of cash for start-ups that cannot attract capital from mainstream venture firms. Most big companies have no desire to buy stock in start-ups that are still too early-stage to have attracted funding from mainstream venture capital firms. Thus, large corporate partners usually pay cash in return for services, products, or IP rights. As long as a start-up does not sell its future prematurely by out-licensing key IP too early in the game, doing an all-cash partnering deal with a big company can bring in much-needed funding that, may be non-dilutive to equity.[33]

Like fundraising, corporate partnering can be time-consuming and frustrating, but, unlike fundraising, the range of discourse in corporate partnering almost always includes substantive scientific or technical matters and can reveal a wealth of useful information. Following are some of the interesting and useful things that start-up founders, entrepreneurs and investors can learn during the course of corporate partnering discussions:

- The key challenges and opportunities that are on the minds of corporate scientists, managers, and executives
- Where and how corporations are investing their research dollars
- How large companies organize their research and development operations
- What types of products and services appeal to potential partners
- How large companies differ in their decision-making
- What is the prevailing mood at different companies within a particular industry

13.4   How to Approach Potential Corporate Partners

The process of pursuing corporate partners takes organization, persistence, and patience. Corporate partnering efforts cannot be rushed. Logically enough, start-ups that are new to the corporate partnering game usually begin with telephone calls and e-mails to the business development departments of large companies. The problem with this approach is that it is backwards. In my experience, the right place to begin prospecting for corporate partnerships is with corporate scientists and engineers (the "lab coats"), rather than with business managers (the "suits"). Business development managers in large companies often carry titles such as "Alliance Manager," "Manager, External R&D," "Director, Technology Licensing, or "Director, External Collaborations." With these outwardly-focused titles, one would think that the job of corporate business

---

[33] A corporate partnering deal that is "non-dilutive to equity" means that the corporate partner does not acquire any equity as part of the transaction, thereby avoiding dilution of existing investors' ownership positions.

development managers is to scout the horizon, proactively searching for promising new technologies to show the cloistered scientists back at headquarters. In reality, most corporate business development managers function more as gatekeepers than as technology scouts. Business development managers at large companies are bombarded daily by inquiries from eager start-ups that are looking for opportunities to present their revolutionary discoveries and breakthrough technologies to potential corporate partners. Being on the receiving end of this onslaught of inquiries, corporate business development managers can become jaded rather quickly. Consequently, most business development managers are loath to let down their guard when start-ups make un-invited solicitations. Rather than serving as the ideal point of entry into big companies, business development managers are more likely to act like sentries at the drawbridge, defending the castle against the barbarians of Start-Up Land.

Seasoned business development managers at big companies do not waste much time chasing down unsubstantiated leads. Instead, they take their cues from in-the-know company scientists and engineers who are the ultimate customers for externally sourced technologies, and who are usually better qualified to assess their employers' scientific and technical needs. Consequently, the most productive way for a start-up to approach a potential corporate partner is first to seek the input of corporate scientists and engineers, and then to identify a scientific or technical champion—preferably one at the level of director or project leader (if not higher)—who will direct his or her counterpart(s) in business development to engage the start-up in a business discussion. In general (there will always be exceptions), prospecting for corporate partners should proceed according to the following sequence of events:

1. Make initial contacts with corporate scientists or engineers who are prospective customers for or users of the start-up's technology or products.
2. Seek substantive feedback on the scientific or technical merits of the start-up's offerings, and establish the basis for productive dialogue and trust-building.
3. Identify a real and present need within the target company, solicit internal support, and cultivate an internal champion.

4. Seek the scientific or technical champion's advice about how to engage the target company in a business discussion. This typically means identifying the appropriate business development contact that would be responsible for "opening the gate" and for helping the start-up to navigate the target company's customary procedures and processes for vetting new technology and formulating plans for a business relationship.
5. Make contact with the business development manager, having already established a basis for discussion through prior dialogue with the target company's scientists or engineers.

As can be seen from the preceding five-step process for business development, the key to establishing a solid foundation for corporate partnering discussions is to establish a good relationship with the prospective partner's scientists or engineers *first*. Only then is the start-up likely to find an open door at the business development manager's office.

Once this five-step process has been initiated, it is best to let discussions proceed at their own natural pace. Big companies have a slow metabolism, and cannot digest new information, or form new business relationships, quickly. Such things take time, and trying to speed up the process can be ineffective at best, and counterproductive at worst. Start-ups can find it hard to understand why big companies can move so slowly, and are quick to attribute big-company slowness to lack of interest, intentional foot-dragging, or more nefarious intentions. But, the fact is, big companies move slowly because they are big. Therefore, it is often good advice for a start-up company that is experiencing slow decision-making by a potential corporate partner simply to move on to something else for a while—whether that means pursuing other potential partners, focusing on internal projects, or simply letting time pass. In these "wait-and-see" situations, finding the proper balance between being proactive, and simply biding one's time, can make the difference between driving oneself a little crazy with impatience, and simply taking the corporate partnering process in stride.

Having a system for keeping track of corporate partnering prospects can help to reduce the angst and lack of control start-ups often feel about the corporate partnering process. Exhibit 13, below, is an example of a spreadsheet used to track strategic partnering contacts.

Exhibit 13
Strategic Partnering Prospect List

Company	Next Step	Their Key Contact(s)	Our Contact	History
#1 TARGETS				
Company A	Karl to e-mail sample data for management meeting	_____ Ph.D., VP of Global Discovery Research;_Sr. Group Leader, Department of Integrated Pharmacology; _____, Vice President of Neuroscience, xyz@drugco.com	Karl	Karl met _____ at conference, sent brochure, left things open for discussion, _____. Send brochure to VP of Neuroscience as follow-up.
Company B	Revise latest work plan to be attached to master agreement, once we receive list of compounds from _____	_____, Senior Vice President of Discovery Research, xyz@pharmaco.com; _____ (licensing in U.K.); abc@pharmaco.com, in U.K.	Rob	High interest in collaboration. Requested proposal for screening 60 compounds.
Company C	Discussions are stalled. Need to elevate to VP level to secure management buy-in to pursue collaboration	_____, Director, Corporate Business Development, _____, head of U.K. CNS research group; _____, Director of Medicinal Chemistry	Rob	Met at ACS poster session. Completed videoconference with their CNS discovery group on _____.
Company D	Set up video conference to go through presentation and resolve technical issues	_____ PhD, Director of Pharmacology (Cambridge, MA). _____ Ph.D., Director of Chemistry. _____, Associate Director of Business Development and Licensing	Rob	_____ Contacted Rob after ACS meeting. Requested PDF of poster.
Company E	Left message with Dr. _____ to arrange video conference next month	_____ Ph.D., Head of Medicinal Chemistry; _____ Sr. Director, Alliance Management	Jim	Met at last year's Neuroscience annual meeting. Had expressed interest in our discovery platform.

Corporate Partnering

13.5 The Corporate Partnering Proposal

Corporate partnering proposals have many variants,, but they all follow the same general outline. This outline usually includes a statement of goals, a work plan that describes a specific set of experiments or tasks, as well as the division of responsibilities; a set of deliverables, a timeline, a budget, and a payment schedule. Exhibit 14, below, provides an example of a typical corporate partnering proposal.

Exhibit 14
Example of Corporate Partnering Proposal

Proposal for Super-Chip Research and Development Collaboration

<u>Submitted to:</u> Dr. _____
Vice President, Global Strategic Alliances
Major Global Technology Corporation

_____
_____
Tel. _____

<u>Submitted by:</u> Dr. _____
President and CEO
Bio-Widgets, Inc.

_____
_____
Tel. _____

___(Month)___(Day), ___(Year)___

SUBJECT: Proposal for Product R&D Collaboration between MAJOR GLOBAL TECHNOLOGY CORPORATION and TECHNO-WIDGETS, INC. to develop prototype SUPER-CHIPs with improved power consumption and performance characteristics.

GOALS:

1) Test materials identified by Major Global Technology Corp. for the SUPER-CHIP under existing standard fabrication conditions;

2) Jointly identify and augment a set of materials for the fabrication of the SUPER-CHIP;

3) Techno-Widgets will manufacture functional SUPER-CHIP prototypes using the set of materials provided by Major Global Technology Corp. Prototypes will be made using ____(Method A) and ____(Method B)_____;

4) Results from these experiments will be shared, analyzed, and modeled and the performance characteristics of the SUPER-CHIP prototype will be improved upon by both parties;

5) With a full understanding of the SUPER-CHIP, Techno-Widgets will make devices using _____based on the _____ materials developed by Techno-Widgets and Major Global Technology Corp.;

6) Major Global Technology Corp. will investigate other techniques for the manufacturing of functional SUPER-CHIP prototype devices.

The following development plan outlines the steps to achieve the GOALS mentioned above and the responsibilities of each party involved. The Plan is subject to mutually agreeable modifications in light of the potential undefined and unforeseen scientific obstacles in characterizing the complicated nature of_____. This document covers the resources, full-time-equivalents (FTEs), materials, and equipment requirements for the Collaboration for ____(period)_____only.

Techno-Widgets also proposes to create a Joint Project Management Committee consisting of Major Global Technology Corp. and Techno-

Corporate Partnering

Widgets personnel to help define and/or modify the path of this Collaboration as necessary and with the intent to achieve realizable commercial products by the end of this or subsequent extensions of this Collaboration. The Joint Project Management Committee will meet ____(frequency)___, at a mutually convenient location to discuss and update the Collaboration and business goals.

Major Global Technology Corp.'s Responsibilities:

- Major Global Technology Corp. will assign one materials expert and one device physics expert to help identify the material-set used for _____;

- These Major Global Technology Corp. experts will help analyze results from Techno-Widgets's experiments and share this analysis with the team members at Techno-Widgets;

- Major Global Technology Corp. will further contribute _____ design know-how from its third party project as far as it is possible within the respective contractual agreements.

Techno-Widgets's Responsibilities:

- Techno-Widgets will test the initial material-set identified by Major Global Technology Corp. using the existing standard fabrication process for the SUPER-CHIP;

- Techno-Widgets will work with Major Global Technology Corp. to identify and augment, if and as necessary, a new _____ material-set;

- Techno-Widgets will make the SUPER-CHIP using the _____ material-set, if and as necessary;

- Techno-Widgets will share the results from these experiments with Major Global Technology Corp. on a regular basis, as the results become available, and or as requested by Major Global Technology Corp. for analysis and modeling to improve these devices;

- Techno-Widgets will submit ___(frequency)___ reports of the progress of the research to Major Global Technology Corp.;

- Techno-Widgets will add resources, within the availability and without significantly draining Techno-Widgets's resources, to supplement these studies as necessary. These resources may include additional material, equipment from _____ lab, and/or FTEs. Any additional funding needs arising from adding resource require written approval from Major Global Technology Corp.

MILESTONES:

Milestone	Elapsed Time
Demo SUPER-CHIP under controlled conditions	__ months
Identify set of new materials for the SUPER-CHIP	__ months
Model device with new materials and process	__ months
Demo improved device for standard use conditions	__ months

PAYMENT SCHEDULE: To accomplish the collaboration's GOALS during the Collaboration, it is proposed that Major Global Technology Corp. fund Techno-Widgets in the amount of $_____ per year; of which, $_____ is used to support ___ FTEs and $_____ for equipment and materials (see Appendix A, Tables 1 & 2). Funding from Major Global Technology Corp. shall be remitted quarterly to Techno-Widgets in the amount of $_____ per quarter. The first quarter payment shall also include $_____ for equipment and materials acquisition cost.

14

Appendices

14.1 Confidentiality Agreement

CONFIDENTIALITY AGREEMENT

This Agreement, dated _____ is made by and between Bio-Widgets, Inc. ("Company"), having a principal place of business at 123 Startup Street, Anywhere, California, 45678 and _____ of _____ ("Recipient").

1. <u>Definition of Confidential Information</u>. "Confidential Information" as used in this Agreement shall mean any and all technical and non-technical information including patent, copyright, trade secret, and proprietary information, techniques, sketches, drawings, models, inventions, know-how, processes, apparatus, equipment, algorithms, software programs, software source documents, biological material, and formulae related to the current, future and proposed products and services of Company, and includes, without limitation, its respective information concerning research, experimental work, development, design details and specifications, engineering, financial information, procurement requirements, purchasing manufacturing, customer lists, business forecasts, sales and merchandising and marketing plans and information.

2. <u>Nondisclosure and Nonuse Obligations</u>. Recipient agrees that it will not make use of, disseminate, or in any way disclose Confidential Information to any person, firm or business, except to the extent necessary for negotiations, discussions, and consultations with personnel or authorized representatives of Company and any purpose Company may hereafter authorize in writing. Recipient agrees that it shall treat all

Confidential Information of Company with the same degree of care as it accords to its own Confidential Information and Recipient represents that it exercises reasonable care to protect its own Confidential Information. Recipient will immediately give notice to Company of any unauthorized use or disclosure of the Confidential Information. Recipient agrees to assist Company in remedying any such unauthorized use or disclosure of the Confidential Information.

3. <u>Exclusions from Nondisclosure and Nonuse Obligations</u>. Recipient's obligations under Paragraph 2 ("Nondisclosure and Nonuse Obligations") with respect to any portion of Confidential Information shall terminate when Recipient can document that: (a) it was in the public domain at or subsequent to the time it was communicated to Recipient by Company through no fault of Recipient; (b) it was rightfully in Recipient's possession free of any obligation of confidence at or subsequent to the time it was communicated to Recipient by Company; (c) it was developed by employees or agents of Recipient independently of and without reference to any information communicated to Recipient by Company; or (d) the communication was in response to a valid order by a court or other governmental body, was otherwise required by law, or was necessary to establish the rights of either party under this Agreement provided, however, that Recipient first gave written notice of such required disclosure to the Company, made a reasonable effort to obtain a protective order requiring that the Confidential Information so disclosed be used only for the purposes for which disclosure was required, and took reasonable steps to allow the Company to seek to protect the confidentiality of the information required to be disclosed.

4. <u>Ownership of Confidential Information and Other Materials</u>. All Confidential Information, and any Derivatives thereof whether created by Company or Recipient, remains the property of Company and no license or other rights to Confidential Information is granted or implied hereby. For purposes of this Agreement, "Derivatives" shall mean: (i) for copyrightable or copyrighted material, any translation, abridgement, revision or other form in which an existing work may be recast, transformed or adapted; (ii) for patentable or patented material, any improvement thereon; and (iii) for material which is protected by trade secret, any new material derived from such existing trade secret material,

including new material which may be protected by copyright, patent and/or trade secret. All materials (including, without limitation, documents, drawings, models, apparatus, sketches, design and lists) furnished to Recipient by Company, and which are designated in writing to be the property of Company, shall remain the property of Company and shall be returned to Company promptly at Company's request, together with any copies thereof.

5. <u>Disclosure of Third Party Information</u>. Neither party shall communicate any information to the other in violation of the proprietary rights of any third party.

6. <u>No Warranty</u>. All Confidential Information is provided "AS IS" and without any warranty, express, implied or otherwise, regarding its accuracy or performance.

7. <u>No Export</u>. Recipient will not export, directly or indirectly, any technical data acquired from Company pursuant to this Agreement or any product utilizing any such data to any country for which the U.S. Government or any agency thereof at the time of export requires an export license or other governmental approval without first obtaining such license or approval.

8. <u>Term</u>. This Agreement shall govern all communications between the parties that are made during the period from the effective date of this Agreement to the date on which either party receives from the other written notice that subsequent communications shall not be so governed, provided, however, that Recipient's obligations under Paragraph 2 ("Nondisclosure and Nonuse Obligations") with respect to Confidential Information of Company which it has previously received shall continue unless terminated pursuant to Paragraph 3 ("Exclusions from Nondisclosure and Nonuse Obligations").

9. <u>No Assignment</u>. Recipient will not assign or transfer any rights or obligations under this Agreement without the prior written consent of Company.

10. <u>Notices</u>. Any notice required or permitted by this Agreement shall be in writing and shall be delivered as follows with notice deemed given as indicated: (i) by personal delivery when delivered personally; (ii) by overnight courier upon written verification of receipt; (iii) by telecopy or facsimile transmission upon acknowledgement of receipt of electronic transmission; or (iv) by certified or registered mail, return receipt requested, upon verification of receipt. Notice shall be sent to the addresses set forth above or such other address as either party may specify in writing.

11. <u>Governing Law</u>. This Agreement shall be governed in all respects by the laws of the United States of America and by the laws of the State of California; as such laws are applied to agreements entered into and to be performed entirely within California between California residents.

12. <u>Severability</u>. Should any provisions of this Agreement be held by a court of law to be illegal, invalid or unenforceable, the legality, validity and enforceability of the remaining provisions of this Agreement shall not be affected or impaired thereby.

13. <u>Waiver</u>. The waiver by Company of a breach of any provision of this Agreement by Recipient shall not operate or be construed as a waiver of any other or subsequent breach by Recipient.

14. <u>Remedies</u>. Because unauthorized disclosure of Confidential Information will diminish the value to the Company of the proprietary interests that are the subject of this Agreement, if Recipient breaches any of its obligations hereunder, the Company shall be entitled to equitable relief to protect its interests therein, including but not limited to injunctive relief, as well as money damages. In the event that the Company seeks an injunction under this Agreement, Recipient waives any requirement that the Company post a bond or other security.

The prevailing party shall be entitled to recover from the losing party its reasonable attorneys' fees and costs incurred in any action brought to enforce any right arising from this Agreement.

15. <u>Entire Agreement</u>. This Agreement constitutes the entire agreement with respect to the Confidential Information disclosed herein and supersedes all prior or contemporaneous oral or written agreements concerning such Confidential Information. This Agreement may only be changed by mutual agreement of authorized representatives of the parties in writing.

IN WITNESS WHEREOF, the parties have executed this Agreement as of the date first written above.

<u>Bio-Widgets, Inc.</u>   <u>Recipient</u>

Name: _____   Name: _____

Signed: _____   Signed: _____

Title: _____   Title: _____

14.2 Due Diligence Checklist

Following is a checklist of items investors may request to assist in the due diligence process. Some of the items listed may not be available or required. Investors may specify those specific items they will need.

<u>Promotional and Fundraising Materials</u>

- [ ] Business plan
- [ ] PPM (private placement memorandum) or other type of offering documents
- [ ] Brochures, technical briefs
- [ ] Web site
- [ ] Press releases and business articles

<u>Corporate Formation Documents and Records</u>

- [ ] Original formation agreement or MOU (memo of understanding) between founders
- [ ] Certificate of incorporation
- [ ] Articles of incorporation
- [ ] Certificate of qualification of foreign corporation (if operating in a state other than state of incorporation)
- [ ] Corporate bylaws
- [ ] Corporate minutes since date of incorporation
- [ ] List of stockholders
- [ ] Stock certificate record book
- [ ] Capitalization table (authorized and issued stock, by class, and all authorized and issued options)
- [ ] DUNS number (Dun & Bradstreet)
- [ ] Federal EIN (employer identification number)
- [ ] State employer number
- [ ] City business license/tax permit

<u>Employment and Consulting Agreements</u>

- [ ] Any agreements with founders
- [ ] Agreements with SAB members (scientific advisory board)

Appendices

- [ ] Employment or consulting agreements with key executives and managers
- [ ] Consulting or employment agreements with staff
- [ ] Confidentiality, invention assignment, and non-compete agreements for employees or consultants
- [ ] Stock option awards for employees, consultants, board members, or SAB members

Landlord, Vendor, and Service Provider Agreements and Contracts

- [ ] Office or lab lease
- [ ] Equipment leases or financing agreements
- [ ] Engagement letters for attorneys, accountants, or other professional services firm
- [ ] Recent statements for utilities (power, water, telephone, Internet)
- [ ] Other agreements or contracts that could have a material effect on the company
- [ ] Building permits, fire code certification, ADA certification

Technology Transfer and Intellectual Property Agreements and Documents

- [ ] Technology option or license agreements with academic institutions or corporations
- [ ] Patent applications or patents
- [ ] Invention assignment agreements with founders
- [ ] Employment agreements of academic founders with their institutions
- [ ] Policy statements of academic institutions regarding faculty start-ups and consulting
- [ ] Agreements of any kind between company founders and other companies

Insurance Policies and Benefits Plans (may not exist for a seed-stage company)

- [ ] Key-man life insurance policy
- [ ] Business liability policy
- [ ] Workers compensation insurance policy

- [ ] Directors and officers insurance policy
- [ ] Errors and omissions insurance policy
- [ ] Board indemnification agreements
- [ ] Company health, dental, vision insurance policies
- [ ] Company retirement savings plan

Banking and Financial Information

- [ ] Copies of bank statements (six months)
- [ ] Annual and current month financial statements (QuickBooks or similar format okay)
- [ ] Annual tax returns since formation
- [ ] Prior financing agreements and documents
- [ ] Recent payroll records (ADP, QuickBooks, or similar format okay)
- [ ] Current budget projection
- [ ] List of capital equipment and cost/method of payment/balance outstanding
- [ ] Accounts payable and receivable aging reports
- [ ] Copies of any grants awarded
- [ ] Use of proceeds statement for current round of financing sought
- [ ] Financing agreements, credit lines
- [ ] Company credit card statements (six months)
- [ ] Names and titles of authorized signatories for banking and business agreements

Personal Information about Founders and Senior Executives

- [ ] Residential address, marital status, name of spouse
- [ ] Signed consent to credit report and background check (standard forms to be provided)

Personnel and Operations

- [ ] CVs or résumés of founders and proof of credentials
- [ ] CVs or résumés of key scientists, engineers, and business managers and proof of credentials
- [ ] CVs or résumés of board of directors or SAB members
- [ ] Company organizational chart

Appendices

- [ ] Employee manual
- [ ] Statements of laboratory procedures or SOPs (standard operating procedures)
- [ ] Operating permits (lab animals, hazardous materials, controlled substances, radiation, etc.)
- [ ] Contracts, NDAs, and licenses with business partners, clients, or academic collaborators

Market, Scientific, Business Development, and Investor Prospecting Information

- [ ] Market research reports, investment research reports, and business analyses
- [ ] Scientific and technical publications
- [ ] Trade and professional affiliations
- [ ] List and status of business development contacts and activities
- [ ] Pricing and technical information for any important technology purchases planned
- [ ] Statement of near-term and long-term risk factors and plans for risk mitigation
- [ ] List and status of other investor contacts

14.3 Certificate of Incorporation

CERTIFICATE OF INCORPORATION
OF TECHNO-WIDGETS, INC.

1. The name of the corporation is **Techno Widgets, Inc.**

2. The address of its registered office in the State of _____ is _____. The name of its registered agent at such address is _____.

3. The nature of the business or purposes to be conducted or promoted is to engage in any lawful act or activity for which corporations may be organized under the General Corporation Law of _____.

4. The total number of shares of stock which the Corporation shall have authority to issue is _____ **shares** comprised of _____ **shares of Common Stock with a par value of $0.001** per share (the "Common Stock") and _____ **shares of Preferred Stock with a par value of $0.001 per share** (the "Preferred Stock").

A description of the respective classes of capital stock and a statement of the designations, preferences, voting powers (or no voting powers), relative, participating, optional or other special rights and privileges and the qualifications, limitations and restrictions of the Preferred Stock and Common Stock are as follows:

A. <u>Preferred Stock</u>. The Preferred Stock may be issued in one or more series at such time or times and for such consideration or considerations as the Board of Directors may determine. Each series shall be so designated as to distinguish the shares thereof from the shares of all other series and classes.

The Board of Directors is expressly authorized, subject to the limitations prescribed by law and the provisions of this Certificate of Incorporation, to provide for the issuance of all or any shares of the Preferred Stock in one or more series, each with such designations, preferences, voting powers (or no voting powers) relative, participating, optional or other special rights and privileges and such qualifications, limitations or restrictions thereof as shall be stated in the resolution or resolutions adopted by the Board of Directors to create such series, and a certificate of said resolution or resolutions shall be filed in accordance with the DGCL. The authority of the Board of Directors with respect to each such series shall include, without limitation of the foregoing, the right to provide that the shares of each such series may be: (i) subject to redemption at such time or times and at such price or prices; (ii) entitled to receive dividends (which may be cumulative or non-cumulative) at such rates, on such conditions, and at such times, and payable in preference to, or in such relation to, the dividends payable on any other class or classes or any other series; (iii) entitled to such rights upon the dissolution of, or upon any distribution of the assets of, the Corporation; (iv) convertible into, or exchangeable for, shares of any other class or classes of stock, or of any other series of the same or any other class or classes of stock of the Corporation at such price or prices or at such rates of exchange and with such adjustments, if any; (v) entitled to the benefit of such limitations, if any, on the issuance of additional shares of such series or shares of any other series of Preferred Stock; or (vi) entitled to such other preferences, powers, qualifications, rights and privileges, all as the Board of Directors may deem advisable and as are not inconsistent with law and the provisions of this Certificate of Incorporation.

B. <u>General</u>. All preferences, voting powers, relative, participating, optional or other special rights and privileges, and qualifications, limitations, or restrictions of the Common Stock are expressly made subject and subordinate to those that may be fixed with respect to any shares of the Preferred Stock. No holder of shares of the Corporation of any class, now or hereafter authorized, shall have any preemptive rights to subscribe for or purchase any additional, unissued or treasury shares of capital stock or other securities of the Corporation.

5. The board of directors is authorized to make, alter or repeal the by-laws of the corporation. Election of directors need not be by written ballot.

6. The name and mailing address of the incorporator is:

Techno Widgets, Inc.
_____(Address)_____
_____(Address)_____

7. A director of the corporation shall not be personally liable to the corporation or its stockholders for monetary damages for breach of fiduciary duty as a director except for liability (i) for any breach of the director's duty of loyalty to the corporation or its stockholders, (ii) for acts or omissions not in good faith or which involve intentional misconduct or a knowing violation of law, (iii) under Section ____ of the _____ General Corporation Law, or (iv) for any transaction from which the director derived any improper personal benefit.

8. Each shareholder shall be entitled to as many votes as shall equal the number of votes which he would be entitled to cast for the election of directors with respect to his shares of stock multiplied by the number of directors to be elected, and he may cast all of such votes for a single director or may distribute them among the number to be voted for, or any two or more of them, as he may see fit.

9. The corporation shall indemnify its officers, directors, employees and agents to the extent permitted by the General Corporation Law of _____.

10. The business of the corporation shall be managed by or under the director of its board of directors which may exercise all such powers of the corporation and do all such lawful acts and things as are not by statute or by the certificate of incorporation or by these by-laws directed or required to be exercised or done by the stockholders.

I, THE UNDERSIGNED, being the incorporator hereinbefore named, for the purpose of forming a corporation pursuant to the General Corporation Law of Delaware, do make this certificate, hereby declaring and certifying that this is my act and deed and the facts herein stated are true, and accordingly have hereunto set my hand this_____day of_____, 200X.

14.4 Term Sheet

MEMORANDUM OF TERMS FOR THE PRIVATE PLACEMENT OF SERIES A CONVERTIBLE PREFERRED STOCK

> THIS TERM SHEET SUMMARIZES THE PRINCIPAL TERMS OF THE PROPOSED FINANCING OF TECHNO-WIDGETS, INC. ("TECHNO WIDGETS" OR THE "COMPANY"). THIS TERM SHEET IS FOR DISCUSSION PURPOSES ONLY; THERE IS NO OBLIGATION ON THE PART OF ANY NEGOTIATING PARTY UNTIL ALL PARTIES SIGN A DEFINITITVE STOCK PURCHASE AGREEMENT. THE TRANSACTIONS CONTEMPLATED BY THIS TERM SHEET ARE SUBJECT TO THE SATISFACTORY COMPLETION OF DUE DILIGENCE. THIS TERM SHEET DOES NOT CONSTITUTE EITHER AN OFFER TO SELL OR AN OFFER TO PURCHASE SECURITIES.

FIRST ROUND OF FINANCING:

Amount to be Raised:	$_____
Type of Security:	Series A Convertible Preferred Stock ("Series A Preferred").
Number of Shares:	_____ shares
Purchase Price:	$_____ per share (the "Purchase Price")
Investors:	Seed-Stage Investors, LLC **("Seed-Stage Ventures")** and other Qualified Investors (Collectively, the **"Qualified Investors"**).
Closing Date:	The closing of the sale of the Series A Preferred (the "Closing") will be on or before _____.

Post-Financing Capitalization:

Class	# of Shares	%
Common Stock	_____	____%
Stock Option Pool	_____ (_____ un-issued)	____%
Series A Preferred Stock	_____	____%
Total	_____	100%

Rights, Preferences, Privileges and Restrictions of the Preferred Stock:

Dividends: The holders of shares of Series A Preferred Stock shall be entitled to receive non-cumulative dividends in preference to the holders of Common Stock at an annual rate of ___% of the Purchase Price per share from legally available funds and when, as and if dividends are declared by the Board of Directors.

Voluntary Conversion: Each holder of Series A Preferred will have the right, at the option of the holder, at any time, to convert shares of Series A Preferred into shares of Common Stock at an initial conversion ratio of one-to-one, subject to adjustment as provided below.

Automatic Conversion: The Series A Preferred will be automatically converted into Common Stock, at the then applicable conversion rate, in the event of either (i) the election of holders of a majority of the then outstanding Preferred Stock, voting together as a class, or (ii) the closing of an underwritten initial public offering of the Company's Common Stock under the Securities

Act of 1933 ("IPO") with aggregate proceeds of at least $___ million at a public offering price of at least three (3) times the Purchase Price (a "Qualified IPO").

Redemption: Commencing five (5) years after the Closing, at the request of the holders of at least two-thirds (2/3) of the then outstanding Series ___ Preferred, the Company will redeem the Series ___ Preferred at a redemption price equal to the Purchase Price plus any accrued and unpaid dividends.

Anti-Dilution Provisions: The conversion price of the Preferred Stock shall be subject to adjustment to prevent dilution on a broad-based weighted average basis (based on all outstanding shares of Preferred Stock and Common Stock) in the event that the Company issues additional shares of Common Stock or securities convertible into or exercisable for Common Stock at a purchase price less than the then-effective conversion price; except, however, that without triggering anti-dilution adjustments, Common Stock and/or options therefor (net of repurchases or expired options) may be sold or reserved for issuance to (1) employees, officers, directors, consultants, contractors or advisors of the Company pursuant to stock purchase or stock option plans or agreements or other incentive stock arrangements approved by the Board, or (2) shares of Common or Preferred Stock (or options or warrants therefore) issued to leasing companies, landlords, lenders and other providers of goods and services to the Company, in each case approved by the Board (including the Series A Designee) or (3) entities in connection with joint ventures, development projects or other strategic transactions in each case approved by the Board (including the Series A Designee), or (4) certain other customary exceptions approved by the Board (including the Series A Designee).

Liquidation Preference: In the event of any liquidation or winding up of the Company, the holders of Series A Preferred shall be entitled to receive prior and in preference to the holders of Common Stock an amount equal to their original purchase price per share (as adjusted for stock splits, stock dividends, recapitalizations, etc.), plus any declared but unpaid dividends (the "Liquidation Preference"). After the payment of the Liquidation Preference to the holders of Preferred Stock the remaining assets shall be distributed ratably to the holders of Common Stock. A merger, acquisition, sale of voting control, sale of substantially all of the assets of the Company or any other transaction or series of transactions in which the shareholders of the Company do not own a majority of the outstanding shares of the surviving corporation shall be deemed to be a liquidation or winding up.

Voting Rights: The holders of shares of Series A Preferred will have the right to that number of votes equal to the number shares of common stock issuable upon conversion.

Protective Provisions

The consent of the holders of at least two-thirds (2/3) of the outstanding shares of Series A preferred stock (voting as a single class on an as converted basis) shall be required for any action that (i) effects a merger or sale of the Company, (ii) changes the rights, preferences or privileges of Series A Preferred Stock, (iii) increases or decreases the authorized number of shares of any series of preferred stock, (iv) creates a new class of stock or shares with a preference over or on parity with the Series A Preferred with respect to voting, dividends, redemption, or upon liquidation, (v) amends the Company's charter or bylaws in a manner that adversely affects the rights of the holders of the Series A Preferred Stock, (vi) redeems or repurchases any shares of preferred or common stock (other than from an employee or consultant upon termination of services), or (vii) pays cash dividends on the Company's common stock.

Information Rights: The Company shall deliver to the Major Investors (A "Major Investor" is a holder of 5% or more of the Company's Preferred Stock or 5% or more of the Company's Common Stock issued upon conversion of the Preferred Stock, or a combination of both) audited annual and unaudited quarterly financial statements prepared in accordance with GAAP, consistently applied. In addition, the Company will furnish Major Investors with monthly financial statements compared against plan and will provide a copy of the Company's annual operating plan within 30 days prior to the beginning of the fiscal year. Each Major Investor shall also be entitled to standard inspection and visitation rights. These provisions shall terminate upon a Qualified IPO

Right of First Offer: Each holder of Series A Preferred will have a right of first offer in the event the Company proposes to offer equity securities to any person (other than (i) the issuance of capital stock to employees, consultants, officers or directors of the Company pursuant to stock purchase or stock option plans or agreements approved by the Board (including options granted prior to the Financing), (ii) the issuance of securities in connection with acquisition transactions, (iii) the issuance of securities to financial institutions or lessors in connection with commercial credit arrangements, equipment financings or similar transactions, (iv) shares issued upon conversion of the Series A Preferred, (v) the issuance of securities in a public offering, (vi) the issuance of securities pursuant to currently outstanding options, warrants, notes, or other rights to acquire securities of the

Company; or (vii) stock splits, stock dividends or like transactions (collectively, the "Permitted Issuances") to purchase that portion of such equity securities equal to (a) the number of shares of Common Stock issued or issuable upon conversion of the Series A Preferred held by such holder of Series A Preferred divided by (b) all of the Company's Common Stock then outstanding or issuable upon exercise of options or warrants or conversion of Preferred Stock. Such equity securities shall be purchased within 20 days from notice by the Company and on the same terms as the securities are purchased by other third party purchasers of the equity securities. Such right of first offer will terminate upon vote of majority in interest of the Series A Preferred, an IPO, or the acquisition of the Company.

The Company shall have a right of first refusal to purchase Common Stock held by any holder of 5% or more of the Company's Common Stock (a "Significant Common Stock Holder") prior to a transfer to a third party. Each of the holders of Series A Preferred and the Common Stock holders shall have the right to purchase the shares not purchased by the Company on a pro-rata basis. Such right of first refusal will terminate upon vote of majority in interest of the Series A Preferred, an IPO or the acquisition of the Company.

Registration Rights:

Registrable Securities: All shares of Common Stock issuable upon conversion of the Series A Preferred Stock shall be deemed "Registrable Securities."

Demand Registration: After the earlier of five years of the closing or six months after the Company has completed an IPO, holders of at least two-thirds (2/3) of the Registrable Securities shall have one (1) demand registration right to request that the Company file a registration statement under the Securities Act of 1933, in order to permit such holders to sell their shares (subject to pro-rata cutbacks at the underwriter's discretion).

Piggyback Registration Rights: The holders of Registrable Securities shall have unlimited piggyback registration rights, subject to pro rata cutback to a minimum of 20% of the offering (complete cutbacks on the IPO) at the underwriter's discretion.

Registration on Form S-3: Once the Company has completed an IPO, the holders of at least 20% of the Registrable Securities will have the right to require the Company to register their shares of Registrable Securities on the abbreviated registration statement on Form S-3, if available for use by the Company and only if such holders are not otherwise eligible to sell their Registrable Securities under Rule 144 of the Securities Act. The Company will not be obligated to effect more than one S-3 registration statements in any twelve-month period. There shall be a limit of a total of three such S-3 registrations.

Registration Expenses: Registration expenses (exclusive of underwriting discounts and commissions, stock transfer taxes and fees of counsel to the selling stockholders) will be borne by the Company for all demand, piggyback and S-3 registrations. The Company will also pay the reasonable fees and expenses of one special counsel to the selling stockholders.

Transfer of Rights: The registration rights set forth herein may be assigned to a transferee or assignee who after such assignment holds at least 2% of Registrable Securities; provided the Company is given written notice thereof, such transferee or assignee agrees in writing to be bound by and subject to the terms and conditions of an Investor Rights Agreement and such agreement shall be effective only if immediately following such transfer the future disposition of such securities by such transferee or assignee is restricted under the Act.

Lock-Up Provision: If requested by the Company and its underwriters, no Investor will sell its shares for a specified period not to exceed 180 days following the effective date of the Company's initial public offering; provided that all officers, directors and 1% shareholders of the Company are similarly bound.

Termination of Registration Rights: The registration obligations of the Company will terminate on the earlier of (i) five years after the Qualified IPO, or (ii) with respect to any holder of registration rights, at such time as all Registrable Securities of such holder may be sold within a three month period pursuant to Rule 144.

Other Provisions: Other reasonable provisions with respect to registration rights shall be contained in an Investor Rights Agreement, including without limitation cross-indemnification, the period of time in which a Registration Statement shall be kept effective and underwriting arrangements.

Board of Directors: Upon closing of the financing, the Bylaws of the Company shall provide that the Board of Directors of the Company shall consist of ___ directors. The holders of Series A Preferred (excluding shares held by Seed-Stage Ventures) shall be entitled to elect two directors (the "Series A Designees). The holders of Common Stock, voting as a separate class, shall be entitled to elect the remaining directors, one of which shall be the CEO of the Company and two of whom shall be designees of Seed-Stage Ventures.

Option Pool: Upon the Closing of this financing there will be _____ shares of Common Stock reserved and available for issuance pursuant to options to employee, directors, consultants and other service providers.

Stock Options: Unless otherwise approved by the Board (including the Series A Designee), options issued after the Closing to employees, directors, consultants and other service providers of the Company generally will be subject to vesting as follows: 25% to vest on the first anniversary of the date of grant (or the employee start date with respect to new employees, if earlier), with the remaining 75% to vest monthly over the next 36 months thereafter.

Employee and Consultant Agreements: Each employee or consultant of the Company shall have entered into an acceptable proprietary information and inventions agreement.

Purchase Agreement: The sale of the Series A Preferred will be made pursuant to a stock purchase agreement reasonably acceptable to the Company and the Investors, which agreement will contain such terms as are usual and customary for agreements between sophisticated venture capital investors and the companies in which they invest, including, among other things, appropriate representations and warranties of the Company, its principal common stockholders and the Investors, covenants of the Company reflecting the provisions set forth in this term sheet and appropriate conditions to closing which will include, among other things, the filing of an Amended and Restated Certificate of Incorporation.

Finders: Neither the Company nor the Investors shall have an obligation for any finder's fees in connection with this transaction.

Confidentiality: This Term Sheet and any related correspondences from Seed-Stage Ventures are to be held in strict confidence and not disclosed to any party other than the Company employees who reasonably need to know and their professional advisors without prior approval of Seed-Stage Ventures.

Legal Counsel and Fees: The Company and Seed-Stage Ventures agree to use their reasonable efforts to close Seed-Stage Ventures's purchase of Series __ Preferred Stock on or before _____. Except for this provision and the provisions contained herein entitled "Confidentiality" and "Legal Counsel and Fees," which are explicitly agreed by Seed-Stage Ventures and the Company to be binding upon execution of this Term Sheet, this Term Sheet is not intended as a legally binding commitment by Seed-Stage Ventures or the Company, and any obligation on the part of Seed-Stage Ventures or the Company is subject to the following conditions precedent: 1. satisfactory completion of due diligence related to the Company, and 2. completion of legal documentation of terms set forth herein to the reasonable satisfaction of Seed-Stage Ventures in its sole discretion.

The Company shall bear its own legal fees and expenses and shall pay, solely if the Closing occurs, the reasonable fees and expenses of counsel to Investors, not to exceed $_____.

TECHNO-WIDGETS, INC.   SEED-STAGE VENTURES, LLC

By: _____   By: _____
Name: _____   Name: _____
Title: _____   Title: _____
Date: _____   Date: _____

14.5   Stock Purchase Agreement

TECHNO-WIDGETS, INC.
SERIES A PREFERRED STOCK PURCHASE AGREEMENT

This Series A Preferred Stock Purchase Agreement, dated as of _____ __, 200X (this "**Agreement**"), is entered into by and among TECHNO-WIDGETS, INC., a _____ corporation (the "**Company**"), and each of the undersigned purchasers (collectively the "**Purchasers**" and individually a "**Purchaser**") listed on the Schedule of Purchasers attached hereto as Exhibit A.

RECITAL

On the terms and subject to the conditions set forth herein, the Purchasers are willing to purchase from the Company, and the Company is willing to sell to the Purchasers, up to an aggregate of _____ shares of the Series A Preferred Stock, par value $0.001 per share (the "**Shares**") at one or more closings.

AGREEMENT

NOW, THEREFORE, in consideration of the foregoing, and the representations, warranties and conditions set forth below, the parties hereto, intending to be legally bound, hereby agree as follows:

1. Purchase and Sale of Shares.

    1.1   Authorization of Series A Preferred Stock. The Company has authorized the issuance and sale to Purchasers of an aggregate of _____ (_____) shares of Series A Preferred Stock (the "Series A Preferred Stock"), having the rights, restrictions, privileges and preferences set forth in the Restated Certificate of Incorporation, as amended to date, in the form attached hereto as Exhibit B (the "Restated Certificate"), on the terms and conditions herein set forth.

1.2 Sale and Issuance of Shares.

(i) First Closing. At the First Closing (as hereinafter defined), the Company shall severally sell to the Purchasers and the Purchasers shall severally acquire from the Company up to an aggregate of _____ (_____) at a purchase price of $0._____ per share (the "Purchase Price") and each Purchaser not already a party thereto shall become a party to the Rights Agreement and the Voting Agreement (as such terms are defined below). The number of Shares to be acquired at the First Closing by each Purchaser at the First Closing is set forth opposite the name of such Purchaser on Exhibit A attached hereto.

(ii) Additional Closings. Subject to the terms and conditions of this Agreement, the Company may sell at an additional closing or closings on or before _____ (each an "Additional Closing"), up to the balance of the shares of Series A Preferred Stock reserved for issuance hereunder but unissued as of the First Closing (not to exceed the total number of shares set forth in clause (i) of this Section 1.2) at a per share price equal to the Purchase Price to such persons as the Board of Directors of the Company may determine (the "Additional Shares"). Any such sales shall be on the same terms and conditions as those contained herein. Purchasers at any Additional Closing, if not already a party hereto or thereto, shall become a party to this Agreement, to that certain Investors' Rights Agreement by and among the Company, certain existing stockholders of the Company, and the Purchasers in the form attached hereto as Exhibit C (the "Rights Agreement"), and to that certain Restated Voting Agreement by and among the Company, certain existing stockholders of the Company and the Purchasers in the form attached hereto as Exhibit D (the "Voting Agreement") and shall have the rights and obligations hereunder and thereunder. The purchasers of such remaining shares of Series A Preferred Stock, upon delivery of an additional counterpart to this Agreement dated as of the date of such Additional Closing, shall be deemed "Purchasers" and such shares purchased by them shall be deemed "Series A Preferred Stock" for purposes of this Agreement. The Additional Closings shall take place at any time or from time to time at such time(s) on or before _____ and such place(s) as the Company and such additional Purchasers may agree. The Purchasers already a party to this Agreement hereby irrevocably waive any preemptive rights or rights of first offer they may possess now or hereafter with respect to any sale of shares of Series A Preferred Stock made pursuant to this Agreement after the First Closing. The First Closing together with each Additional Closing are sometimes referred to as the "Closing" or the "Closings."

    1.3   <u>Closings</u>.

        (i)   <u>First Closing</u>. The initial purchase and sale of the First Closing Shares shall take place at the offices of <u> (Law Firm) </u>, <u> (address) </u>, on _____, 200X, at 10:00 a.m. or at such other place and time as the Company and the Purchasers thereat may mutually agree (which date, time and place are designated the "First Closing"). At the First Closing, the Company shall deliver to each Purchaser thereat a certificate representing the shares of Series A Preferred Stock being acquired by such Purchaser at the First Closing against payment of the purchase price therefor by check payable to the Company, by wire transfer to the Company's bank account, cancellation of indebtedness or any combination of the foregoing.

        (ii)   <u>Additional Closings</u>. At each Additional Closing, the Company shall deliver to each Purchaser thereat a certificate representing the Additional Shares being acquired by such Purchaser at the such Additional Closing against payment of the purchase price therefor by check payable to the Company, by wire transfer to the Company's bank account, cancellation of indebtedness or any combination of the foregoing together with an executed counterpart of this Agreement, the Rights Agreement and the Voting Agreement.

2.   <u>Representations and Warranties of the Company</u>. The Company hereby represents and warrants to the Purchasers that the statements contained in the following paragraphs of this Section 4 are all true and correct as of the date hereof.

Appendices

2.1 <u>Corporate Organization and Authority</u>. The Company:

(i) is a corporation duly organized, validly existing, authorized to exercise all its corporate powers, rights and privileges, and in good standing in the State of _____;

(ii) has all requisite corporate power and corporate authority to own, lease and operate its properties and to carry on its business as now conducted and as proposed to be conducted and possesses all business licenses, franchises, rights and privileges material to the conduct of its business; and

(iii) is qualified as a foreign corporation and is in good standing in the State of California.

2.2 <u>Capitalization</u>. The authorized capital of the Company consists of:

(i) <u>Series A Preferred Stock</u>. _____(number of shares)_____ shares of Series A Preferred Stock, of which _____(number)_____ shares are issued and outstanding. Each share of Series A Preferred Stock is convertible into one (1) share of Common Stock.

(ii) <u>Series A Preferred Stock</u>. _____(number)_____ shares of Series A Preferred Stock, of which _____(number)_____ are issued and outstanding. Each share of Series A Preferred Stock is convertible into one (1) share of Common Stock.

(iii) <u>Common Stock</u>. _____(number)_____shares of Common Stock, of which_____(number)_____ shares are issued and outstanding. All such issued and outstanding shares of Common Stock have been duly and validly issued (including, without limitation, issued in compliance with applicable federal and state securities laws), and are fully-paid, non-assessable.

(iv) The Company has reserved _____(number)_____ shares of Common Stock for issuance to the Company's employees, officers, directors or outside consultants or contractors pursuant to the 200X Stock Option Plan of the Company, _____(number)_____ shares of Common Stock for issuance upon exercise of certain issued and outstanding warrants to purchase common stock of the Company and _____(number)_____ shares of Common Stock for issuance upon conversion of the Series A and Series A Preferred Stock.

 2.3 <u>Subsidiaries</u>. The Company does not presently own, have any investment in, or control, directly or indirectly, any corporation, limited liability company, limited partnership or other business entity. The Company is not a participant in any joint venture or general partnership.

 2.4 <u>Authorization</u>. All corporate action on the part of the Company, its directors and stockholders necessary for the authorization, execution, delivery and performance of all obligations under this Agreement and for the issuance and delivery of the Shares and the Common Stock issuable upon conversion of the Shares has been taken, and this Agreement constitutes a valid and legally binding obligation of the Company enforceable in accordance with its terms, except as limited by applicable bankruptcy, insolvency, reorganization, moratorium or other laws of general application relating to or affecting enforcement of creditors' rights and rules of law concerning equitable remedies.

 2.5 <u>Validity of Shares</u>. The Shares, when issued, sold and delivered in accordance with the terms and for the consideration expressed in this Agreement, shall be duly and validly issued (including, without limitation, issued in compliance with applicable federal and state securities laws), fully-paid and non-assessable and neither the Company nor the holder thereof shall be subject to any preemptive or similar right with respect thereto. Subject to the accuracy of the Purchasers' representations in Section 3 hereof, the offer, sale and issuance of the Shares and the Common Stock issuable upon the conversion of the Shares, constitute transactions exempt from the registration requirements of Section 5 of the Securities Act of 1933, as amended (the "**Securities Act**").

 2.6 <u>Brokers and Finders</u>. The Company has not retained any investment banker, broker, or finder in connection with the transactions contemplated by this Agreement.

3. <u>Representations and Warranties by the Purchasers</u>. Each Purchaser represents and warrants to the Company as of the time of issuance of the Shares as follows:

3.1 <u>Investment Intent</u> The Shares and the Common Stock issuable upon conversion of the Shares (collectively, the "**Underlying Securities**; the Underlying Securities and the Shares collectively referred to herein as the "**Securities**") will be acquired for each Purchaser's own account, for investment and not with a view to, or for resale in connection with, any distribution or public offering thereof within the meaning of the Securities Act or the California Corporate Securities Law of 1968, as amended (the "**California Law**").

3.2 <u>Securities Not Registered</u>. Each Purchaser understands that the none of the Securities has been registered under the Securities Act by reason of their issuance in a transaction exempt from the registration and prospectus delivery requirements of the Securities Act pursuant to Section 4(2) thereof, that the Company has no present intention of registering any of the Securities, that the Securities must be held by such Purchaser indefinitely, and that such Purchaser must therefore bear the economic risk of such investment indefinitely, unless a subsequent disposition thereof is registered under the Securities Act or is exempt from registration. Each Purchaser further understands that the Securities have not been qualified under the California Law by reason of their issuance in a transaction exempt from the qualification requirements of the California Law, which exemption depends upon, among other things, the *bona fide* nature of such Purchaser's investment intent expressed above.

3.3 <u>Full Disclosure</u>. Each Purchaser and its representatives has been given all such information as has been requested in order to evaluate the merits and risks of the prospective investment contemplated herein. Notwithstanding the foregoing, such due diligence investigation shall not limit the representations and warranties made by the Company in Section 2 hereof.

3.4 <u>Accredited Purchaser</u>. Each Purchaser (i) is an "**Accredited Purchaser**" as that term is defined in Rule 501 of Regulation D promulgated under the Securities Act or has such knowledge and experience in financial and business matters as to be capable of evaluating the merits and risks of such Purchaser's prospective investment in the Securities; (ii) has the ability to bear the economic risks of such Purchaser's prospective investment, including a complete loss of such Purchaser's investment in the Securities; and (iii) has not been offered the Securities by any form of advertisement, article, notice or other communication published in any newspaper, magazine, or similar media or broadcast over television or radio, or any seminar or meeting whose attendees have been invited by any such media.

3.5 <u>Authority</u>. Each Purchaser has the full right, power and authority to enter into and perform such Purchaser's obligations under this Agreement, and this Agreement constitutes a valid and binding obligation of such Purchaser enforceable in accordance with its terms except as limited by applicable bankruptcy, insolvency, reorganization, fraudulent conveyance, moratorium, usury or other laws of general application relating to or affecting enforcement of creditors rights and rules or laws concerning equitable remedies. No consent, approval or authorization of or designation, declaration or filing with any governmental authority on the part of such Purchaser is required in connection with the valid execution and delivery of this Agreement.

3.6 <u>No Transfer</u>. Each Purchaser understands that if the Company does not (i) register its Common Stock with the Securities and Exchange Commission pursuant to Section 12 of the Exchange Act, (ii) become subject to Section 15(d) of the Securities Exchange Ac of 1934, as amended, (iii) supply information pursuant to Rule 15c2-11 thereunder, or (iv) have a registration statement covering the Securities (or a filing pursuant to the exemption from registration under Regulation A of the Securities Act covering the Securities) under the Securities Act in effect when such Purchaser desires to sell the Securities, such Purchaser may be required to hold the Securities for an indeterminate period. Each Purchaser also understands that any sale of the Securities that might be made by such Purchaser in reliance upon Rule 144 under the Securities Act may be made only in limited amounts in accordance with the terms and conditions of that rule.

3.7 **Legend Requirements**. All certificates for the Shares shall bear substantially the following legend:

> "THE SHARES REPRESENTED BY THIS CERTIFICATE HAVE BEEN ACQUIRED FOR INVESTMENT PURPOSES ONLY AND HAVE NOT BEEN REGISTERED UNDER THE SECURITIES ACT OF 1933. THE SHARES MAY NOT BE SOLD OR TRANSFERRED IN THE ABSENCE OF SUCH REGISTRATION OR AN EXEMPTION THEREFROM UNDER SAID ACT."

The certificates evidencing the Shares shall also bear any legend required by any other agreement executed in connection herewith and any legend required by the Commissioner of Corporations of the State of California or pursuant to any state, local or foreign law applicable to such securities or the sale and issuance thereof.

4. **Miscellaneous**.

4.1 **Covenant to Reserve Shares**. The Company covenants to take all such necessary action to authorize and reserve an adequate number of shares of Common Stock to be issued upon conversion of the Series A Preferred Stock.

4.2 **Waivers and Amendments**. Any provision of this Agreement may be amended, waived or modified upon the written consent of the Company and the Purchasers holding a majority in interest of the then-outstanding Shares acquired pursuant to this Agreement. Notwithstanding the foregoing, the Company shall amend the Schedule of Purchasers as of each Closing to reflect the Purchasers thereat.

4.3 **Governing Law**. This Agreement and all actions arising out of or in connection with this Agreement shall be governed by and construed in accordance with the laws of the State of _____, without regard to the conflicts of law provisions of the State of _____ or of any other state.

4.4 *Entire Agreement*. This Agreement constitutes the full and entire understanding and agreement between the parties with regard to the subjects hereof and thereof.

4.5 *Notices, etc.* All notices and other communications required or permitted hereunder shall be in writing and shall be sent via facsimile, overnight courier service or mailed by certified or registered mail, postage prepaid, return receipt requested, addressed or sent (a) if to a Purchaser, at the address or facsimile number of the Purchaser set forth on such Purchaser's signature page to this Agreement, or at such other address or number as the Purchaser shall have furnished to the Company in writing, or (b) if to the Company, at _____(Address)_____, or at such other address or number as the Company shall have furnished to the Purchaser in writing.

4.6 *Validity*. If any provision of this Agreement shall be judicially determined to be invalid, illegal or unenforceable, the validity, legality and enforceability of the remaining provisions shall not in any way be affected or impaired thereby.

4.7 *Counterparts*. This Agreement may be executed in any number of counterparts, each of which shall be an original, but all of which together shall be deemed to constitute one instrument.

IN WITNESS WHEREOF, the parties have caused this Agreement to be duly executed and delivered by their proper and duly authorized officers as of the date and year first written above.

COMPANY:
TECHNO-WIDGETS, INC.
a _____ corporation
By: _____
    _____, President & CEO

PURCHASERS COUNTERPART SIGNATURE PAGE TO TECHNO-WIDGETS, INC.
SERIES A PREFERRED STOCK PURCHASE AGREEMENT

SEED-STAGE VENTURES, LLC

By: _____

Address: _____
_____
_____

$_____
Amount of Subscription

PURCHASERS COUNTERPART SIGNATURE PAGE TO TECHNO-WIDGETS, INC.
SERIES A PREFERRED STOCK PURCHASE AGREEMENT

PURCHASERS:
CO-INVESTOR CORPORATION

By: _____

Address: _____
          _____
          _____

$ _____
Amount of Subscription

PURCHASERS COUNTERPART SIGNATURE PAGE TO TECHNO-WIDGETS, INC.
SERIES A PREFERRED STOCK PURCHASE AGREEMENT

_____

Name of Subscriber (Please Print)

_____

Signature of Subscriber

$_____
Amount of Subscription

Address:
_____
_____
_____

SCHEDULE OF PURCHASERS

PURCHASER	NO. OF SHARES OF SERIES A PREFERRED STOCK	TOTAL PURCHASE PRICE
Seed-Stage Ventures, LLC		$_____
Co-Investor Corporation		$_____
TOTAL:	_____	_____

14.6 Stock Option Award

TECHNO-WIDGETS, INC.
STOCK INCENTIVE PLAN
INCENTIVE STOCK OPTION AGREEMENT

THIS INCENTIVE STOCK OPTION AGREEMENT (this "**Option Agreement**") by and between Techno Widgets, Inc., a Delaware corporation (the "**Corporation**"), and _____ (the "**Participant**") evidences the incentive stock option (the "**Option**") granted by the Corporation to the Participant as to the number of shares of the Corporation's Common Stock, $0.001 par value, first set forth below.

Number of Shares of Common Stock:[1] _____ **Award Date:** _____

Exercise Price per Share:[1] $_____ **Expiration Date:**[1,2] _____

Vesting[1,2] The Option shall become vested as to 12.5% of the total number of shares of Common Stock subject to the Option on the six month anniversary of the Award Date. The remaining 87.5% of the total number of shares of Common Stock subject to the Option shall vest in 42 substantially equal monthly installments, with the first installment vesting on the last day of the month following the month in which the six month anniversary of the Award Date occurs and an additional installment vesting on the last day of each of the 41 months thereafter.

The Option is granted under the Techno Widgets, Inc. Stock Incentive Plan (the "**Plan**") and subject to the Terms and Conditions of Incentive Stock Option (the "**Terms**") attached to this Option Agreement (incorporated herein by this reference) and to the Plan. The Option has been granted to the Participant in addition to, and not in lieu of, any other form of compensation otherwise payable or to be paid to the Participant. The Option is intended as an incentive stock option within the meaning of Section 422 of the Code (an "**ISO**"). Capitalized terms are defined in the Plan if not defined herein. The parties agree to the terms of the Option set forth herein. The Participant acknowledges receipt of a copy of the Terms and the Plan, specifically acknowledges and agrees to Section 14 of the Terms, and agrees to maintain in confidence all information provided to him/her in connection with the Option.

"PARTICIPANT" TECHNO-WIDGETS, INC.,
a Delaware corporation

_____
Signature

By:_____

_____
Print Name

Its:_____

_____
Address

_____
City, State, Zip Code

CONSENT OF SPOUSE

In consideration of the Corporation's execution of this Option Agreement, the undersigned spouse of the Participant agrees to be bound by all of the terms and provisions hereof and of the Plan.

_____   _____
Signature of Spouse   *Date*

14.7 Executive Search Agreement

The author wishes to thank Bench International for the following example of a performance-based retained search agreement, which is used with permission.[34]

RETAINER AGREEMENT

EXECUTIVE SEARCH COMPANY, Inc. (hereinafter, "ExecSearchCo") agrees to perform a search on behalf of **Bio-Widgets, Inc.** (hereinafter, "Client") for the position of ____**(Job Title)**____, commencing upon the date of execution of this agreement and under the following terms and conditions:

(1) RETAINER FEE

The ExecSearchCo Retainer Fee rate is _____ (___%) of Annual Compensation. Annual Compensation shall be defined as base salary, sign-on bonuses and other bonuses actually paid to candidate in the first full year of employment, it being understood that if a bonus is paid to the ____(Job Title)____ during the course of the first year, ExecSearchCo will be entitled to receive an amount equal to _____ (___%) of such bonus, when paid. Annual Compensation shall not include relocation, house hunting, house acquisition, housing allowance or other reimbursements, stock, stock options or loans. ExecSearchCo shall reduce the total fee by _____, by crediting $_____ against each payment under Paragraph 2, below.

(2) RETAINER FEE PAYMENT SCHEDULE

(a) A first payment of $_____ equal to one-third of the estimated Retainer Fee of $_____, less $_____ based upon a projected Annual Compensation of $_____ shall be due and payable upon execution of this Agreement.

---

[34] Bench International, 120 South Doheny Dr., Beverly Hills, CA, 90211. See www.benchinternational.com

(b) A second payment of $_____, less $_____ shall be due and payable upon the presentation by ExecSearchCo to CLIENT of résumés and written assessments of the first _____ (__) valid candidates.

(c) A third and final payment equal to the difference between the total of the first two retainer payments and the total Retainer Fee adjusted based upon actual Annual Compensation as outlined in the offer letter, less $_____, shall become due and payable upon offer by CLIENT and acceptance by candidate of the position described herein, and candidate has commenced work on-site at Bio-Widgets's location, or off-site in an arrangement satisfactory to Bio-Widgets. Provided performance obligations of ExecSearchCo under this Paragraph 2, Section (b) have been met, a third and final payment shall become immediately due and payable which payment shall equal the payment in this Paragraph 2, Section (b) upon either (i) termination of this Agreement by CLIENT later than three (3) months after the date of execution of this Agreement or (ii) filling the position internally or by other independent means by CLIENT

Any Retainer Fees paid under this Agreement are non-refundable to CLIENT.

(3)   **ADDITIONAL PLACEMENTS**

Should Client hire any additional candidates identified by and presented to Client by ExecSearchCo under this Agreement within one year after the date of termination of this Agreement, Client will be billed and shall pay to ExecSearchCo a fee of _____ (__%) of Annual Compensation for each such hire, as outlined in the offer letter. No additional expenses will be incurred by ExecSearchCo or billed to Client in support of such hires without Client's approval. The structure of such payment as cash or a combination of cash and equity, will be determined in good faith between the parties.

(4)   **TERMINATION**

This Agreement shall terminate (i) upon written notice by Client or (ii) on the date of hire of a candidate for the position and consistent with Paragraph (2), section (c), subsections (i) and (ii).

(5) EXPENSES

Client agrees to pay ExecSearchCo the amount of _____ dollars ($_____) per month while the Agreement is in effect to cover office and other incidental expenses in the routine conduct of this search. In addition, Client shall be responsible for additional major expenses, including without limitation, coach-class travel, registrations and advertising, which expenses shall not be incurred or billed to Client without Client's prior approval. Such additional expenses shall be due and payable upon presentation of invoice.

(6) WARRANTY

ExecSearchCo warrants executive placement for _____ (___) days from the Start Date. Should candidate placed by ExecSearchCo leave Client within ___ (___) days of the Start Date due to termination-for-cause, termination for poor performance or by resignation, ExecSearchCo agrees to replace candidate for no additional Retainer Fee. However, Client shall reimburse ExecSearchCo for travel and other expenses during the course of the replacement search pursuant to Paragraph 5 of this Agreement. Notwithstanding, ExecSearchCo shall be under no obligation to replace an employee placed by ExecSearchCo who is no longer able to perform in the position because of loss due to injury, death, reductions-in-force by Client, other terminations-not-for-cause by Client, or events beyond the control of either party.

(7) CONFIDENTIALITY

Résumés, candidate identities, references and other correspondence of ExecSearchCo is confidential information of ExecSearchCo provided to Client for the sole and exclusive use of Client and may not be disclosed by Client to any third party without ExecSearchCo's written approval. Nothing in this agreement shall prohibit or limit Client's use of confidential information received from ExecSearchCo which (i) is at the time of the disclosure by ExecSearchCo was already rightfully in the possession of Client; (ii) is at the time of the disclosure by ExecSearchCo in the public domain or thereafter becomes part of the public domain other than as a result of disclosure or other fault of Client or its representatives; (iii) has been lawfully received by Client from a third party without restriction on use or disclosure where, to the knowledge of Client, such third party has the legal right to so disclose the information to Client; or (iv) is generated by Client independently of and without reference to any confidential information communicated to Client by ExecSearchCo. In addition, Client shall be entitled to disclose confidential information received from ExecSearchCo as required by law, governmental rule, regulation or court order or in connection with litigation between the parties; provided however, that before making any such disclosure, Client shall: (A) give ExecSearchCo reasonable notice thereof; and (B) use commercially reasonable efforts to limit the extent and scope of such disclosure, including without limitation, requesting a protective order or an agreement from the applicable party to limit disclosure and maintain confidentiality.

(8) GOVERNING LAW AND VENUE

This Agreement shall be governed by and construed in accordance with the laws of the State of _____ for contracts entered into within the State of _____. ExecSearchCo operates under and subscribes to the equal opportunity practices of the United States Government. All actions relating to this agreement shall be venued solely within the State of _____, and the parties hereto commit to the jurisdiction of such state.

(9) COUNTERPARTS

This agreement may be executed in counterparts, each of which shall be deemed to be an original, but all of which taken together shall constitute one and the same agreement.

Executed this _____ th day of _____, 200X:

EXECUTIVE SEARCH CO., INC.	**CLIENT**
By:	By:
Name:	Name:
Title:	Title:

Appendices

14.8 Letter of Invitation to Join Scientific Advisory Board

_____, 200X

Dr. _____
_____
_____

Dear Dr. _____:

On behalf of the Board of Directors of Bio-Widgets, Inc., I would like to extend to you this formal invitation to join the company's inaugural Scientific Advisory Board (the "SAB"). We are quite pleased to have been introduced to you by _____, scientific co-founder of Bio-Widgets, and would be honored by your acceptance of our invitation.

This letter confirms the terms of compensation that we would like to offer in return for your commitment and your active participation as an SAB member. Although Bio-Widget's scientific and management team is still small, we expect to grow rapidly as we establish initial corporate collaborations and close our next round of funding. Our management philosophy is guided by the principle that those who contribute to Bio-Widget's growth should receive timely and generous rewards for their efforts. We have begun to put appropriate incentives in place for current and future team members at Bio-Widgets, and we consider our SAB members to be part of this team. For your agreement to provide active service as a member of Bio-Widgets's SAB, the Board of Directors has granted to you, subject to your acceptance of this offer, an option to purchase_____ shares of Bio-Widgets's common stock at an exercise price of $___ per share pursuant to, and subject to the terms of, Bio-Widgets's Stock Incentive Plan and the enclosed Nonqualified Stock Option Agreement. The option will vest according to the following schedule: 25% of the shares subject to the option will be vested as of the date of grant, and the remaining 75% of the shares subject to the option will vest in equal monthly installments over four years. In the future, the Board of Directors may issue additional stock options to SAB members, at its sole discretion.

Each member's service on the SAB will be reviewed annually, based upon his or her level of involvement during the prior year, and his or her ongoing ability to serve actively. We anticipate that active SAB members will attend one SAB meeting per year in person, and three meetings per year via teleconference and/or video-conference. We would also expect that SAB members be available from time to time, by prior request of the SAB co-chairs, for individual telephone or e-mail interaction.

In addition to equity compensation, each SAB member will be paid an honorarium of $_____ per in-person SAB meeting and $_____ per SAB meeting via teleconference or videoconference. Bio-Widgets will reimburse all SAB members for personal out-of-pocket expenses incurred in relation to SAB meetings, including airfare, local transportation, meals and accommodations.

Furthermore, we expect that situations may arise in which Bio-Widgets may wish to engage individual members of its SAB as consultants to the company. In such cases, Bio-Widgets would be glad to arrange for additional compensation on mutually agreeable terms.

Once all SAB members have confirmed their acceptance, we will begin the task of scheduling our first meeting.

Next Steps

If these terms are agreeable to you, please indicate your acceptance by signing both copies of this letter, in the spaces indicated. In addition, please sign the enclosed Award Agreement (and have your spouse sign as well, if married) and return it to us, along with one signed copy of this letter, in the enclosed, pre-addressed envelope.

Upon our receipt of your signed acceptance and Award Agreement, we will countersign the Award Agreement and return a copy to you, along with a copy of the disclosure statement for the Stock Incentive Plan, for your files.

If you have questions, please do not hesitate to contact me at my office phone number _____, or at my e-mail address, _____.

I look forward to meeting you in person in the near future and welcome you to the Bio-Widgets team.

Sincerely,

_____
Chairman, Board of Directors

Confirmation of Acceptance

By my signature below, I accept this invitation to join Bio-Widgets's Scientific Advisory Board.

_____
Signed

14.9   Job Offer Letter

_____(Date)_____

_____(Name)_____ Ph.D.
_____(Address)_____
_____(Address)_____

Dear ____(Name)_____:

On behalf of Bio-Widgets, Inc., I am delighted to extend to you a formal offer to join the company as Vice President, _____. In this capacity, you will direct and supervise research operations that are central to product development, and to Bio-Widgets' corporate collaborations, business development plans and grant-supported research projects. In addition, you will play an important role in managing the interface between Bio-Widgets's various research groups.

As Vice President, _____, you will supervise_____ and will be responsible for _____, in accordance with Bio-Widgets's overall strategic plan. Subject to the general direction established by the Board of Directors and its final approval, you will be responsible for developing, monitoring and modifying biology research plans, budgets, staffing plans, work plans, corporate and academic collaborations, fee-for-service projects and grant programs, as well as for proposing and guiding intellectual property development and the preparation of publications and scientific presentations within your areas of expertise.

In addition, you will represent and support Bio-Widgets in equity fund raising efforts and in management and board matters that call upon your scientific and industrial expertise.

Appendices

The Board of Directors of Bio-Widgets has approved the terms of your offer, as described below. Upon your acceptance, we can begin immediately to assist you with your living arrangements and with your transition into the company. We will be glad to answer any questions you may have about this offer.

Compensation

Your starting salary will be $_____ per month and will be subject to annual review. In addition, upon commencement of your full-time employment on premises at Bio-Widgets, the Board of Directors shall award you an initial stock option grant of _____ stock options. Twelve and one-half percent (12.5%) of the options shall vest on the six-month anniversary of the award date which shall coincide with your commencement date. The remaining 87.5% shall vest in 42 substantially equal monthly installments. Upon your joining the company, we will provide you with a copy of the Bio-Widgets, Inc. Stock Incentive Plan ("Plan") and related paperwork for your signature. Additional stock option grants will be reviewed annually.

Re-location Expense Reimbursement

To assist you with your anticipated re-location to _____ from _____, Bio-Widgets will reimburse you for your reasonable out-of-pocket expenses related to your re-location, up to $_____, net of taxes. Bio-Widgets will reimburse you upon your submission to the Company of receipts for personal expenses related to your re-location.

Short-Term Living Arrangements

To assist you with short-term living arrangements in the _____ area, Bio-Widgets will pay for your extended-stay hotel or monthly apartment rental, up to $_____ per month, for the ___-month period from _____ through _____. You will be responsible for making your own living arrangements, but Bio-Widgets will pay your rental cost upon presentation of an invoice.

Personal Travel Expense to (_____) from (_____)

To assist you with the disposition of your current home in _____, Bio-Widgets will pay for up to ____ round-trips by air between _____ and _____ between _____ and _____. Bio-Widgets will pay for up to $____ per round-trip, inclusive of coach class airfare, auto rental or transfers. When feasible, you agree to link your personal travel to _____ with other Bio-Widgets-related business travel that may coincide with your personal trip(s). Such linked trips will count toward your total number of company-paid personal round trips. You agree to schedule your trips so as to minimize loss of business days, and will present receipts to Bio-Widgets for reimbursement.

Performance Bonus

Because you will lead and manage a significant portion of Bio-Widgets's scientific operations, your work will affect Bio-Widgets's ability to complete revenue-generating projects successfully and on time, to generate strategically valuable new business or awarded grants and to raise growth capital. To provide you with a strong incentive to excel in your position and to help Bio-Widgets achieve its operational and financial goals, Bio-Widgets is offering you a performance-based. This bonus will be tied to your impact upon Bio-Widgets's recognized revenues, signed fee-for-service or co-development contracts, awarded grants and completed fund raising transactions during your first year at Bio-Widgets.

To be eligible to receive a performance bonus, you must remain under Bio-Widgets's full-time employment throughout the year and through your first anniversary. In addition, your individual job performance, as documented in your written annual review, as well as in any interim reviews conducted during your first year, must be judged to be satisfactory and without material negative comments that could call into question your ability to continue managing your job responsibilities effectively.

Provided that you are bonus-eligible, you will, at the discretion of the Board of Directors, receive a cash bonus equal to:

- ___% of up to first $___ million of contract revenues recognized by Bio-Widgets during the first year of your employment and generated as a result of your management, and

- ___% of up to the next $___ million of recognized contract or grant revenue so generated, and

- ___% of up to the next $___ million of recognized revenue or revenue backlog from any combination of completed or newly contracted projects or awarded grants so generated, and, finally,

- ___% of up to the next $___ million of recognized revenue, revenue backlog or growth capital from any combination of completed or newly contracted projects, or awarded grants so generated, or equity financing from new investors.

Your bonus shall be subject to annual review.

Benefits Program

During your employment at Bio-Widgets, you will be entitled to participate in the company's benefits program, as made available generally to Bio-Widgets employees. At present, Bio-Widgets offers a Company-sponsored health insurance plan and a Company-sponsored 401K retirement savings plan. If you decide to participate in the Company health insurance plan, it is important that you maintain your existing health insurance benefits, until your enrollment in Bio-Widgets's insurance plan is confirmed by the plan provider.

Vacation Days

You will be entitled to _____ (___) weeks paid vacation plus _____ (___) fixed holidays per year. You will accrue one vacation day per month for the first _____ (___) months of your employment, which you may begin to use upon completion of your sixth month. You will also be entitled to _____ (___) personal days per year, which you may use at your discretion. Personal days may not be carried over from year to year.

Start Date

Your start date will be _____, pending your ability to provide written verification of your right to work in the United States by that time.

Proprietary Information

This letter confirms our understanding that you are not subject to any employment agreement that would preclude you from joining Bio-Widgets, and that you are legally entitled to work in the United States. This letter also confirms that you will not be asked to disclose to us any proprietary information from your prior places of employment. In addition, you will agree to execute a Proprietary Information and Inventions Agreement as a condition of employment.

Employment at Will

This letter confirms our understanding that your employment at Bio-Widgets is not for a specific term, is at the mutual consent of you and Bio-Widgets, is at will in nature, and can be terminated at any time by you or Bio-Widgets.

Severance Package

In the event that your position at Bio-Widgets is terminated three months or more after your first date of employment as a result of a merger, acquisition or loss of control, and not for cause, you shall be entitled to receive severance pay for a period of up to three months, or until you accept a full-time position with another employer, whichever comes first. Your severance pay would be based on your highest monthly salary at the time of your termination. Bonuses you have accrued up through the day of your termination will still apply. In addition, upon your termination under the above-stated conditions, the un-vested portion of those stock option awards made to you prior to the date of termination would, subject to the terms of the Plan, automatically vest.

Appendices

Empoyee Manual

Upon commencement of your employment, we will provide you with a copy of Bio-Widgets's Employee Manual, including an Acknowledgement of Receipt Form for your signature.

Entire Agreement

This letter constitutes the entire agreement between you and Bio-Widgets and supersedes all prior agreements between the parties regarding employment. Please review these terms to ensure they are consistent with your understanding. If so, please sign and date both copies of this letter and confirm your planned start date. This offer of employment will terminate if not accepted by _____.

We believe that you will be able to make a significant contribution to the growth and development of Bio-Widgets and look forward to receiving your acceptance of our offer. Please do not hesistate to call me if you have any questions.

Sincerely,

_____
Chief Executive Officer

Accepted: _____

Date: _____

cc: _____ (Corporate Counsel)

14.10 Inventions Assignment Agreement

INVENTIONS ASSIGNMENT AGREEMENT

(Consultants, Advisors, and/or Collaborators)

This Inventions Assignment (this "**Agreement**") is entered into as of this ___ day of _____, by and between Bio-Widgets, Inc., a _____ corporation with offices at _____ (the "**Company**") and _____ with an address at _____ ("**You**").

During the course of providing consulting services, advisory services or collaborative services to Company, and in consideration of Your services and the compensation paid to You, You hereby agree as follows:

1. <u>Ownership</u>. You agree to assign and hereby assign to Company all right, title and interest (including without limitation, all intellectual property rights) in and to any and all inventions, works of authorship, designs, know-how, ideas, concepts, techniques, discoveries, developments, innovations, improvements and information made or conceived, in whole or in part, by You during the term of this Agreement which either: (a) arise out of or relate to any services You provide to Company; (b) involve or are related to Company's actual or demonstrably anticipated research or development or core business; or (c) incorporate or are based on, in whole or in part, any of Company's Confidential Information (collectively, "**Inventions**"). You agree to promptly disclose and provide all Inventions to the Company. You have read the California Goggin Act attached hereto as Schedule A and understand that under its provisions You may retain ownership of inventions that You may make entirely on Your own time and not using Company's equipment, supplies, facilities, or trade secret information except for inventions that either (i) relate at the time of conception or reduction to practice of the invention to Company's business or actual or demonstrably anticipated research or development or (ii) result from any work performed by You for Company.2. <u>Further Assurances</u>. You agree to assist Company, at Company's expense but at no additional compensation to You, to further evidence, record and perfect the assignments described

Appendices

in Section 3, and to perfect, obtain, maintain, enforce and defend any rights assigned.

3.   Representations and Warranties. You warrant and represent: (i) that You have full right, power and authority to enter into this Agreement and perform all of Your obligations under this Agreement, and that in performing those obligations You will not knowingly violate any agreement or obligation between You and any third party, including without limitation any agreements or policies of any university or corporation for which You provide services; (ii) that neither the services You provide to Company, the Inventions, nor any use thereof will, to the best of Your knowledge, violate or in any way infringe upon the rights of third parties; (iii) that You have no reason to believe You do not have full right and authority to transfer the Inventions as set forth in this Agreement and that no authorization, consent, waiver or approval of any public body, authority, or any third party is necessary for You to transfer the Inventions or to consummate any transaction contemplated by this Agreement; (iv) that in Your performance of all the terms of this Agreement and the creation of the Inventions, You will not knowingly breach any agreement to keep in confidence proprietary information or trade secrets acquired by You in confidence or in trust from a third party.

4.   Remedies. You acknowledge that the Company will be irreparably harmed and have no adequate remedy at law if You violate the terms of Section 2, 3 or 4 of this Agreement. In such event, the Company will have the right, in addition to any other rights and remedies it may possess, to seek and obtain equitable relief in any court of competent jurisdiction.

5.   No License. Nothing in this Agreement is intended to grant any rights to You under any patent, copyright, or other intellectual property right of Company, nor shall this Agreement grant You any rights in or to Confidential Information except as set forth herein.

6.   Term. This Agreement shall survive until such time as You and Company terminate all relationships. Notwithstanding the foregoing, Sections 2, 4, 5, 6, 7, 8 and 9 shall survive the expiration or termination of this Agreement. Section 3 shall survive the expiration or termination of this

Agreement with respect to Inventions made or conceived during the term of this Agreement.

7. <u>General</u>. This Agreement and the schedule hereto constitute and contain the entire agreement and final understanding concerning Your relationship as an employee of Company. This Agreement supersedes and replaces all prior negotiations and agreements proposed or otherwise concerning the subject matter hereof. If any provision of this Agreement is determined by a court to be illegal or unenforceable, then the remainder of this Agreement shall remain in full force and effect. This Agreement will be construed and enforced in accordance with the internal laws of the State of California, excluding that body of laws relating to conflicts of law. Any dispute arising out of this Agreement shall be resolved in state or federal courts located in _____, California, and the parties expressly waive any challenge to the jurisdiction or venue of such courts. No changes or modifications or waivers to this Agreement will be effective unless in writing and signed by both parties.

"Company"
Bio-Widgets, Inc.

By: _____

Name: _____

Title: _____

"You"

By: _____

Name: _____

Schedule A
THE GOGGIN ACT
Sections 2870, 2871, and 2872 of the California Labor Code

2870. (a) Any provision in an employment agreement which provides that an employee shall assign, or offer to assign, any of his or her rights in an invention to his or her employer shall not apply to an invention that the employee developed entirely on his or her own time without using the employer's equipment, supplies, facilities, or trade secret information except for those inventions that either: (1) Relate at the time of conception or reduction to practice of the invention to the employer's business, or actual or demonstrably anticipated research or development of the employer; or (2) Result from any work performed by the employee for the employer;

(b) To the extent a provision in an employment agreement purports to require an employee to assign an invention otherwise excluded from being required to be assigned under subdivision (a), the provision is against the public policy of this state and is unenforceable.

2871. No employer shall require a provision made void and unenforceable by Section 2870 as a condition of employment or continued employment. Nothing in this article shall be construed to forbid or restrict the right of an employer to provide in contracts of employment for disclosure, provided that any such disclosures be received in confidence, of all of the employee's inventions made solely or jointly with others during the term of his or her employment, a review process by the employer to determine such issues as may arise, and for full title to certain patents and inventions to be in the United States, as required by contracts between the employer and the United States or any of its agencies.

2872. If an employment agreement entered into after January 1, 1980, contains a provision requiring the employee to assign or offer to assign any of his or her rights in any invention to his or her employer, the employer must also, at the time the agreement is made, provide a written notification to the employee that the agreement does not apply to an invention which qualifies fully under the provisions of Section 2870. In any suit or action arising thereunder, the burden of proof shall be on the employee claiming the benefits of its provisions.

14.11 Useful Web Sites

Following is a list of Web sites that company founders, entrepreneurs and investors will likely return to frequently for official information, essential forms, and useful business services. Some of the Web sites are specific to California.

Federal Web Sites

www.irs.gov, Internal Revenue Service

http://grants.nih.gov/grants/funding/sbirsttr_programs.htm, NIH Office of Extramural Research Web site, for information about SBIR (Small Business Innovation Research) and STTR (Small Business Technology Transfer) grants.

www.sba.gov, Small Business Association of the U.S. Government

www.sec.gov, Securities and Exchange Commission

www.uspto.gov, U.S. Patent and Trademark Office

State Web Sites

www.edd.ca.gov, California Employment Development Department

www.ftb.ca.gov, California Franchise Tax Board

www.ss.ca.gov/business, California Secretary of State Business Portal

www.state.de.us/corp, State of Delaware Division of Corporations (many companies incorporate in Delaware, due to the state's corporation-friendly legal environment)

Corporate and Trade Association Web Sites

www.angelcapitalassociation.org, Organization of angel investment groups in North America.

Appendices

www.bizfilings.com, Company providing incorporation and state-registered agent services

www.fedex.kinkos.com, Document printing and processing services

www.nvca.com, National Venture Capital Association

www.open.americanexpress.com, Small business financial services

www.pwcmoneytree, PriceWaterhouseCoopers' quarterly survey of venture capital investing activity in the U.S.

www.radford.com, Company providing compensation surveys

www.ventureone.com, Dow Jones' resource for venture capital business intelligence, publications and conferences

14.12 Inspirational and Motivational Books

Starting and investing in new companies requires constant inspiration and motivation. When you feel as if you are carrying the weight of the start-up world on your shoulders, and even when things are going well, it can be helpful and calming to draw upon the wisdom of great thinkers and gifted authors. I find that the best reading selections are those that have withstood the test of time. (Fifty years is my usual cutoff.) Some titles I recommend include:

Meditations, by Marcus Aurelius (For the stoic in you.)

How to Stop Worrying and Start Living, by Dale Carnegie (When things look bad, ask yourself: What's the worst that could happen?)

How to be Rich, by J. Paul Getty (When traveling on business, take time to visit museums and take in the local culture.)

Think and Grow Rich, by Napolean Hill (Definiteness of purpose, positive mental attitude.)

Extraordinary Popular Delusions and the Madness of Crowds, by Charles MacKay (History is replete with tales of speculative excess.)

The Power of Positive Thinking, by Norman Vincent Peale (It works, if you think about it.)

For the pleasure of reading great business writing, I also recommend *Soul of a New Machine*, to which I was introduced in a business school course on entrepreneurship. This book, for which author Tracy Kidder won a Pulitzer Prize, tells the true story of the team that developed Data General's entry into the hotly contested market for minicomputers during the 1970s. To understand what drives engineers at high-tech companies to stay up all night debugging code, read this book.

ABOUT THE AUTHOR

William L. Robbins is a founder and managing director of Convergent Ventures, a seed-stage life science and technology venture investment and development firm in Los Angeles. Mr. Robbins has more than twenty-three years of experience as a venture investor, entrepreneur, start-up executive, and manager in the pharmaceutical, biotechnology, medical technology, and high technology industries. Mr. Robbins serves as chairman of the board, president, and chief executive officer of Neurion Pharmaceuticals Inc. He is also a founder and director of ORFID Corporation and Encode Bio, Inc. Previously, Mr. Robbins founded Convergent Management Inc., a business development consulting firm focused on early-stage life science companies. Previously, he served as vice president of business development at Bio-Imaging Technologies, a medical imaging and clinical research company that went public during his tenure. He also held marketing and new product development positions at Warner-Lambert Company, and account management positions at the health care division of Grey Advertising in New York.

In the not-for-profit sector, Mr. Robbins is chairman of the board of Israel Cancer Research Fund's Los Angeles chapter and a director of the American Technion Society's Southern California chapter. Mr. Robbins is an occasional guest lecturer and panelist at industry conferences and in academic programs, and a frequent mentor to undergraduate and graduate students. He served as president of the Columbia Business School Club of Southern California and is a director of the Dartmouth Club of Los Angeles. Mr. Robbins holds an M.B.A. from Columbia Business School and an A.B. in psychology, modified with biology, from Dartmouth College.

Mr. Robbins is married to Hila Robbins, D.M.D., a board-certified pediatric dentist in private practice, and adjunct associate professor of pediatric dentistry at the UCLA School of Dentistry. The Robbins reside in Los Angeles.

The Raising Venture Capital Collection Published by Aspatore

▶**Pitching to Venture Capitalists** – Essential Strategies for Approaching Venture Capitalists, Making Presentations, Entering Into Negotiations, and Securing Funding – Written by Leading Venture Capitalist Patrick Ennis – $49.95

▶**Raising Capital for Entrepreneurs** – Industry Insiders on Angel Funding, Venture Capital, and Growth Money from Private Investors – Includes Highlights on Advantages and Disadvantages of Each – $49.95

▶**Term Sheets and Valuations** – Best-Selling Venture Capital Book of 2005 – Line-by-Line Descriptions of Each Clause and Negotiation Points – $14.95

▶**Deal Terms** – The Finer Points of Venture Capital Deal Structures, Valuations, Stock Options, and Getting Deals Done – Wilmerding's Follow-On Book to Term Sheets and Valuations, and the Current Second Best-Selling Venture Capital Book – $49.95

▶**Venture Debt Alternatives and Evaluation Guidelines** – A Comprehensive Look at the Venture Debt Marketplace Along with a Systematic Framework for Approaching the Debt Capital Markets, Increasing Transaction Transparency, and Avoiding Common, Costly Mistakes – An Option Every Entrepreneur Should Consider in Addition to Venture Capital – $249.95

▶**Venture Capital Best Practices** – Leading Venture Capitalists and Lawyers Share Keys to Success in Doing Venture Capital Deals – $49.95

▶**Compensation Structures for Venture-Backed Companies** – How Venture Capitalists Want to See the Structure of Management and Employee Compensation, Stock Options, Retirement, Debt, and Bonus Plans – $119.95

▶**The Role of Board Members in Venture-Backed Companies** – Rules, Responsibilities, and Motivations of Board Members – From Management and Venture Capitalist Perspectives – $99.95

▶**Venture Capital Valuations** - Top Venture Capitalists on Step-by-Step Strategies and Methodologies for Valuing Companies at All Stages – $99.95

▶**The Venture Capital Legal Handbook** – Industry Insiders on the Laws and Documents that Govern Venture Capital Deals, Raising Capital, Mergers and Acquisitions, and More – Includes Every Major Document Used in Venture Capital Deals with Analysis and Negotiation Points – Save Thousands in Legal Fees – 820 Pages – $299.95

Buy All Ten Titles Above – Save 40%
(The Equivalent of Four Books for Free) – $999.95
Call 1-866-Aspatore (277-2867) – Phone Order Rate Only

Buy All Ten Titles Above Plus the CD-Rom of Venture Capital Documents and Financial Modeling
Save $1,000 (The Equivalent of All Ten Books for Free) – $1,999.95

Ready-to-Use
Venture Capital Financial Modeling

In Microsoft Excel that Can Be Customized for Your Use

When it comes to venture capital investment, each company is unique. There is no single model that can cover all situations. The good news is that there are certain underlying, well-known concepts and methods that can be brought together into a cohesive model to help automate and improve the decision-making process in analyzing an investment. In *Venture Capital Financial Modeling*, Praveen Gupta, one of the top modelers in venture capital, attempts to bring these concepts together, explaining and applying them to various financial models used by venture capitalists in evaluation of their investments.

The models analyzed in *Venture Capital Financial Modeling* provide immeasurable financial benefit to entrepreneurs and venture capitalists and will save both groups countless hours of analysis. Entrepreneurs will be better able to perform a financial analysis on their companies and get a realistic view of possible decisions by venture capitalists. Venture capitalists will be able to perform a similar analysis, resulting in smoother negotiations with educated entrepreneurs.

All interactive financial models described in this book—**valuation modeling, dilution modeling, investment return analysis modeling, and merger and acquisition distribution modeling**—are available on the accompanying CD-ROM. These models can be adapted to individual company requirements based on the number of investors and founders by adding or removing appropriate line items. For more detailed information, please visit www.aspatore.com/vcfinancialmodeling.asp.

The table of contents for *Venture Capital Financial Modeling* includes:
Chapter 1) Overview–Venture Capital Financial Modeling
Chapter 2) Valuation Modeling
- Method 1: Desired Ownership; - Method 2: Financial Ratios
Chapter 3) Dilution Modeling
- Method 1: No Adjustment; - Method 2: Broad-Based Weighted Average
- Method 3: Middle-of-the-Road Weighted Average; - Method 4: Narrow Based Weighted Average; - Method 5: Full Ratchet
- Dilution Method Comparison
Chapter 4) Investment Return Analysis Modeling
- Initial Public Offering; - Merger & Acquisition
Chapter 5) Exit Analysis Modeling
- Initial Public Offering; - Merger & Acquisition

Available via CD-Rom or E-mail
$995 – Individual License
$2495 – Firm-Wide License

Call 1-866-Aspatore (277-2867) to Order Today!

Ready-to-Use Venture Capital Documents CD-ROM
In Microsoft Word that Can Be Customized for Your Use

Every Major Document and Legal Agreement Used in Venture Capital Deals

The Venture Capital Documents Collection is the definitive resource for venture capital and the only reference material you will need for understanding, drafting, and negotiating deals. This CD-ROM features every major document and legal agreement used in venture capital deals. Included are more than 1,200 pages of the most up-to-date information used by leading venture capitalists—written by top venture capitalists and private equity lawyers—that collectively provide a thorough examination of every aspect of any document/contract used in venture capital. The CD-ROM also features every venture capital-related contract/document published in any of the books published by Aspatore, ready to use in Microsoft word and be customized to fit your needs.

The CD-ROM includes the following documents:

- Term Sheets
- Stock Incentive Plan
- Stock Option Award Agreement
- Due Diligence Documents
- Board of Directors Contract
- Investor Questionnaires
- Subscription Agreement
- Summary of Terms for Financing
- Independent Contractor Agreement
- Subordination Provisions
- Merger Agreement
- Board Meeting Minutes
- Shareholders Agreement
- Employment and Stock Purchase Agreements
- Confidentiality and Non-Competition Agreements
- Private Placement Memorandum
- Contents of Corporation Bylaws
- Charter
- Public Company Registration Information
- Letter of Intent
- Investor Rights Agreement
- Stock Appreciation Rights Agreement
- Conference and Assignment
- Certificate of Designation
- Operating Agreement for Venture Funds
- Convertible Preferred Stock Purchase Agreement
- Special Employment Terms and Management Employment Agreements and Many More…

Within these documents lies a wealth of critical information that every entrepreneur, venture capitalist, and lawyer should have at their fingertips.

Available via CD-ROM or E-Mail
$995 – Individual License
$2495 – Firm-Wide License

Best-Selling Seminar CDs and Books from Aspatore Books

The Financial Strategies for Venture Capital-Backed Companies Seminar

CFOs of Venture Capital-Backed Companies on Strategies for Financial Tools, Controls, and Growth Strategies Planning – Four Hours of Speeches, Interactive Workbook, and Book – $499.95

In this seminar, you will learn answers to questions such as the following:

- How do you set financial goals for your company? Do you have a "checks and balances" system to ensure that those goals are being met and that expenses are being kept in check?
- What qualities do a CEO and CFO of a venture-backed company need to have to be successful and to have long-term success?
- What is your vision on managing the financials of your company? How do you keep a firm grip on what is happening financially at your company?
- What do you look for in the financials that tells you the company is on the right track? What statistics or numbers do you look most closely at?
- What alerts you to a red flag in the financials of your company?
- During a time of rapid growth, how do you determine what an "okay" level of money to be losing is for the company?

The M&A Strategies for Venture Capital-Backed Companies Seminar

Top Venture Capitalists on Strategies for Successfully Completing Mergers and Acquisitions at the Right Valuation – Three Hours of Speeches, Interactive Workbook, and Book – $499.95

In this seminar, you will learn answers to questions such as the following:

- What is the ideal way to structure M&A deals? How do management teams try to structure M&A deals?
- What are the items that are most often negotiated with the acquiring company or management team?
- What factors most affect the deal structure (such as stage of company, management team, profitability, etc.)?
- What is the right way to approach valuations?
- What aspects are the most negotiable, or what creates a situation where negotiation is possible?
- How can a management team validate the valuation they are looking for? What research/data should they use to support their valuation?
- What should a management team look most closely at when deciding whether to accept a deal (such as purchase price, earn-out clauses, employment contracts for management staying on, etc.)?
- When is the right time for a venture capital-backed company to pursue an M&A-type event?

To Order, Call 1-866-Aspatore (277-2867) or Visit www.Aspatore.com

ASPATORE BOOKS